Imagining Manila

Imagining Manila

Literature, Empire and Orientalism

Tom Sykes

BLOOMSBURY ACADEMIC
LONDON • NEW YORK • OXFORD • NEW DELHI • SYDNEY

BLOOMSBURY ACADEMIC
Bloomsbury Publishing Plc
50 Bedford Square, London, WC1B 3DP, UK
1385 Broadway, New York, NY 10018, USA
29 Earlsfort Terrace, Dublin 2, Ireland

BLOOMSBURY, BLOOMSBURY ACADEMIC and the Diana logo are trademarks of
Bloomsbury Publishing Plc

First published in Great Britain by I.B. TAURIS 2021
This paperback edition published by Bloomsbury Academic 2022

Copyright © Tom Sykes, 2021

Tom Sykes has asserted his right under the Copyright, Designs and
Patents Act, 1988, to be identified as Author of this work.

For legal purposes the Acknowledgements on p. viii constitute an extension
of this copyright page.

Cover design by Rebecca Heselton
Cover image: A street in Manila, Philippines, circa 1930.
(© Denniston/Royal Geographical Society/Getty Images)

All rights reserved. No part of this publication may be reproduced or transmitted
in any form or by any means, electronic or mechanical, including photocopying,
recording, or any information storage or retrieval system, without prior
permission in writing from the publishers.

Bloomsbury Publishing Plc does not have any control over, or responsibility for, any
third-party websites referred to or in this book. All internet addresses given in this
book were correct at the time of going to press. The author and publisher regret
any inconvenience caused if addresses have changed or sites have ceased to
exist, but can accept no responsibility for any such changes.

A catalogue record for this book is available from the British Library.

A catalog record for this book is available from the Library of Congress.

ISBN: HB: 978-1-7883-1831-0
PB: 978-0-7556-4039-3
ePDF: 978-0-7556-0287-2
eBook: 978-0-7556-0288-9

Typeset by Deanta Global Publishing Services, Chennai, India

To find out more about our authors and books visit www.bloomsbury.com
and sign up for our newsletters.

For my father Simon Sykes, a man with many gifts. I'm proud to have inherited at least some of them.

Contents

Acknowledgements	viii
Introduction: Manilaism as an Orientalism	1
1 'A Seething Cauldron of Evil': Hispanophobia, Manila-as-hell and third world blues	19
2 'Known to All Students of History': Adventure, imperial mythology and Orientalist rhetoric in Manilaism of the US conquest of the Philippines	37
3 'The Pious New Name of the Musket': Language, gender, race and benevolent assimilation	53
4 'She Can Take on American Ideas': Desire, capital and flawed simulation in twentieth-century Manilaism	69
5 The making of a supranational stereotype: Western constructions of the Chinese in Manila and Beyond	81
6 Call of Duterte: *Cacique* despotism and Western (neo)liberal crisis	99
7 Towards an anti-Manilaism	111
Conclusion: Liberal Orientalism versus humanism, socialism and internationalism	133
Notes	141
Bibliography	181
Index	201

Acknowledgements

Although over the last decade-and-a-half I've written and edited several books in various genres, this is my first academic monograph. Embarking on it filled me with trepidation. I'm therefore indebted to innumerable people who smoothed the research and writing process with their moral and intellectual support.

The person who contributed most to this book's chances of ever being realized is Tamar Steinitz, my secondary doctoral supervisor at Goldsmiths, University of London. When I began working with Tamar, I hadn't written anything in the academic register for ten years. By the time I'd finished working with her, I'd learned an extraordinary amount about structure, style, argumentation, epistemology and much else essential to the craft. I am also thankful to the late Bart Moore-Gilbert, a colossus in the field of postcolonial studies, who supervised me briefly but adroitly until he sadly passed away in 2015. Ardashir Vakil, my primary supervisor, gave me wise counsel on the creative practice element of my PhD, aspects of which have found their way into the book you're about to read.

Had Tomasz Hoskins of Bloomsbury/I.B. Tauris not commissioned *Imagining Manila*, much of the material in it would never have found an audience. Deepest thanks to him and his colleague Nayiri Kendir, who among many other important things, recruited peer reviewers and proposed the alluring front cover.

I am also grateful to colleagues at the University of Portsmouth: Oliver Gruner for reading through the entire manuscript and making many erudite suggestions; Sudip Sen for his constructive criticism of certain chapters; Stephen Harper for discussions about everything from US imperialism to Sinophobic stereotyping, and for his recommending texts that turned out to be indispensable to my project, including Martin Green's *Dreams of Adventure, Deeds of Empire* and Alain Grosrichard's *The Sultan's Court*; Sophia Wood for lending me books on the representation of Jews in British literature; Sally Shaw for chats about research ethics; and Lincoln Geraghty for his insider's knowledge on pitching books to academic publishers (clearly it worked or you wouldn't be reading this now).

The editors of the *Journal of Postcolonial Writing* and *Social Identities* in addition to Karl Bell, leader of the Supernatural Cities research project, gave me opportunities to publish articles that laid the groundwork for this book.

Others across the world have made important contributions. Thank you Gene Alcantara for teaching me so much about the expatriate Filipino community in the UK. Filipinos in the Philippines who kindly shared their contacts with me and suggested research pathways include Douglas Candano, Avie Olarte, Charlson Ong, Victor Paz, Nina Somera, Joel Toledo and 'Taja Villanueva'.

Last but not least, thanks to my family who – generally, most of the time – put up with my foibles and risky sojourns without complaint.

Introduction
Manilaism as an Orientalism

I lived in Manila in 2009–10 and have been travelling back there frequently ever since. Over this time, I have grown weary of reading and hearing the countless stereotypes, half-truths, myths and misperceptions that Westerners have about the city in particular and the Philippines in general. If I'd been given a proverbial pound for every time a British person has asked me if I go to the Philippines because I am a sex tourist, I could have retired in luxury by now. The ubiquity of child prostitution is brought up almost as often. In 2015, when my then-partner, a Filipina, accompanied me to view some properties for sale in my hometown of Portsmouth, the white British female estate agent asked if we had met online. Perhaps realizing that she might have implied that I had paid a fee for my girlfriend via some sordid 'Asian brides' website, the estate agent hurriedly qualified her question with the claim that most romances begin on the internet these days anyway. She then offered what I am sure she, albeit in her cack-handed way, intended to be a compliment but that was nonetheless grounded in problematic assumptions about the sexual willingness and availability of Asian women: 'They're all beautiful over there,' she said to my girlfriend, and then, looking at me, added, 'aren't they?'

During a spell in a British hospital a few years earlier, I met two white middle-aged male patients who had holidayed in and around Manila. Both condemned the grinding poverty of the city while commending the zero-tolerance approach to crime and the effectiveness of strongman leaders within the police, the judiciary and politics. They felt that overly liberal, namby-pamby Britain could do with a dose of the same. One of the men remarked on the extraordinary optimism of Filipinos, especially in the teeth of adversity, violence and exploitation. The other man had, perhaps inevitably, dated a Filipina during his trip which had stoked mixed feelings in him. 'These girls are naturally caring,' he said, raising his eyebrows at one of the numerous Filipina migrant nurses as she rushed past our beds. 'Trouble is,' he went on, 'they're all a bit simple, a bit superstitious'. He then tried to corroborate his homogenizing allegation about *all* 50 million

Filipinas with an anecdote about just one of them: his date had accused him of 'treading on her grave' when he had stepped over her while she was sitting on the floor of their hotel room watching TV.

From these and other encounters with Westerners and from popular Western books, films and TV programmes, I started to form a mental image of Manila that was irreconcilable with my lived experience of the city as a foreigner who had formed close friendships there; made professional connections with some of its universities, NGOs and media outlets; interviewed a wide range of Manileños for both journalistic and academic assignments; and undertaken archival research in its libraries and museums. The Manila constructed by the estate agent, the hospital patients, po-faced documentaries and sensationalist novels was a miserable landscape of crime, corruption, deprivation, sleaze, authoritarianism and backward beliefs. Although of course not without its social, political and economic problems, the Manila I knew was considerably more nuanced than that. (I will delve into the nature of this nuance later, as it is one of the guiding themes of this book.) I then started to wonder exactly why my appraisal of the city so diverged from the perspectives above. Was it merely because my engagement with Manila had been more focused and sustained than other Westerners'? But then how to account for the peculiar notions of those, like the estate agent, who had never been to Manila and were never likely to? How had their guesses and generalizations been informed by cultural, political and ideological factors? I wondered how old were these boilerplates of people – highly sexualized women, tyrannical kingpins, simpering paupers – and places – slums, crime scenes, red light districts. Given that the Philippines was a Spanish colony from the late sixteenth to the late nineteenth centuries, then was indirectly ruled by the United States and, since 1946, has been economically and politically subordinate to the United States and, increasingly, regional powers including China and Japan, I assumed that these tropes were epiphenomena of certain pre-eminent Global Northern attitudes towards the Global South. But what were the exact mechanics of that process? How have these tropes then fed back into the popular consciousness in both the West and in the Philippines? In which ways has this time- and culture-specific episteme accorded with – and deviated from – other, what we might call 'Orientalist' discourses, that have tried to explicate peripheral spaces elsewhere? Given that, in other contexts, oppressive discourses always necessarily spawn resistance and opposition, how successfully have cultural producers – in the Philippines and elsewhere – been in countering, satirizing or deconstructing these hegemonic paradigms?

This book attempts to answer these sorts of questions albeit within the confines of literary history. I focus on literature for several reasons. While over the years, films, television programmes, advertisements, public relations brochures, political speeches, online content and other media have helped to manufacture external perceptions of Manila and the Philippines, there have not been enough of them over a lengthy enough period to constitute a coherent discourse as such. However, my research over the last decade has revealed that Westerners have been writing novels, travelogues, memoirs and works of literary journalism set in Manila since the early eighteenth century, and that common concepts, sentiments and symbolic devices can be traced through them up to the present day.

* * *

The objective space of a house – its corners, corridors, cellar, rooms – is far less important than what poetically it is endowed with, which is usually a quality with an imaginative or figurative value we can name and feel; thus a house may be haunted or homelike, or prisonlike or magical. So space acquires emotional and even rational sense by a kind of poetic process, whereby the vacant or anonymous reaches of distance are converted into meaning for us here.[1]

In his pioneering study *Orientalism* (1978), Edward Said uses the above analogy to illustrate his notion of an 'imaginative geography' of 'a geographical, cultural, linguistic, and ethnic unit called the Orient'[2] that, since the fourteenth century, has been 'made by the mind[s]' of European writers and scholars labouring under the hypothesis that 'both their [the Orientals'] territory and their mentality are [. . .] different from "ours"'.[3] Furthermore, Said argues that Orientalist representations of the Orient are defined by 'typical encapsulations: the journey, the history, the fable, the stereotype, the polemical confrontation',[4] and that, by the 1800s, the Orientalist project came to be 'tinged and impressed with' the project of European empire-building in Asia and Africa: 'an Englishman in India or Egypt in the later nineteenth century took an interest in those countries that was never far from their status in his mind as British colonies.'[5] While in *Orientalism* Said's critical purview encompasses mainly French and British discursive constructions of North Africa and the Middle East, in the almost forty years since the book was first published, other scholars have adapted its theoretical framework to cross-examine imaginative geographies relating to the Indian Subcontinent, Sub-Saharan Africa, East Asia and Latin America. In the same spirit, this book applies some of the techniques of Orientalist discourse analysis to a lineage of signifying practices related to Manila, a part of the world largely overlooked by critics working in Said's slipstream.[6] In a conscious allusion to *Orientalism*, I have coined the term 'Manilaism' to describe a trajectory of Anglo-American writing on Manila from roughly the early eighteenth century to the present day, which imagines the city as a textual space founded on a number of (neo-)imperialist, (neo-)colonialist and ethnocentric assumptions. Over the course of Manilaism so far, these assumptions have compelled writers to pass generally negative value judgements on a host of issues affecting Manila such as class, gender, race, ethnicity, religion, culture, business, labour, human development and governmental policy. As with other Orientalisms, such judgements are a concomitant of, as Robert J.C. Young terms it, 'the project and practice of colonial modernity [. . .] constituting and generated by a specific historical discourse of knowledge articulated with the operation of political power'.[7]

While this book is indebted to Said's methodology, it is also mindful of the tension between Said's 'social constructivism and his epistemological realism' which causes him to oscillate between post-structuralist claims about the inherent instability of all linguistic apprehensions of reality and a more materialist approach that evaluates the truth status of propositions about the Orient.[8] I am therefore more aligned with the materialist dimension of Said's thought because I practise what the postcolonial critic Benita Parry calls 'intertextual confirmation'[9] – wherein the validity of a data source is established by comparing it to other relevant sources – in order to test the credibility of Manilaist adumbrations against Western and Filipino texts that, in the Argentine historian Walter D. Mignolo's formulation, can be termed 'decolonial' because they defy Manilaism's reactionary and supremacist sentiments.[10] Furthermore, in Parry's view, Said and those other trailblazers of postcolonial theory, Homi K. Bhabha and Gayatri Chakravorty Spivak, advance 'an essentially textualist account of culture'[11] that foregrounds the 'discursive violence' of signifying practices to the detriment of interrogating the repressive, real-life colonial apparatuses that produce such discursive violence.[12] Thus, informed by the 'philological' discipline of literary criticism in which 'the historical context of a literary work [. . .] is integral to a proper understanding of it'[13] and Jennifer M. McMahon's suggestion that postcolonial analyses of 'culture and language' should be 'grounded by historically contextualizing these phenomena and always keeping in mind both the physical and cultural violence of [. . .] colonization',[14] I have tried to reconcile these textualist and materialist modes by closely reading the tropes and techniques of Manilaist texts while positing their affiliations with the wider social, political and economic conditions of their originating periods. This could be a boundless, endless exercise, of course; indeed, an entire monograph could be written about, say, the confluence of material-historical forces undergirding just one American author's slur against the Chinese Filipinos in 1929. Therefore, while this study cannot pursue in full every line of enquiry sparked by the subject matter, I hope it can convey to the reader some sense of the complex interplay between the world and its literary epiphenomena as it relates to Manila.

If someone were able to time travel from mid-nineteenth-century Manila to the modern-day city, she would of course see that much had changed. She would also notice that other aspects had not changed enough. Then as now, Manila is assuredly located in the Global South, its rates of poverty, unemployment, overcrowding, pollution and disease far higher than in most of Europe and North America. Furthermore, our time traveller might gather that, while Manila is no longer the nexus of an official colony of a Western empire, it suffers in myriad ways from an unjust globalized capitalist system that some commentators deem 'neocolonial'[15] because the wealthier, mostly Western nations reap immense profits from the exploitation of Global Southern markets, resources and labour. If our temponaut was also au fait with Western books about Manila from her own century, she would recognize that some of these texts' preoccupations had survived into the next millennium, if not quite in their original guises. The nineteenth-century othering of Manila's human populations and geographical features as qualitatively inferior to their counterparts in the West was rooted in, to use Martin Green's phrase, an imperial 'ideology in which freedom and morality were the main values; freedom and morality in religion meaning Protestantism; in commerce meaning capitalist enterprise; in politics meaning a gentry republic or constitutional monarchy'.[16] This ideology fed into the construction of peripheral spaces like Manila as sites where 'anything goes, morally and politically [. . .] once you're far from the core countries geographically'.[17] After the Philippines' relationship with the United States altered in the 1940s from one of formal colonial subjugation to one of financial, military and political dependency, the earlier attitudes mutated according to the twists and turns of real history, and they continue to shape representations of Manila up to the present day.

My methodology for tracking the evolution of these imaginative geographies draws partly upon Jonathan Crush's literary-historical analysis of the South African city of Johannesburg. In its early days (the 1880s and 1890s), Johannesburg was portrayed in European life writing as a utopian metropolis of industrial progress. However, as 'Euroimperial' influence declined after 1930 (the Union of South Africa gained independence from Britain in 1931), the city was limned as a dystopian site of ethnic discord and economic catastrophe.[18] Correspondingly, I have found that Western visitors to Manila in the US colonial period (1898–1941), such as the American literary journalist George A. Miller, praise the city's modernity, rational planning and spry development ('it has joined the ranks of the world's big business centres', he writes),[19] while, later on, travelogues by DeLoris Stevenson, P.J. O'Rourke and others construct Manila less charitably after the Philippines has gained independence from the United States in 1946.

I have used several criteria to designate and delimit Manilaist texts. I chose to consider material that reflects on Manila rather than on other regions of the Philippines because, as the British author James Hamilton-Paterson argues, 'Manila remains the nipple from which the world takes most of its information about the Philippines'.[20] Hamilton-Paterson wrote that in 1987, but even a cursory glance of the foreign sections of contemporary newspapers, magazines and websites shows that it is just as true today. Moreover, the vast majority of Anglo-American writing on the Philippines has engaged to some degree or other with the capital city, and much of it exclusively so. These authors' fixation on the city is attributable to its significance to Philippine, Southeast Asian and world history. Manila was, in many respects, the site in which certain key turning points occurred in the history of Western imperialism, among them the rise of colonial mercantilism in Asia (in 1697, the English seaman William Dampier thought Manila a 'place of great strength and trade')[21] and the extinction of the Spanish Empire that precipitated the ascendancy of the United States to global imperial hegemony. Manila was also a strategic desideratum for both sides in the Pacific theatre of the Second World War and underwent such intense fighting that, by February 1945, 'an American investigation team thought Manila was the second most devastated city after Warsaw'.[22] Come the Cold War, when the Philippines shifted from being a US overseas possession to a subject of what Pankaj Mishra dubs America's 'informal empire [. . .] shown up by military bases, economic pressures and military coups',[23] Manila became the epitome of a Global Southern urban sprawl in the clutches of 'dollar-imperialism', both as a font of human and natural resources and as a market for US-manufactured commodities.[24] From the late twentieth century up to the present day, Manila has been something of a bellwether for what Niall Ferguson has determined as 'the descent of the West' and the 'reorientation of the world'[25] towards Asia; the city's economic ties to the United States and Europe have loosened – though not vanished – as the Philippines has established commercial relationships with Japan, South Korea and, most recently, China and Russia. That said, as we will see later in this book, there is a risk of overstating Manila's 'pivot'[26] to these other nations, for, despite the current President Duterte's populist anti-American bluster, the Philippines remains economically intimate with the United States and American troops are deployed in counter-insurgency operations against Islamist and Maoist rebels in what Mesrob Vartavarian characterizes as a continuation of 'American dominance in the Philippines':

> Through close involvement with Philippine security forces, American policy makers have maintained high levels of influence in an ostensibly independent country. When electoral inclinations veer the country in directions deemed unacceptable by national elites and American overseers, imperial directives and personnel are deployed through capillary connections to correct deviations.[27]

This study uses a spatial definition of Manila that is sensitive to the transformations the city's built environments and land area boundaries have undergone over the centuries. In 1823, just before the first Manilaists were writing, the city of Manila had 38,000 denizens and consisted of 16 districts covering 16.56 square miles of territory on the eastern bank of Manila Bay.[28] In 1978, to reflect the swelling population and the creation of new conurbations around Manila such as Quezon City, the Marcos administration established the National Capital Region (more colloquially known as 'Metro Manila') which was to incorporate 239.22 square miles and almost 6 million residents by 1980.[29] For this study I have chosen texts that engage with Manila as it would have been officially delineated at the respective historical moments from which these texts emerged. Be that as it may, I have occasionally afforded myself the liberty of 'zooming out' of the textual-geographical borders of Manila in order to consider propositions more generally made about the Philippines and Southeast Asia, but only when such propositions contribute to a comprehension of political and aesthetic questions relevant to the Manilaist symbolic order. At the same time, I have left out a fair sum of Western fiction and life writing that, while taking the Philippines as its subject, has nothing to do with neither Manila nor the discursive coordinates of Manilaism.

If some texts are omitted from the Manilaist frame due to their geographical scope, so others must be by reason of their authors' nationalities and attendant political allegiances. Although I discuss the specific lineaments of Anglo-American Manilaism at length later, at this point it may be useful to summarize what distinguishes these writers from their Spanish, Russian and German counterparts. Whereas British and American men of letters – and most are men – routinely offered uncompromising opinions on topics such as ethnicity, culture, class, religion, labour, enterprise, human development and governmental protocols, a plethora of Spanish epistles, news articles, histories and journal entries from the late sixteenth to late nineteenth centuries[30] provided relatively constative descriptions of military or missionary expeditions to outlying provinces and of the administrative niceties of the colonial church and state.[31] By contrast, Anglo-American Manilaist writing – at least from the 1840s until 1898 – is full of opprobrium towards Spanish rule and the archaic, under-developed society it has produced. This, as I argue in great depth later, is a corollary of British and American imperial ambitions in the Philippines that were to culminate in the amphibious invasion of Manila by the United States in May 1898. Be that as it may, some early Spanish observers promulgate hetero-stereotypes about Malay Filipinos and Chinese Filipinos that later Anglo-American writers will repurpose for their own ideological ends. Writing in 1570, Miguel López de Legazpi, the founder of Spanish Manila and the first governor of the Philippines, conceives of the indigenes as unacceptably blithe about the crucial task of gold-mining: 'Thus does their idleness surpass their covetousness'.[32] Legazpi's bigotry is typical of European thought of the early modern period, which gave rise, according to Robin Blackburn, to racism as an international apparatus of domination legitimated materially by the Atlantic slave trade (of which Spain was a pioneer) and ideologically by new exclusionary conceptions of European modernity, identity and political economy.[33] Legazpi's outrage at the natives' reluctance to fulfil their natural roles as menial labourers is explained in economic terms by the Filipino historian Renato Constantino. Since mineral wealth extraction, he notes, was of little monetary value to the subsistence agricultural societies of Luzon island of the time, indifference to gold-mining had less to do with idleness than with 'the absence of an exploitative class as such'.[34] There was a religious as well as a pecuniary logic behind this contempt towards the natives due to 'the imperative of gaining converts to the Catholic faith' that fostered a 'keeping the Filipinos in line' mood within the Spanish establishment, argues Luis H. Francia.[35] Three centuries after Legazpi, the Spanish literary journalist Pablo Feced Temprano, who owned a farm in the Casmarines Sur province and was a regular visitor to Manila in the 1880s, slandered members of the Tagalog ethnic group as both 'indolent' and so paganistic that it would be difficult to 'elevate [them] [. . .] to the height of the most cultured and civilised people'.[36] Moreover, Richard Chu has written extensively about derogatory Spanish constructions of Chinese Filipinos, elements of which influenced Anglo-American Manilaist Sinophobia. Chapter 5 grapples with this topic in-depth.

At any rate, testimonies such as Legazpi's and Temprano's are rare. If, as John Newsome Crossley notes, there is a 'blind spot' in Spanish colonial historiography then there is an equivalent paucity of primary narrative sources from the Spanish era.[37] The central reason for this, according to historian Paul A. Kramer, is the Spanish Empire's 'stunning metropolitan ignorance of the archipelago' and its accompanying qualms about extracting cultural artefacts and natural specimens for placement in Spanish museums.[38] This disposition was markedly contrary to the thirst for knowledge-as-power that galvanized American botanists, sociologists, anthropologists and 'race scientists' to research the Philippines after the genocidal takeover of the islands by the United States in 1898–1902.[39] Whereas American intellectual curiosity produced copious popular books on the territory, Spanish apathy produced notably few.

In addition, my demarcation of Manilaism has a temporal dimension. For instance, the travelogue *A New Voyage Round the World* (1697) by the English explorer William Dampier and *A New Voyage Round the World by a Course Never Sailed Before*, Daniel Defoe's 1725 roman à thèse, should be considered 'pre-Manilaist' for two reasons. First, they are temperamentally more akin to the generally dispassionate outlook of the early Spanish texts mentioned earlier. Second, they typically avoid the stereotypes and evaluative criticisms of Manilaism proper. Dampier's comment that the 'Spaniards have no place of much strength in all these islands'[40] is a purely descriptive statement and there is no evidence elsewhere in his account that he believes this tenuous state of affairs to present England's empire with an opportunity to oust the Spanish and take the Philippines for itself. Although Jane H. Jack asserts that Defoe's novel is 'designed to enlist the sympathy of its readers for a serious scheme of colonization',[41] there is no proof of this intention in the sequences set in Manila. The visiting English sailors and merchants who are the protagonists of the narrative hold no opinions good or bad about Manila, do not articulate any desire to appropriate the city and enjoy good relations with the Spanish governor, despite the narrator mildly chiding the 'supercilious punctilio' that prevents trade with the colony on land but permits it to take place on board foreign ships.[42] Akin to this, though in a subtextual fashion, *A New Voyage Round the World* provides some discursive blueprints for how subsequent Manilaists would imagine Chinese Filipinos. This is one of the concerns of Chapter 5.

The Manilaist tone alters considerably in the second half of the nineteenth century, when the UK was the Philippines' top trading partner and the United States was massively increasing its imports of cash crops from the recently liberalized colonial economy.[43] One upshot of this new economic landscape was a growing curiosity about the Philippines among Anglo-American readers that exceeded that of their counterparts in Germany, France, Russia and other nations with weaker links to the archipelago. The Scottish businessman Robert MacMicking appears to be aware of this when, in his 1851 travel memoir *Recollections of Manilla and the Philippines during 1848, 1849 and 1850*, he writes, 'I have attempted to give some idea of the actual state and prospects of this valuable colony [. . .] with the [. . .] object of directing more attention to these islands than has been hitherto paid to them by our merchants and manufacturers.'[44] Considerably more material on Manila was published in the United States and United Kingdom than anywhere else outside of the Philippines; of fourteen Manila-oriented memoirs, novels and travelogues released between 1859 and 1900 now located in the University of Santo Tomas archives, only one originated outside of America or Britain. The Filipinas Heritage Library of the Ayala Museum in Manila holds fifty-eight books written by foreigners dating from 1850 to 1900, and that reference Manila to a greater or lesser extent, only three of which were of non-Anglo-American provenance.

Those few eighteenth- and nineteenth-century chronicles of Manila published outside the United States and United Kingdom are typically more sanguine about encounters with people and places. In 1852–5, the Russian novelist and civil servant Ivan Goncharov travelled the world in his capacity as a naval secretary, recording his sojourn in *The Voyage of the Frigate Pallada*. As he is sailing into Manila Bay in February 1854, Goncharov is seized by 'a pleasant feeling of curiosity'[45] about the distant church bells he can hear and, later on, is glowing about the ecclesiastical architecture of the fortified Spanish quarter of Intramuros.[46] These impressions deviate considerably from the habitual vilification of the Roman Catholic Church by his British and American contemporaries, as will be detailed in Chapter 1. Although Goncharov concurs with the Anglo-American Manilaist assumption that Spanish power is waning inexorably, he does not, as per the Britons and the Americans, regard Manila as a failed city in a failed state that might be redeemed by another imperial power:

> On my way to Manila I thought, truth to tell, that the spirit of a fallen, impoverished power would blow on me that I should see desolation and a lack of strictness and order – in a word, the poetry of disintegration. But I was amazed by the well-organized appearance of the town and its cleanliness.[47]

Unlike British and American visitors in the same era, Goncharov refrains from commercially assaying the city and his elaborate renderings of its 'beautiful' (a recurring adjective throughout his text) outskirts appear to be driven by an artist's yearning for 'magnificence and [. . .] poetry'[48] rather than an imperialist knowledge-gatherer's exaltation of, to use Barbara Korte's phrase, 'landscape aesthetics' as an ulterior rationale for land-grabbing.[49] Furthermore, Goncharov is notably nuanced about questions of race and ethnicity, and, in a gesture that is commendably ahead of its time, is inclined to deconstruct the stereotypes that Anglo-American Manilaism deals in almost automatically: '"Why indeed," I thought, "should a Chinese not have fair hair and a red nose just like a European?"'[50] Rather than inciting scorn or anxiety, such cultural and demographic 'incongruities [. . .] very much aroused my curiosity'.[51] Moreover, a note of compassionate pathos rings out in Goncharov's observations of dehumanized *indio* natives: 'they looked exactly like some sort of victuals put out for show between sides of mutton and gammons of ham.'[52] His more balanced dissections of the church, the colonial establishment and Manila's social mélange could have been motivated by several dynamics. He was a radical political liberal and a supporter of the Russian Decembrist movement which stood for republicanism, social equality and the replacement of feudalism with public ownership of land.[53] In addition, his own nation – of which he was a loyal servant – had no interventionist designs on the Philippines and therefore no vested interest in the outcome of the rivalries hatching in the power vacuum opening up as Spanish authority was crumbling. Indeed, according to Martin Green, 'Not until the second half of the nineteenth century did they [the Russians] become English-style merchants, entrepreneurs, and engage in capitalist expansion.'[54] Besides that, Green continues, Russia's limited 'continental imperialism' in Eastern Europe and Central Asia 'was not reflected in the imaginative literature in any way' because 'the conscience' of radical writers like Goncharov, Pushkin and later Tolstoy and Herzen 'was against it'.[55] While the German ethnologist and explorer Fedor Jagor's *Travels in the Philippines* (1875) is less forgiving than Goncharov of the 'uneducated, improvident, and extravagant Spaniards,'[56] it is closer to Goncharov's sensibilities when it eulogizes the 'wonderfully gentle' Spanish laws.[57] Furthermore, that 'it would be difficult to find a colony in which the natives, taken in all, feel more comfortable than in the Philippines' is down, Jagor writes, to the 'uncivilised inhabitants' having 'quickly adopted the rights, forms and ceremonies' of Catholicism.[58] Like Goncharov, Jagor's respect – though qualified – for Spanish governance and his resistance to appraising Manila as a potential conquest is partly determined by the fact that his mother empire had only a slight presence in Asia in the 1870s and would not express a strategic interest in the Philippines until the Spanish–American War two decades later.[59]

If Manilaist texts can be so-designated according to their British and American provenance, they also share certain formal affinities with one another. Whereas in *Orientalism* Said engages with what he admits is a 'broadly construed "field"' of 'theories, epics, novels, social descriptions, and political accounts',[60] my emphasis is somewhat narrower: on popular literary genres – mostly memoirs, travelogues and novels – that have been the Anglo-American public's main source of information about Manila. The novels in particular have, according to Morton J. Netzorg, 'appealed to a mass audience' and had 'some chance of shaping American public ideas or impressions about the Philippines'.[61] As well as prose fiction, Western colonialist travelogues have, so argues Debbie Lisle, a special capacity for 'disseminating the goals of empire' because 'stories of "faraway lands" were crucial in establishing the unequal, unjust and exploitative relations of colonial rule'.[62] As Patrick Holland and Graham Huggan contend, such travel narratives textually produce the non-European world according to Western fixations. The examples Holland and Huggan give include the Congo having been for Joseph Conrad 'a mirror to the dark side of the soul'[63] and plucky Western adventurers regarding the Amazon as a 'happy hunting ground'.[64] Nineteenth-century autobiographical travel writing (which constitutes the majority of early- to mid-Manilaist texts) was particularly effective in this enterprise because it reached a capacious audience and, as Said observes of analogous texts on the Near East, 'contributed to the density of public awareness of the Orient'.[65] I have excluded a number of reference books, scientific studies and other specialist works from the Manilaist trajectory because they do not belong to the popular genres mentioned earlier.

The functions and intentions of Manilaist novels, memoirs and travelogues vary immensely. The American Associated Press[66] correspondent Walter Robb's *The Khaki Cabinet and Old Manila* (1926) uses the format of a travel chronicle to chastise – albeit from a liberal reformist rather than anti-colonial standpoint – the American political class's questionable assertion that the Philippines is not directly run by the United States (see Chapter 5 for further elaboration of this point)[67] while Edward Stratemeyer, author of the boy's own adventure novel *The Campaign of the Jungle, or Under Lawton through Luzon* (1900), declares that he hopes his fictional portrait of the Philippine–American War will have a 'general usefulness [. . .] from a historical standpoint'.[68] Other texts, such as *United States Colonies and Dependencies Illustrated* (1914) by William D. Boyce, are self-professed taxonomies of architecture, urban districts, ethnic groups and civic structures, if heavily infused with personal anecdote. (In the specific case of Boyce, this formal eclecticism may be explained by his career transition from 'the original yellow journalist', who established the *Saturday Blade* newspaper in 1887 to disseminate gossip, scandal and true crime stories, to his later more 'laudable journalistic enterprises' as a didactic Orientalist travel writer dedicated to informing foreigners about 'how the other half live', as a contemporary critic put it.)[69] More heterogeneous still, Robert MacMicking's *Recollections of Manilla and the Philippines during 1848, 1849 and 1850* is something of a patchwork of narratives about notable people and places; polemical screeds on geopolitics and economics; and catalogues of information on media, etiquette, transport, food, drink and accommodation. Whichever ways these books differ superficially in terms of style, structure or aims, they share enough of the same social, political and cultural postulations to together constitute an imaginative geography of Manila in the sense that Said means in his Orientalism thesis. For him, it matters less that Lord Byron wrote poetry, Karl Marx treatises on political economy or Edward William Lane lexicographical guides, and more that these authors viewed the Orient through the prism of – to some extent or another – Western superiority. The same is true of the Manilaist sub-species of Orientalism.

While this book is not a literary history structured in strict chronological order, its earlier chapters tend to engage with Manilaist tropes that originated at the beginning of Manilaism or on historical phases or events of the nineteenth and early twentieth centuries (e.g. Spanish religious rule and the Philippine–American War). Later chapters on the Chinese Filipino community and the Duterte presidency focus more on recent or current affairs. My aim is that the reader will have a good grasp of the full timeline of Manilaism by the penultimate section of this book, which outlines some of the ways creative writers have critiqued or rejected the discourse over many years. If Chapters 1 to 7 try to map out Manilaism's past and present, the somewhat polemical conclusion offers some thoughts about its future, especially with regard to how it may intersect with other Orientalisms in our new age of global political, economic, social and environmental crisis.

Chapter 1 concerns what I dub 'Manila-as-Hell', which is perhaps the most memorable, dramatic and enduring lens through which Manilaists have gazed at the city over almost 300 years. In the mid- to late-1800s, British and American imperial rivalries with Spain and other European states produced a race-based 'Anglo-Saxon' consciousness which regarded Spanish politics, culture and religion (the Roman Catholic Church was a dominant force in the Hispanic Philippines) as fundamentally inferior. These prejudices percolate into the dark, corrupt and supernaturally unsettling visions of writers including the American adventurer Charles Wilkes and the British trader and diplomat Nicholas Loney. In the first third of the twentieth century, when the United States had supplanted Spain as the colonial overlords of Manila, George A. Miller and Walter Robb draw on similar imagery to reinforce a contrast between the barbaric residues of Spanish cultural influence and American promises of moral, social and technological improvement. During and after the Second World War, Western fiction writers, memoirists and correspondents construct a war-torn 'Manila-as-hell' in which the heretical, atavistic Japanese destroyed everything precious that liberal, magnanimous American imperialism had ostensibly introduced to the city: freedom, the rule of law, political progress and Protestantism. When, after the war, the Philippines was recast as a politically unstable client state of the United States, Manilaist demonology finds fresh targets: the toxic ubiquity of superstition; cruel, Faustian hoodlums and *caciques* (thuggish political chiefs); and diabolical scenes of third world (as it was starting to be deemed at the time) poverty caused by Western-directed globalized inequality (although these causes are seldom recognized by Manilaists). Manilas-as-hell at the turn of the millennium coincide with new neuroses about the Philippines' drift away from exclusively Western cultural-economic domination, then-new movements in Western literature such as postmodernism and a keenness to contain the city within primitive, pre-industrial symbolism despite other Asian nations (chief among them China and Japan) now being portrayed as excessively 'Techno-Orientalist'[70] thanks to their perceived contestation of Western economic and scientific regnance.

Chapter 2 discusses Manilaist fiction and travel writing published in the prelude to and during the American conquest of the Philippines, arguably the foundational event in US imperialism, which bore chilling parallels with later campaigns in Vietnam and Iraq. Guided by a number of colonialist and ethnocentric suppositions, William Henry Thomes, Charles King, Edward Stratemeyer, Archibald Clavering Gunter and others mobilize rhetorical devices and narrative strategies to, first of all, subtly enjoin the overthrow of the Spanish in Manila and, later on, omit, distort or excuse the often brutal conduct of the US armed forces in the Spanish–American and Philippine–American Wars. The bulk of these texts belong to what Martin Green, in his exhaustive survey of colonial fiction, *Dreams of Adventure, Deeds of Empire* (1981), defines as the Western 'adventure' novel, whose propagandistic purpose was to mythologize empire and prepare 'young men [. . .] to go out to the colonies, to rule, and their families to rejoice in their fates out there'.[71] The political raison d'être of these myths, Green writes, was to make imperialism 'palatable' to Western readerships by 'obscuring' its flaws, excesses and injustices.[72]

Chapter 3 begins by dissecting Manilaism's Janus-faced stereotypes of Filipinos throughout the US invasion and 'pacification'[73] phases. These representations oscillate in tandem with the United States' rapid revisions of its military and diplomatic strategy; the protean positionality of Filipino and Asian immigrants in Western society; and hegemonic stances towards other socio-ethnic groups in Manila. When the first Manilaists, among them Robert MacMicking and Charles Wilkes, came to the city they regarded the Filipinos they met in much the same way as the Spanish, that is unreliable, docile and ultimately benign 'lazy native[s]'.[74] However, by the time of the boy's own novels of the Spanish–American War of 1898, when the United States was fighting alongside Filipino insurgents against the Spanish, the lazy natives have metamorphosed into brave, decent freedom fighters in stark contrast to the ruthless, totalitarian Spanish. After the overthrow of the Spanish, it became clear that American forces would not be leaving the Philippines and a new conflict broke out between the United States and the Filipino rebels. Some of the same adventure novelists who just a year or two before portrayed Filipinos in a positive light now condemn them as terrorists, torturers and war criminals. At this time, a moral panic gripped US media and literary schema of Americans 'going native'[75] in Manila, risking their physical health and civilizational advantages through exposure to the savage, treacherous behaviour of disease-carrying Filipinos. Over the first half of the twentieth century, Filipinos return to their status as supine lesser beings in line with elite perceptions of the rapidly growing Filipino diaspora in the United States, itself a consequence of the extraction of migrant labour that was a lucrative 'dividend' from the colonial project in the Philippines. Such modelling of Filipinos is also contoured by pseudoscientific racist theories positing '*Homo philippinensis*', the indigenous Filipino, as being close to 'Neanderthal' man.[76] This chapter then conveys how, after the United States had consolidated its control over Manila and the Philippines, travel writers such as William D. Boyce and Frank G. Carpenter apply the same techniques as Stratemeyer, Gunter et al. to discursively negotiate the contradictions of the new American interventionist ideology of 'benevolent assimilation',[77] which depended somewhat uneasily on tropes of modernization, partnership, tutelage and the re-imagining of the Philippines as a submissive, feminized space willing its own exploitation and domination by a foreign aggressor.

Having secured the Philippines from its own people, the Americans set about renovating Manila's roads, homes, businesses, public buildings, parks and canals in order to, as the chief architect of this enterprise Daniel Burnham wrote in a 1905 letter, 'create a unified city equal to the greatest of the Western world with the unparalleled and priceless addition of a tropical setting'.[78] Chapter 4 examines almost a century of writers, from Mary H. Fee in the early 1910s to Timothy Mo in the late 1990s, who imagine Manila as a simulation of an American city, albeit one with imperfections. The notion that Manila, in trying to replicate the best of Western urbanity, has instead been a crude, kitsch spoof of New York or Los Angeles, has always suited Manilaist agendas borne from the Philippines' junior status in international power structures and its role as a heavy importer of US cultural commodities. Transfixed by the Americophile Marcos dictatorship, Manilaists of the 1970s and 1980s seek to legitimize their observations about Manila's 'Pepsicolonisation'[79] by emphasizing the ways in which Manileños have internalized – and are therefore supposedly welcoming towards – the codes of Western simulation. By the 1990s, an almost century-old model of feminine allure has been re-configured by Western memoirists and foreign correspondents who portray Manila as a salacious paradise catering to the Western male libido. As with previous simulations, this one is the logical outgrowth of the Philippines' political and economic subject position as 'hooked up' as the Filipina cultural theorist Neferti Xina M. Tadiar argues,

> to the US desiring machine through a system of flows of labor and capital in the guise of free exchange (export-oriented, capital and import-dependent) but functioning in the mode of dialysis, which gives one the strength and life depleted from the other. As such, the Philippines is, in other words, a hospitality industry, a hostess to 'American' desires, a hooker.[80]

Chapter 5 examines the historical development of a 'supranational stereotype' of Chinese people in the Manila context, which draws on various cultural and ethnic canards about Chinese communities in China, wider Asia and the West. These depictions are highly convoluted because the Chinese community in Manila has historically been demonized by Western visitors, Spanish colonialists and the Malay Filipino population for a variety of contradictory reasons. The Chinese as skinflint entrepreneur is perhaps the oldest hetero-stereotype in the Manilaist repertoire, reaching back to Daniel Defoe in 1725, and bearing common attributes with the anti-Semitic modelling of Jews in Europe. A century or more later, Charles Wilkes and William Henry Thomes conflate disquiet about Chinese migration to the United Kingdom and United States with disquiet about Chinese economic activity in Manila. While these authors revere the enterprising spirit of the Chinese, they are also anxious that the Chinese are depriving other ethnic groups of jobs and opportunities to prosper; a paradoxical formulation not unlike one that British and American newspapers of the time applied to

Chinese migrant workers in London and California. A new paradox came into play towards the end of the century when an ascendant middle class of mixed race Chinese *méstizos* produced both the wealthy businesspeople who shored up the socio-economic status quo and the leading personalities of the Philippine independence movement that sought to overturn that status quo. Manilaism invests this ambiguity in Chinese characters who are outwardly respectable yet ultimately untrustworthy when dealing with Westerners. Although such patent Sinophobia lulled as the twentieth century wore on, geopolitical events intervened to ensure that innuendos about Chinese elitism and money-grabbing survived – though faintly – in the work of Raymond Nelson and Timothy Mo. These texts are arguably responding to the swift rise of the People's Republic of China to regional superpower status and the consequences of this new multilateral world order for the Philippines. However, come the election of President Rodrigo Duterte in 2016, the anti-Chinese sentiment re-ignited, hypocrisy a crucial part of the kindling. At the same time as overlooking or vindicating the exercise of American 'hard' and 'soft' power over the Philippines, Jonathan Miller and other liberal Manilaists exaggerate China's military and economic threat to Manila, the rest of Southeast Asia and the West.

Chapter 6 looks more closely at Duterte and how he constitutes a conundrum to the tenets of modern-day Manilaism. In one sense, Duterte is the apotheosis of Manilaist templates across the ages; he is the ultimate *cacique* – vain, brash, impulsive, anti-democratic and unrepentantly violent – and meets most of the criteria Alain Grosrichard proposes for 'Oriental despotism',[81] as it was articulated by French Enlightenment intellectuals fascinated by the Middle East. However, Manilaism's application of these same criteria to Duterte leaves them open to the same criticisms as their Gallic forebears, not to say the Orientalist scholars Edward Said critiques. The journalists Jonathan Miller and Tom Smith, among others, are quick to denounce the fear, populism, political divisiveness, summary executions and administrative catastrophes of Duterte's Manila, but they are oblivious to the complicity of almost forty years of Western neoliberal policy in contributing to this predicament. Furthermore, these writers' centrist insistence on categorizing Duterte as yet another 'authoritarian populist' more or less interchangeable with Vladimir Putin, Narendra Modi et al. betrays a profound ignorance about the local peculiarities of Duterte's rise and the important differences between his odious politics and those other men's. And, predictably, once again these analyses are hampered by Orientalist double standards, from the assumption that Duterte's mass-murder of 20,000 drug addicts and pushers is qualitatively worse than the millions killed by recent

Western wars of choice, to the notion that Duterte's crimes are more deserving of Western ire than, for instance, Modi's connivance in communal massacres and political assassinations.

In a 2003 retrospective of his career, Edward Said argued that writers and researchers native to the Middle East can contest the 'semi-mythical construct' of Orientalism because 'history is made by men and women, just as it can also be unmade and rewritten, so that "our" east, "our" orient becomes "ours" to possess and direct'. As for those non-natives who want to avoid the problematic simplifications of Orientalism, it is, Said states, perfectly possible to obtain 'knowledge of other peoples' that 'is the result of understanding, compassion, careful study and analysis for their own sakes'.[82] The final chapter of this book evaluates a counter-hegemonic lineage of texts, produced by both Filipinos and foreigners, that have opposed, subverted or deconstructed many Manilaist paradigms. The lyrical essayist Luis H. Francia and the travel writer Maslyn Williams exhibit a refreshing self-reflexivity that acknowledges the fallibility of their observations, research ethics and (in the case of Williams at least) status as Western professional writers reporting on a postcolonial site. This provides a welcome counterweight to Manilaism's arrogant trust in the authority and authenticity of its own gaze. Furthermore, novelists Jessica Hagedorn and Gina Apostol and polymathic author Nick Joaquin defy Manilaism's generalizing caricatures of people and places by subverting those images or writing in the 'shadow'[83] of Filipino rather than Western authors who 'reduce' or 'excise'[84] those aspects of Manila they find distasteful. In this chapter I also demonstrate anti-Manilaism's application of parodic idioms and shadowing techniques designed to variously interrogate and provide alternatives to the clichés of Manilaist prose. Other authors such as Tom Bamforth and Jose Y. Dalisay Jr. meditate on the deep and complex material drivers of the poverty, despair and alienation that Manilaist topographies either take for granted or fetishize, while the travel journalist Madis Ma. Guerrero conveys an alternative Manila whose coordinates of working-class hope, agency, solidarity and community are distressingly absent from the Manilaist sign system.

1

'A Seething Cauldron of Evil'

Hispanophobia, Manila-as-hell and third world blues

Western literature has been likening cities to the Christian hell for at least 700 years. At one end of this spectrum of representations are urban spaces that are mildly redolent of hell or that have hellish features which are explicable rationally in what Tzvetan Todorov, inspired by Sigmund Freud, calls 'the Uncanny'. At the other end of the spectrum are cities that are closer imitations of hell – such as the fiery metropolis of Dis in Dante Alighieri's fourteenth-century poem *Inferno* – as it has been limned in religious texts, and that therefore belong to Todorov's category of 'the Fantastic', where people and places in narratives are only comprehensible in supernatural terms.[1] Furthermore, each textual city-as-hell is shaped by cultural and material determinants specific to its historical moment of origin; for example, Joan M. Ferrante observes that Dante populated Dis with suffering heretics because that sin was 'intimately associated with politics for Dante's audience'. The politics of the time were notable for Pope John XXII's clampdown on opponents who rejected Christian dogma, and the Holy Roman Emperor Frederick II's conflation of religious dissent with sedition.[2]

This chapter analyses how, since the early Victorian era, a significant current within Manilaist writing has marshalled the city-as-hell motif in its constructions of Manila. These representations share many of the characteristics Todorov mentions and, like Ferrante's critique of Dante, can be understood with reference to their various economic, social and political contexts. Moreover, they cohere with Orientalist idées fixe about the inferiority of Eastern beliefs, mores and political-economic structures, as articulated by Edward Said and, more specifically to the thesis of this chapter, Alain Grosrichard, who asserts that French Enlightenment commentators on the Arab world conceived of a 'despotic state' that 'tends to reduce itself to one vast single city, surrounded by an infinity of ruins and fallow land'.[3] Aside from targeting the 'savage' Asians that are the staples of Said's and Grosrichard's Orientalisms, the early exponents of

Manila-as-hell are strongly critical of the reputedly illiberal, impious and arcane Spanish colonial regime in Manila.

The Manila-as-hell model emanated from the mid-nineteenth century when Britain, France, Germany and the United States were expanding their imperial influence over parts of Africa, Asia and the Americas while the Spanish Empire was disintegrating in a process that had begun centuries before. According to Martin Green, right from its genesis in the late fifteenth century the Spanish Empire was plagued with internal divisions and revolts. When King Charles V abdicated the Spanish and Holy Roman thrones in 1554–6, the 'idea of [Spanish] empire was discredited' in the eyes of England, which was at this time starting its own imperial ascent.[4] The Reformation added a theological dimension to England's perception of Spain as a geopolitical adversary and fuelled negative portrayals of Spanish behaviour abroad. As Green avers, 'The cruelty of the Spaniards to their Indian subjects was a constant theme of Protestant moralists everywhere.'[5] The growth of Protestantism was of course synchronous with the growth of capitalism, and Protestant England was able to industrialize in the sixteenth century while the Catholic Spanish Empire could not. In the 1690s, England 'made itself the source of financial credit' and saw itself as a consummate 'mercantile state, and a mercantile world power'.[6] Thus, the nation was well-prepared for the crucial next phase of Euro-imperialism, in which empires '[competed] against each other for the profits to be derived from exploiting the periphery and trading with the arena surrounding the system'.[7] Woefully unprepared for this next phase, Spain lost its West African possessions to Portugal in 1778 and its territories in North America, including West Florida, to the United States in the 1810s and 1820s. By 1865, all of Spain's colonies in Latin America save Cuba and Puerto Rico had gained their independence.

Although Spain was still clinging on to its Philippine colony by the time the first Manilaists Charles Wilkes, Nicholas Loney and Robert MacMicking were active in the 1840s and 1850s, Spanish authority had been rocked by a series of religious-inspired native revolts and the temporary occupation of Manila by the British (1762–4).[8] Until the late 1840s, the British took full advantage of Spain's inability to repress the *Moro* Muslims in the southern Philippines by 'encroaching' on these 'territories' with their navy.[9] Predictably perhaps, these defeats and humiliations informed a consensus among early Victorian Manilaists that Spain was grievously mismanaging Manila due to a combination of anachronistic fiscal policies, administrative incompetence and authoritarian oppressiveness. These writers caricatured *peninsulares* (citizens born in Spain now holding influential posts in Manila society) as brutally and corruptly holding on to undeserved power in a marginal backwater. In 1851, the British trading company Kerr & Co. (which at the time also employed Robert MacMicking's older brother Thomas) sent its rising star Nicholas Loney to Manila to evaluate its investment potential. In his letters – collected and published in 1964, almost a century after his death – he decries the decadence, greed and inertia of the then-governor of Manila, symbolized by his ownership of an excessive '25 horses'.[10] A disciple of free-market dynamism and rationalization, Loney would later run his own firm, Loney & Kerr Co., which sought to increase the efficiency of Philippine sugar production by making loans to farmers and importing state-of-the-art machinery from Europe. Loney embodied a new nexus between Western economic aspirations and political imperatives regarding the Philippines given that, simultaneous to these business activities, he served as the first British vice consul to the Philippines with special responsibility for advising foreign companies on how to penetrate local markets. With similar repugnance towards the Spanish leadership of Manila, Charles Wilkes complains of cigar-smoking officials who devote their three-year terms to enriching themselves,[11] behaving in ways 'so cruel as to be a disgrace to the records of the nineteenth century'.[12] Wilkes was the commander of the United States Exploring Expedition (1838–42), a colossal operation comprising seven ships ranging from 250 to 780 tonnes in size that transported sailors, soldiers, botanists, cartographers, naturalists, a mineralogist and a philologist to dozens of destinations in the Pacific and Atlantic Oceans. The expedition signalled the United States' ambitions to increase its global power by gathering scientific knowledge about 'all doubtful islands and shoals'[13] and by ruthlessly subjugating native populations in Fiji and elsewhere. Funded by Congress and authorized by presidents John Quincy Adams and Andrew Jackson, this staunchly patriotic mission invested Wilkes with a sense of superiority over all the regimes that he visited, Spanish Manila included.

For Orientalists of Wilkes's stripe, having Spaniards ruling in Asia was no less rebarbative than having Asians ruling in Asia. To understand this mentality we can return to Grosrichard's observations about other Asian polities located nearer to the West than the Philippines. 'The despotic City' of the Arab world, he writes, was envisaged by French intellectuals as 'an absurd economy, its only goal the jouissance of the One [the vizier or king], not the country's enrichment'.[14] Rampant graft at the highest level causes an 'internal haemorrhage of wealth' and disincentivizes the masses: 'they do not work, they make no improvement in anything'.[15] This iniquitous and dehumanizing order produces a hellish textual space, 'a silent, dismal desert, haunted by a flock of dispirited victims'.[16] Similarly, the lower-class Malay Filipinos of Spanish Manila are 'idle' in the view of Loney,

Wilkes and Robert MacMicking, because there is little hope of social mobility within this backwardly bureaucratic peripheral site. Like Grosrichard's diabolical *terra nullius* bereft of European modernity, Loney's Manila is a miserably inert environment where 'Energy grows listless and benumbed'.[17]

The common defects between Loney et al.'s Manila and the Grosrichardian despotic city might be explained by the fact that, while the Spanish in Manila were of Western heritage and therefore ought to belong to the same prestigious civilization as the British and the Americans, Manilaism casts them as a lower breed of Westerner. But why? At this time, a variety of politicians and intellectuals were setting forth the doctrine of Anglo-Saxon exceptionalism. One of them, the British Liberal parliamentarian Sir Charles Dilke, proposed the concept of 'Greater Britain' as 'a cohesive racial and political structure for the global diaspora of an Anglo-Saxon race which continued to share the same language and institutions', as Robert J. C. Young views it.[18] According to this conception, Greater Britain included the United States, New Zealand, Australia and parts of Canada, but did not extend to colonies or ex-colonies of other Western European nations (even, it would appear, a nation such as Germany, which could reasonably lay claim to the nomenclature 'Saxon').[19] Anglo-Saxon exceptionalism is covert throughout MacMicking and overt in Loney, who writes, 'Spanish and Anglo-Saxon ideas are so radically different about many things there can seldom be any sympathy.'[20] His conclusion is based on his 'never [having] formed anything approaching to a friendship with a Spaniard' and several personal observations about the demerits of the Spanish 'dons' he has encountered. They are not interested in expanding their knowledge of the world through travel, he claims, and he considers socially inferior those who have retired from employment in the navy to set up as small businessmen.[21] Presumably, given Loney's personal aspirations for high-ranking officialdom and involvement in large-scale commerce, it would be ungentlemanly to abandon honourable service to one's country in favour of low-level petit bourgeois money-making. His more suggestive later remark that Spaniards have too many 'French ideas' and lament that he is 'the only specimen of his race on the island'[22] would appear to be couched in a dichotomy between Spanish and Anglo-Saxon cultural consciousnesses. At the same time as Anglo-Saxonism was being articulated by influential Atlantic Westerners, a corresponding phenomenon known as *Latinidad* was emerging in both Latin America and those Euro-imperialist states whose languages were Latin based. As the Argentine historian Walter D. Mignolo elaborates, the Colombian diplomat José Maria Torres Caicedo drew a cultural and political boundary between 'Anglo-Saxon America,

Danish America, Dutch America' and 'Spanish America, French America and Portuguese America', while French 'intellectuals and state officers [used *Latinidad*] to take the lead in Europe among the configuration of Latin countries involved in the Americas (Spain, Italy, Portugal and France itself), and allowed it also to confront the United States' continuing expansion toward the south'.[23] Tensions between *Latinidad* and non-*Latinidad* interests in the Americas would result in 'the imperial imaginary' regarding 'Latin Americans as second-class Europeans'.[24] Such prejudices towards Spaniards and 'Latins' deriving from the Americas may have been exported to Manila, given the Philippines' colonial ties with Latin America (from the 1560s until the 1820s it was governed indirectly by Spain via the Mexican Viceroyalty) and the fact that many Manilaist writers of this phase and later were widely travelled sailors, traders and diplomats who would likely have been aware of the Latinidad-Anglo-Saxon binary. Certainly, other British and American commentators of the period were. 'The Spaniards of this period,' writes Green, 'were in fact habitually described by nineteenth-century WASP [white Anglo-Saxon Protestant] historians as Visigoths, and as thus full of barbaric vigor'.[25]

It is probable that, in the Manilaist mind, the sloth, greed and tyranny of the Spanish in Manila was not only a congenital fact of their Spanish-ness or Latin-ness but a consequence of their having spent too much time in the East, among Easterners who exhibited those same deficiencies. As MacMicking tellingly writes, 'many of the natives of Spain who are even now selected to fill the highest offices, are about as despotic and as unscrupulous as any Asiatics in their notions of government and in their exercise of power.'[26] In like spirit, Grosrichard shows how European men of letters from Michel Nau to Montesquieu devised 'physical determinist' formulations about climate, biology and racial typology to conclude that Oriental societies are fundamentally authoritarian in character.[27] Tropical weather makes Asians 'excessively sensitive to the least threat of danger' and therefore 'naturally made to be slaves'[28] under sultans who, as a result of the same 'burning-hot climate', suffer from a 'laziness of mind and a lasciviousness of body'.[29] Correspondingly, MacMicking notes that 'the heat of the climate probably disposes' those living in Manila against 'sterner and self-denying mental duties';[30] Spanish soldiers are 'effeminate defenders' and Spanish priests routinely take mistresses despite it 'openly violating' their faith.[31] I unpack the fuller implications of Westerners 'going native' in the Philippines later, for it will become a central component of the long arc of Manilaism.

The more explicitly hellish attributes of Manila come to the fore when MacMicking and his contemporaries turn their gazes towards ambits of the city that bear the stamp of, so these Manilaists construe it, the atavistic and esoteric Roman Catholic Church: Spain's primary hegemonic apparatus in the Philippines. In the tradition of literary adumbrations of cities 'whose forms are systematically distorted to convey a particular mood or quality',[32] these writers describe creepily mystical spaces that confuse and disturb rational, Protestant subjectivity. According to Loney's correspondences from the 1850s, lurid paintings of the inferno inside a church are designed to frighten the public into 'properly attending to their religious duties'. Equally disconcertingly, 'shadows flit [. . .] about' the old walled Spanish quarter of Intramuros 'like unearthly things'.[33] 'Insubstantial shadows' are also to be found in Grosrichard's Oriental terrains, along with 'magic mirrors and talismans', 'deep and silent nights' and other dreamy, not-quite-real phenomena.[34]

Visiting after the United States had annexed the Philippines from Spain in 1898 and established a new colonial state headquartered in Manila, the travel writers George A. Miller and Walter Robb mobilized similarly foreboding imagery but for a slightly different purpose: to elucidate how far the capital has advanced from a backward, Hispanic-Catholic outpost to a modern, (would-be) Protestant-American metropolis. Over the first four decades of the twentieth century, Miller penned a commercially successful series of lavishly descriptive and sometimes nostalgic travel narratives of Panama, China and the Philippines. His *Interesting Manila* (1929) is a portentous-toned recollection of his walks around Intramuros' 'old convents' and 'old monasteries' which barely conceal 'mysteries as dark as black robes'[35] and 'deeds of lust and blood'.[36] He is non-specific about the nature of these mysteries and deeds, alluding only to Spanish-era 'political plotting' and 'ecclesiastical intrigue'.[37] Maybe Miller feels no duty to elaborate given the fundamental incompatibility of this religious and cultural milieu with the mentality of the 'American [. . .] [who] usually turns up his nose because the way of doing things is different from his own'.[38] His final analysis is thus: 'The Anglo-Saxon lives in the concrete, the Oriental in the shadows.'[39] Moreover, although its influence has greatly reduced since the Spanish were ousted, the Catholic Church lingers on like a spectral presence in the new, forward-looking Manila that is connecting itself to international trade and tourism: 'The globe trotter [. . .] has no idea that he treads on the bones of a vanished empire.'[40] In his memoir *The Khaki Cabinet and Old Manila* (1926), Walter Robb suggests that the United States' purportedly more enlightened approach to colonial nation-building – 'a course [that] would entail no injustice upon anyone else, Filipinos least of all'[41] – will preserve a civic infrastructure that had, under the Spanish, been persistently menaced by fires, earthquakes and other, almost biblical *forces majeure*.[42]

Manilaist texts published during and shortly after the Second World War amplify these religious metaphors and employ them against Japan's empire rather than Spain's. On his way home from an assignment in Shanghai, the American Associated Press correspondent Clark Lee stopped off in Manila just before the Japanese invaded it mere hours after their attack on Pearl Harbor. In 1943, he published *They Call It Pacific*, a memoir of that event and his subsequent daring escape through the southern Philippine islands to Brisbane, Australia. A self-proclaimed liberal supporter of the US Democratic Party, Lee is empathetic and even-handed enough to critique the racism of the American colonial state in Manila[43] and acknowledge Japan's economic motives for attacking the Philippines ('To go on playing power politics, they had to gain free access to certain raw materials').[44] However, his descriptions of Japanese air raids on Manila conform to the less progressive paradigms of both faith-driven Orientalism and the city-as-hell repertoire. While the statement 'there was not a time when the night skies of Manila were not brilliant with fires'[45] is borne from a professional journalist's aspiration to disinterestedly document the events he has witnessed, it also recalls the prototypical burning city of Dis in Dante's *Inferno* as well as other textual cities-as-hell set alight by military conflict.[46] Later in the same paragraph, Lee's comparing of the 'death and ruin' caused by the Japanese aggressions to 'Genghis Khan and his hordes of terror'[47] glances back to an earlier generation of Orientalists whose 'view of European superiority over Muslims', holds Felix Konrad, led them to the conviction that Khan was a brutal infidel who would not have conquered large swathes of Asia had Christian 'progress' reached the region in the early Middle Ages.[48] Lee's perspective earned the hegemonic seal of approval from Joseph I. Greene, a US Army colonel who praised *They Call It Pacific*'s 'clearness', 'strength' and 'accuracy' in a glowing review for the *New York Times*.[49]

In his novel *Perla of the Walled City* (1946), the devoutly Christian American author John Bechtel regards war-torn Manila in even more apocalyptic terms: 'blocks – yes, miles – of twisted ruins and grotesque concrete skeletons'.[50] The scene is, in Bechtel's overwrought simile, like 'Mars, the mighty god of War, had tramped down his iron heel and had ground unmercifully The Pearl of the Orient into the dust'.[51] Since Manila – or, more specifically, the church-filled sanctuary of Intramuros – has been desecrated by the heretical Japanese, the beautiful 'Pearl of the Orient' that the Americans constructed between 1898 and 1941 is no more. The severity of Bechtel's approach may have been informed by his lived experience of the Japanese war machine. He was working as a priest for the right-wing, evangelical Christian and Missionary Alliance in Hong Kong when the Japanese invaded in 1941. He and around 3,000 other Westerners were interned for the rest of the conflict.[52] But Bechtel's special sense of hurt and loss about Manila's fate in the war is perhaps related to the fact it had, unlike Hong Kong, Singapore or any other Asian city occupied by the Japanese, been the centre of American power in Asia. Indeed, DeLoris Stevenson in *Land of the Morning* (1956), a chronicle of accompanying her clergyman husband on a post-war mission to the Philippines, regrets how this 'daughter of the American republic'[53] has become a wasteland of 'bombed-out buildings'[54] because the Japanese had blasphemed against the Christian creed by destroying '80% of church buildings' and converting 'churches [into . . .] fortresses during the war'.[55] American 'Popular notions of Japanese religious practices'[56] as barbaric probably influenced Stevenson's faith-based disparagement of the Japanese. Her sentiment is mirrored in US propaganda discourses of the Pacific War, including popular song, which sets up 'a classic struggle of a good (and apparently Christian) United States against an evil enemy in the form of the "heathen" Japanese'.[57] Like Bechtel, Stevenson was a religious conservative (before relocating to the Philippines she was active in Michigan's Capital City Youth Temperance movement), so it is no great surprise that she tacitly endorses this Manichaean, good-versus-evil formula by overlooking American connivance in Manila's destruction when the historical record shows that the 'liberation' of the city in 1945 killed 120,000 and ravaged its built environment, whereas the Japanese invasion of Manila in 1941–2 resulted in considerably fewer casualties and little structural damage.[58] But Orientalist constructions are not necessarily more accurate when they are inspired by 'actual experience of the Orient',[59] as Said contends. Rather, 'the imaginative demonology of "the mysterious Orient"'[60] derives more from a long genealogy of Orientalists cleaving to 'unshakeable abstract maxims about the "civilization" [. . .] [they] had studied; rarely were Orientalists interested in anything except proving the validity of these musty "truths" by applying them, without great success, to uncomprehending, hence degenerate, natives'.[61] In like fashion, Stevenson's commitment to the redemptive capacity of her evangelical beliefs impels her to frame the US church and state in Manila as indisputably positive forces for renewal that are conjuring order from chaos, as in the case of the Union Theological Seminary on Taft Avenue, now 'completely rehabilitated'.[62] It is hard not to uncouple Bechtel's and Stevenson's impressions of Manila as a city doomed by its retreat from Western-Christian hegemony from the historical reality that, as Damon L. Woods argues, 'After World War II, there was an influx of fundamentalist missionaries to the islands' who, taking a typical stance of cultural condescension, 'came to the conclusion that Filipinos were incapable of ecclesiastical leadership'.⁶³ This attitude, too, would appear to be a figment of the American Orientalist imagination given that, in 1902, Filipinos had established the Iglesia Filipina Independiente, a large, influential and well-administrated autonomous church.⁶⁴

Published a year after *Land of the Morning*, a testimony about daily Manila life appearing in the American newspaper *The Catholic Advance*, is a brasher putdown of the city's spiritual waywardness: 'the external activities of [the Philippine Catholic] Church sometimes leave the foreigner wondering if this is the same Catholic Church he knew at home.'⁶⁵ This regrettable misinterpretation of Western Christianity has made Manila a somewhat un-Christian place of 'cacophony',⁶⁶ where men 'shoot craps' behind 'the large figure of the Blessed Virgin' and the parading of the Black Nazarene, a 'black-faced' statue of Jesus, attracts 'an enterprising pickpocket'.⁶⁷ By deploring downtown Manila as a 'seething cauldron of Evil'⁶⁸ for its crime, homelessness and unemployment, the nameless author of this piece implies that the Philippines' sorry excuse for an established church has failed to have a civilizing effect over the populace.

After that *Catholic Advance* story, in the later 1950s and throughout the 1960s, numerous personal accounts of the Second World War in the mould of Clark Lee's were published in the United States. These either construct Manila in much the same fashion as Lee or avoid the city entirely, concentrating instead on military flashpoints elsewhere in the Philippines.⁶⁹ Simultaneously, there were a small number of Anglo-American travel guides, reference books and memoirs – most notably Raymond Nelson's travelogue-cum-history book, *The Philippines* (1968) – that eschewed the city-as-hell mode in favour of Panglossian write-ups of Manila as a vibrant and rapidly developing – if still socially fragmented – urban centre.⁷⁰ It is likely that the authors of these texts – more of whom are addressed in Chapter 4 of this book – were galvanized by a melioristic impulse that the new American-led world order was uplifting the Third World in the face of the (often interrelated) menaces of communism and revolutionary nationalism. When the United States granted the Philippines its formal independence in 1946, leading American politicians were concerned about the new republic gaining too much autonomy over its economy, armed forces and foreign policy. US legislation such as the 'Bell Measure' and the Tydings Rehabilitation Act imposed harmful quotas on Philippine exports while granting preferential treatment to American importers. It also encouraged unfair competition between national and foreign banks which, according to the historian Samuel K. Tan, 'hindered economic development' and 'established the basis of a neo-colonial control of the economy'.⁷¹ Furthermore, the two nations agreed treaties on war veterans' benefits, the absorption of the Philippine military into the US armed forces and the retention of American military bases in the country.[72] As the Cold War was commencing, the stage was set for the new, nominally independent Philippine republic to become a strategic and economic client state of the United States, forming a link in the Asian cordon around communist China and the USSR, and occupying a subordinate role in the 'dollar-imperialist' world order in which '[developing nations] suffered from a degree of dependence on trade with the dollar area'.[73]

However, in life writing of the 1970s and 1980s by P.J. O'Rourke, Ian Buruma, Maslyn Williams and others, the city-as-hell trope is resurrected and infused with what Mary Louise Pratt terms 'third world blues', a tendency within Western travel writing to depict non-Western 'cityscapes' as 'grotesque' and 'joyless'. The attitude is driven by pessimism and unexamined guilt towards societies that had freed themselves from Western colonial oppression, though not from indirect manipulation.[74] Pratt holds that two prime exponents of third world blues, the travel writers Paul Theroux and Alberto Moravia, are oblivious to the global causes of the local quandaries they mention in their respective works because they refuse the 'history tying the North American Theroux to Spanish America or the Italian Moravia to Africa, despite the fact that much of what they are lamenting is the depredations of western-induced dependency'.[75] The more recent research of the urban theorist Tom Angotti elucidates the dynamics of this dependency and how they impact upon Global Southern cities such as Manila. 'Urbanization,' he writes, 'responds to the demand for cheap labor and raw materials in the developed nations of the North' and is at the mercy of 'debt to Northern banks, reliance on oil and other exports, and increasing dependency on food and other products made in the North'.[76] The resulting 'unequal, inefficient sprawled metropolitan growth',[77] Angotti claims, is misunderstood by 'urban orientalist' experts as a problem to be solved by 'the expansion and accumulation of capital in cities' and the 'global marketplace for land and resources', whereas the problem is in actuality produced by those same economic processes.[78]

In exactly the same spirit of denial that Angotti confronts, P.J. O'Rourke in *Holidays in Hell* (1989) portrays a slum in northern Manila as a hell-like 'pile of rotting, burning trash'[79] before holding the actions of President Corazon Aquino, who has recently succeeded the despotic Ferdinand Marcos, responsible for both the regression of living conditions in the slum and for Manila more generally remaining 'the same squalid mess it's always been'.[80] (This comment conforms to Edward Said's contention about Orientalism's 'dogmatic views of "the Oriental" as a kind of [. . .] unchanging abstraction').[81] At no point in his narrative does O'Rourke suggest that blame for the 'mess' could be spread more widely to the Philippines' underling position in the world economic system, which is an epiphenomenon of his own country's global capitalist-imperialist policies. This failure of analysis is almost certainly an upshot of O'Rourke's positioning as 'a former sixties enragé who had turned to democracy, free enterprise, and the American way',[82] as Christopher Hitchens mockingly described him (this being before Hitchens himself made much the same ideological conversion in the early 2000s). Hitchens holds that, despite its global scope with chapters on crises in Africa, Asia and Latin America, *Holidays in Hell* 'repress[es] all flickers of compassion'[83] and is ultimately parochial in its vision: 'everything reminds him [O'Rourke] of California.'[84] However, the posture is unconvincing in an imperialistic world where 'there just haven't been that many international destinations where Ronald Reagan can be made to look any better than he does at home'.[85] In his collection of personal essays on Asia, *God's Dust* (1989; 1991), Ian Buruma, who was later editor of that bastion of US media liberalism, *The New York Review of Books*, offers a diagnosis of Manila's social defects that owes something to his anti-Catholic antecedents in the previous century. After a terse discussion of the Filipino historian Reynaldo C. Ileto's research which 'traces the forms of peasant rebellion back to folk versions of the [Christian] passion', Buruma claims that modern Manileños remain beholden to 'ancestor worship', 'a succession of messiahs' and other primitive customs and beliefs.[86] This is, Buruma hints via the remarks of a Manileño taxi driver he paraphrases, one reason for the prevalence of 'the politicians' quarrelling, the crime, the communists, the lack of any change in the country'.[87] While James Fenton in his book of reportage, *All the Wrong Places* (1988; 2005), is more scathing of American complicity in Manila's political predicaments – he upbraids US foreign policy for making 'the Philippines a nuclear target'[88] and denounces President Reagan's Machiavellian stance towards the Marcos dictatorship as 'absolutely wicked'[89] – his analysis of the regime and its opponents revives a number of problematic religious and supernatural concepts from his literary forebears of the late 1800s/early 1900s. As he tells us in the book, before he goes to the Philippines he is minded by Western press reports to think it a 'strange and fascinating place' where a 'holy war' is being waged by Muslim *Moro* separatists in the south against the Roman Catholic central government in Manila.[90] As with other textual cities-as-hell, vice and corrosive carnality define urban identity, for 'Manila was a brothel'.[91] When Fenton travels to the capital, he discovers that Manileños, rich and poor, powerful and powerless, are fettered by superstition. A group of anti-Marcos protestors who 'quite expected to be shot' take a detour into the Church of Our Lady in Binondo to rest 'under the crucified figure of the Black Nazarene', a dark-skinned statue of Jesus Christ believed by Filipinos to bestow good fortune.[92] When Fenton meets the First Lady, Imelda Marcos, she tells him that her spiritual guide has warned of three omens that will appear before the government collapses: an earthquake that will ravage a church, a volcanic eruption and the seizure of a bridge by opposition activists. After he interrogates the rational validity of this theory – 'some people said [. . .] [the condition] had already been fulfilled [. . .] Others said no'[93] – Fenton asserts his atheism during a conversation with his peasant host – a self-described Christian – in Ilocos Norte province. The meeting ends with his host saying 'firmly: "If you don't believe in religion at all, then there is no reason to discuss these things."'[94] The implication here, perhaps, is that, while Fenton has tried hard – or at least harder than O'Rourke and Buruma – to arrive at an holistic understanding of the political situation in Manila and the Philippines, his Western, rational subjectivity will always prove a barrier to the kind of cross-cultural communication that would permit him to see things as a Manileño or Filipino would. His host appears to acknowledge this bind when, after their tête-a-tête about religious belief, he says, 'You must now start a new subject and we will talk about that.'[95] We will see shortly how this tension about what is knowable and communicable is exacerbated in Manilaist texts published in the 1990s and 2000s.

While the Australian writer and filmmaker Maslyn Williams's 1979 travelogue *Faces of My Neighbour* is a notable exception to the above authors' simultaneous fetish for and distrust of local superstition – not to say their quietism (at least in the cases of O'Rourke and Buruma, if not Fenton) about the neo-colonial damage done to Manila – it is not entirely free of Manilaist ideation. Williams's Manila is, like his contemporaries', permeated by 'strongmen'[96] and 'corrupt and egomanical'[97] officials fawned over by adoring subjects. When Williams is granted an audience with Ferdinand Marcos, he notes that people 'gaze up at him and wait expectantly to be moved, amused, inspired, and made to feel pleased that they have him as their leader'.[98] Likewise, the literary journalist Mark Kram's article on the 'Thrilla in Manila' boxing match from 1975 characterizes Marcos as a 'small brown derringer of a man' whose presence at the Joe Frazier-Muhammad Ali fight compels '28,000' Manileños to brave 'packed and malodorous' public transport to join him there.[99] Congruent assumptions can be found in a discourse of reactionary Western historiography preoccupied with what the Filipino theorist Reynaldo C. Ileto calls '*cacique* democracy'.[100] Ileto argues that mainstream American scholars of the Philippines from the

1950s to the 1990s, such as Stanley Karnow and Alfred McCoy, overstate and exaggerate the problems of 'repressive, manipulative' governance, election-rigging, graft, 'clientilism' and clannish 'factionalism'[101] in order to assert that 'the tragedies and problems of the present are the consequence not so much of American intervention as of the tenacity of Philippine traditions'.[102] In alignment with the third world blues hypothesis, the figure of the tyrannical, impassioned *cacique* chief at once embodies Western cynicism about Filipinos' fitness to govern themselves in the postcolonial era and vindicates Western neo-imperialist meddling in Philippine affairs. While Kram, Williams, O'Rourke and the other life writers of the 1970s and 1980s do not make explicit comparisons between the *cacique* and the Christian Devil, shared traits are discernible. According to Christian demonology, the Devil intimidates mortals into doing his evil bidding[103] or, as in the myth of Faust, manipulates them with offers of magical powers.[104] This dialectic of rule by terror and rule by inducement is, from a Manilaist perspective, not too remote from the mechanics of the cults of personality propagated by Marcos and the other demonic lords of textual Manilas-as-hell.

In novels published after 1989, these and other supernatural images intensify to a degree that eclipses even the fire-and-brimstone theatrics of Lee and Bechtel. After Cold War rivalries ended, the Philippines' geopolitical value to the United States reduced, American bases in the republic were shut down and the Philippines struck a series of aid, trade and credit deals with China,[105] Japan[106] and South Korea.[107] That Manila's deeper descent into hell may be a consequence of such a departure from the Western sphere of influence is indicated by one of the Filipino characters in Alex Garland's thriller novel *The Tesseract* (1998). He says that the Spanish conquistadors of the 1570s had God on their 'side'[108] when they colonized the archipelago; the concomitant point here, perhaps, being that God may be displeased now the Spanish – and other Western powers – have lost control over the territory. Compared to the *caciques* or *cacique*-like characters in Fenton, Buruma and O'Rourke, the antagonists of *The Tesseract* and other Western fictions of the late twentieth/early twenty-first centuries are inordinately cruel, devious and ferocious. Informed by the intertextual and ahistorical conventions of postmodernism, these caricatures belong firmly to the Western pulp horror/thriller genre. The pages of both *The Tesseract* and Timothy Mo's graphically violent picaresque *Renegade or Halo²* (2000) are populated by maladroit, Quentin Tarantino-esque hitmen, while in the latter text a Manileño mobster looks like a 'Mexican bandido, El Jefe from a Sam Peckinpah movie'.[109] These symbolic standards, selected from fifty years of Hollywood film and more than a century of lowbrow paperbacks, reveal more about the political climate and means of cultural production of late-twentieth-century Britain and the United States than anything of import about Manila. Fredric Jameson, in his study of American 'nostalgia films' of the 1980s, asserts that the crime movie *Body Heat*'s (1981) blending of a 1930s aesthetic with 'a contemporary setting' demonstrates that Westerners are 'unable to focus our own present, as though we have become incapable of achieving aesthetic representations of our own experience. But if that is so, then it is [...] an alarming and pathological symptom of a society that has become incapable of dealing with time and history.'[110] Transposing Jameson's thesis to Mo and Garland, we might propose that these writers are incapable of expressing much of value or meaning about the real 'time and history' of Manila because they are engrossed by projecting onto the city idioms cannibalized from representational schemes that are firmly embedded in Western popular culture and that have little or no connection to the Philippines or Asia. So, while Mo and Garland's postmodernist approach marks a new stylistic direction for the canon in one sense, in another it is far from new because, as we have seen, previous generations of Manilaists have also plundered the Western cultural imagination for concepts such as the Judeo-Christian city-as-hell itself.

Furthermore, these 1990s narratives are decidedly less naturalistic and more imaginative in their depictions of the supernatural than any of their (fictional or nonfictional) predecessors. In Garland's Manila, hotels appear 'undead' or remind his British protagonist Sean of 'concrete corpses'.[111] A graveyard is infested with 'an army of ancestral spirits, seething in the still air around the tomb, peering out of the statues' eyes'.[112] Like a merciless Devil type, the *cacique*-like mobster Don Pepe 'moves in mysterious ways' in a turbid moral universe when ordering the maiming of one lieutenant for a petty offence and then forgiving another for the mass-murder of innocents.[113] Various faiths and religions have posited hell as a zone subject to almost inconceivably different physical laws to those of the phenomenal world, including time.[114] Hence, Sean in *The Tesseract* feels as if he is waiting for an eternity in flummoxed anguish to rendezvous with the criminals he has wronged, and that Manila's otherworldly temporality can never be understood, at least not by a Western outsider: 'What about ten minutes ago? Or was it fifteen? Whatever. Ten, fifteen, he'd been a headless chicken.'[115] Ultimately, the entire textual time and space of *The Tesseract* is an unfathomable puzzle articulated by the guiding motif of the novel: 'A tesseract is a four-dimensional object – a hypercube – unravelled.... We can see the thing unravelled, but not the thing itself.'[116] In the same vein, 'Everything [is] thrown into question' in *Ghosts of Manila* (1994), James Hamilton-Paterson's arguably more unsettling conception of the city.[117] Like a splatter movie script, the novel begins with a cinematic sweep across the gruesome preparation of corpses for the illegal trade that, 'smacking of Burke and Hare',[118] supply skeletons to medical researchers: 'Two of the men now take down butcher's knives from a magnetic rack [. . .] . One takes the upper half of the body, the other lower. Deftly they remove the arms and legs.'[119] The environs of this Manila-as-hell are reminiscent of the farthest circles of Dante's hell, with 'water [. . .] bubbling fiercely'[120] in place of the River Styx where 'Beneath the water people are who sigh / And make this water bubble at the surface';[121] and the 'perpetual slime of the squatter areas' and 'noxious black estuaries'[122] in lieu of the Styx's 'putrid water'.[123] Furthermore, like the nightmarish city of Dis, Hamilton-Paterson's Manila is a holding tank for every Dantean sinner imaginable: thieves, liars, pederasts and murderers. Whereas in the post-war novels of Bechtel and Stevenson, Manila is faintly redolent of hell, and its hellish incidents and topographical features situated within the parameters of reason, the Manila of both *The Tesseract* and *Ghosts of Manila* is a more direct, thoroughgoing signifier for the Place of Torment. As Alberto Manguel puts it in his review of *Ghosts of Manila*, 'Hell is the present-day Philippines.'[124] That 'sane people chose'[125] to believe in paranormal creatures such as a hybrid bat-woman (that may have been inspired by the *manananggal* of Philippine mythology) who sucks the livers out of babies suggests that, like Dante's *Inferno*, Hamilton-Paterson's fictional universe belongs to the Todorovian rubric of the 'Fantastic',[126] since it often frames supernatural phenomena as natural and self-evident. At the same time, Hamilton-Paterson's persistent questioning of the veracity of characters who witness or report on preternatural events, such as journalists who write 'vampire stories' to discredit local officials,[127] places *Ghosts of Manila* in the 'Marvellous' camp because, as the Todorovian scholar Andrzej Wicher puts it, 'the reader, and sometimes also the acting characters, cannot feel certain as to the nature of the narrated, or observed, events: they may be supernatural, but this remains only a supposition or hypothesis.'[128] Either way, the novel is a striking departure from the more realist fictions of Bechtel and Stevenson, which deploy hell and the mystical as ciphers for ideas or emotions, as is more typical of 'Uncanny' narratives.[129]

These later writers' appeals to religious argot are at odds with contemporary Western literary and cinematic portrayals of other Asian cities, particularly those in China and Japan. 'Whereas Orientalism as a strategy of representational containment,' write David S. Roh, Betsy Huang and Greta A. Nui, 'arrests Asia in traditional, and often premodern imagery, Techno-Orientalism presents [. . .] an "Orient" undergoing rapid economic and cultural transformations'.[130] In its arresting of Manila in such premodern idioms as hell, sin, curses and mythical beasts, the system of signification into which we can slot Garland and Hamilton-Paterson is in an arrested state itself by not having evolved in step with parallel Techno-Orientalist modes. As with previous iterations of the Manila-as-hell configuration, the disparity might be ascribed to transformations in the power relationship not only between the Atlantic West and the Philippines, but also between East and West over the last thirty years. As Martin Jacques contends, China, Russia, Japan and India have been growing in prosperity, military strength and scientific capability at a rate that poses a substantial threat to United States and Western European global hegemony.[131] As yet, the Philippines lacks the material means to join that order of nations and has not been imagined in the terms of Techno-Orientalism, which often fetishizes and exaggerates progress in 'the East'.

A recent text that stitches many of these past iterations of city-as-hell into a single imagined territory is Dan Brown's cliché-peppered potboiler *Inferno* (2013), the title being a patent reference to Dante. Subtlety is not a priority. Manila is, Brown writes, 'the gates of hell'[132] and as soon as his British doctor character Sienna Brookes enters them she is shocked and appalled by every urban Manilaist boilerplate in the cupboard: the 'shantytown – a city made of corrugated metal and cardboard',[133] the 'masses of people',[134] 'the young men approaching, salivating like wolves',[135] 'the stench of human excrement [hanging] ... in the air',[136] 'the six-hour traffic jams, suffocating pollution, and a horrifying sex trade'.[137] While this vision is nowhere near as vividly imaginative as Garland's and Hamilton-Paterson's, it is considerably more hysterical, not to say more insulting to Manileños. This extreme perspective makes sense if we once again place the lens of third world blues over it, for *Inferno* emerges from a period during which the Philippines was growing financially and diplomatically closer than ever before to non-Western states such as China[138] and Japan.[139]

In this chapter I have examined variations on the city-as-hell motif as they have been overlaid on Manila, from violence of both the interpersonal and large-scale military varieties to sin, corruption, poverty, urban decay, incoherent religiosity and supernatural menace. Like Said's discourse of Orientalism, these ideologically informed constructions 'are particularly valuable as a sign of European-Atlantic power over the Orient'.[140] While the exact extent to which these constructions have 'enabled' – to use another of Said's designations – hostile and/or exploitative Western policy in Manila and the Philippines is hard to ascertain, clearly they have provided an 'accepted grid for filtering through the Orient into Western consciousness'.[141] Even with that in mind, we should not overstate the socio-political influence of the texts I have considered in this chapter. That said, they are components of a popular cultural discourse that was hegemonic and therefore more likely than other, competing discourses to mould public opinion about the Philippines. After reading DeLoris Stevenson, for instance, a member of the American electorate may have been more inclined to support their government's intentions to reconstruct post-war Philippines in America's image, as a semi-dependent, laissez-faire capitalist pseudo-democracy. Forty years later, having read *The Tesseract* an Englishman or woman of a certain ideological bent might well have felt a pang of colonial nostalgia about the days when Western empires dominated cities like Manila, given how the metropolis had deteriorated so dramatically since that time, according to Garland's depiction. In the case of Dan Brown's *Inferno*, the impact was more immediately measurable because it triggered a controversy in Philippine public life. The chairman of the Metro Manila urban region, Francis Tolentino, wrote an open letter accusing Brown of an 'inaccurate portrayal of our beloved metropolis. [. . .] We are displeased [by] how you have used Manila as a venue and source of a character's breakdown and trauma, much more her disillusionment in humanity'.[142] As we have seen, Brown was by no means the first Western author to render Manila as a psychogeographical hell. Indeed, the acuteness and severity of *Inferno*'s imagery shows that neither literary history nor actual history have changed as significantly as some might have hoped. That ethnocentric fear, anxiety, contempt and condescension continue to animate Manilas-as-hell after all these years is not only because some literary conventions die hard but also because, while we are no longer living in the Age of Empires or through the Cold War or the 'New World Order'[143] of the 1990s and early 2000s, Global Northern countries like Britain and the United States continue to exploit Global Southern countries like the Philippines. According to the political theorist M.G.E. Kelly, this 'parasitical' arrangement contributes to the 'pitiful conditions'[144] of many Global Southern cities blighted by hunger, 'environmental devastation'[145] and 'inadequate medical and educational systems'.[146] All of which suggests that the Orientalist city-as-hell is unlikely to disappear from Western letters until these political and economic relations between North and South alter drastically.

2

'Known to All Students of History'

Adventure, imperial mythology and Orientalist rhetoric in Manilaism of the US conquest of the Philippines

'The 1899 Philippine–American War is not the sort of topic the Filipino public likes to talk about', writes Reynaldo C. Ileto.[1] There is an equivalent absence of the event from American political, media and literary discourses and it remains to this day 'The war we forget',[2] according to the economic historian Hugh Rockoff. One reason, Ileto continues, is that 'to imagine Filipinos warring with Americans simply contradicts the dominant tropes of the Philippine–American relationship [. . .] expressed in kinship terms'.[3] When justifying foreign military adventurism over the last century, US elites have preferred the fustian of 'kinship', 'aid' and 'humanitarian intervention'[4] to idioms such as 'imperialism', 'colonialism' or 'conquest'. Arguably, this inclination has been informed by two slightly differing hegemonic perceptions about the Unites States' role in world affairs: first, its reticence to self-identify as an empire at all – as scholars on both the political left and right have contended[5] – and second, its view of itself as an 'international policeman'[6] whose occupations of foreign lands are necessary to confront tyranny and promote democracy, human rights and prosperity. From the conquest of the Philippines to the present day, both perceptions have been underpinned by the conscious efforts of statesmen and policy-makers to distance American conduct abroad from the violence, racism, autocracy, acculturation and exploitation associated with the older European empires that directly ruled large swathes of the globe from the eighteenth century until the middle of the twentieth century. In 1898, shortly after the United States formally took possession of the Philippines, President William McKinley wrote, 'we come, not as invaders or conquerors, but as friends'.[7] Earlier that year, he had explicitly criticized Spanish colonialism in Cuba and its 'cruel, barbarous and uncivilized practices' towards 'a dependent people striving to be free',[8] while claiming that America's mission was 'to put an end to the barbarities, bloodshed, starvation, and horrible miseries now existing there'.[9] Furthermore, said McKinley, 'I speak not of forcible annexation, for that cannot be thought of. That, by our code of morality, would be criminal aggression.'[10] Whenever American presidents since McKinley have ordered military assaults on smaller nations, they have explicitly denied imperialist objectives and invoked McKinley's argot of security, protection and justice. After sending marines to the Isthmus of Panama in late 1903, President Theodore Roosevelt said 'the United States should control, police, and protect the [Panama] canal' and assume 'the position of guarantor of the canal and of its peaceful use by all the world'.[11] In 1965, at the height of European decolonization in Africa and Asia, President Lyndon B. Johnson said of American entanglement in Indochina, 'we want nothing for ourselves, only that the people of South Vietnam be allowed to guide their own country in their own way'.[12] By time of the postcolonial moment of the early twenty-first century, when European-style settler colonialism and military imperialism were widely seen as monstrous and anachronistic, George W. Bush said in the prelude to the 2003 US-led invasion of Iraq, 'If we must begin a military campaign, it will be directed against the lawless men who rule your country and not against you. As our coalition takes away their power, we will deliver the food and medicine you need.'[13] After the NATO bombing of Libya in 2011, Barack Obama announced, 'Confronted by [Qadaffi's] brutal repression [. . .] [we] had a unique ability to stop that violence: an international mandate for action [based on] [. . .] a plea for help from the Libyan people themselves.'[14] Martin Green avers that this yearning to distance the United States from the older imperial powers dates back to at least the time of the romantic author James Fenimore Cooper (1789–1851), when many Americans believed their country could achieve a 'less threatening future greatness' by not emulating the territorially acquisitive modus operandi of 'land-powers' such as France, Russia and Austria. Rather, so this doxa had it, the United States should aspire to Britain's 'sea-power' status, which made it the 'right' kind of empire because it was 'essentially a trading nation, and the home of liberty'.[15] The distinction made here between Britain and the other European empires is highly disputable since the former was not exactly averse to large-scale land-grabbing itself. That said, such special pleading for the superiority of the British was probably due to a feeling of kinship with 'the old country' from where most Americans had emigrated. It was no doubt ethnically and racially informed too; we saw the significance of Anglo-Saxon identity to Manilaism in Chapter 1.

As Bush and Obama were to do later in different contexts, McKinley framed the US attack on the Philippines as a rescue operation to save innocents from the clutches of dictatorship. But, as with Iraq and Libya, the real-life outcomes of the campaign were far from humanitarian. After the United States declared war on the Spanish Empire in April 1898, it informally assured Filipino nationalist rebels led by Emilio Aguinaldo that, if they allied with the Americans to overthrow the Spanish colonial regime in the Philippines, the rebels would be free to found an independent republic.[16] As soon as the Spanish were defeated, the Americans reneged on this offer and a confrontation with Aguinaldo's forces ensued. One-sixth of the population (200,000–250,000 people) was killed in the conflict due to – as was to be the case in the Vietnam War – the US army's reluctance to distinguish between civilians and combatants (villages were routinely torched and some commanding officers explicitly ordered the slaughter of women and children), and its tactic of 'strategic hamleting' that caused widespread starvation and disease.[17] The Philippine–American historian Dylan Rodriguez designates the US operation a 'genocide' stimulated by the same devotion to 'white supremacy' that signalized the massacres of Native Americans in the late nineteenth century.[18]

With very few exceptions, US popular novels, memoirs and travelogues of the period omit, downplay, distort or offer 'obfuscatory justifications'[19] for US misconduct in the war. This should come as no surprise when we recognize that these texts align with Martin Green's category of the colonial adventure novel, which typically portrays

> a series of events [...] in settings remote from the domestic and probably from the civilized (at least in the psychological sense of remote), which constitutes a challenge to the central character. In meeting this challenge, he/she performs a series of exploits which make him/her a hero, eminent in virtues such as courage, fortitude, cunning, strength, leadership, and persistence.[20]

At the same time as foregrounding these ideals, Manilaist adventure stories deploy various technical devices in order to, among other things, reassure young male readerships of the historical verisimilitude of their truth claims and to 'excise' and 'reduce' morally and politically uncomfortable aspects of the conflict.[21]

To grasp the full historical and ideological impact of these formal approaches, it is necessary to begin by investigating a current of Manilaism that predates the American assault on the Philippines but nonetheless evinces annexationist ambitions over the territory. Such ambitions are latent in the cocksure fashion by which Manilaist writers delineate the imaginative geography of Manila. The narratologist H. Porter Abbott notes that 'narrative is always a matter of selecting'; a writer's gaze will never encompass everything about the site he or she is trying to represent nor offer a fully rounded, balanced or neutral transcription of that site.[22] In colonial discourses, the 'commanding view' metropolitan writers take of peripheral sites, argues the literary critic David Spurr, is a conscious act of selection intended to 'convey a sense of mastery over the unknown and over what is often perceived by the Western writer as strange and bizarre'.[23] The consequence is 'the organisation and classification of things [that] takes place according to the writer's own system of value'.[24] Although for Spurr the commanding view is used by ethnocentric travel writers to stress their racial-cultural advantages over what they perceive as unevolved societies, the concept can, I think, be repurposed to comprehend the authorial perspective of Nicholas Loney, whom I first discussed in Chapter 1. Rather than assuming mastery over a primitive, native-ruled location, Loney takes a 'monarch of all I survey'[25] standpoint on the social and economic stagnation of late Spanish colonial governance of Manila. He frames the city by structuring his narrative as, so to speak, a virtual tour that he as narrator leads the reader on: 'Let us in imagination cross together the fine bridge. [. . .] Do you see those provincial crafts of queer shape and dimension?'[26] Loney's direct addressing and rhetorical questioning of the reader implies an interactivity between author and reader, which in turn might convince the reader to trust in the veracity of Loney's observations, whether they are trivial asides about a 'not ignoble looking building by the river side' or damning value judgements about the retardation of Manila's development by Spanish bureaucracy: 'Enterprise grows faint and languid.'[27] Free of self-doubt or self-questioning, Loney's commanding view is symptomatic of Manilaist representations and is a mechanism by which discourses of imperial power, argue Ashcroft, Griffiths and Tiffin, operate under the illusion that their significations of the periphery are 'authentic' and 'normative'.[28] Thus, when Loney makes his mild jibes at the Spanish – as per the quote earlier about enterprise – he does it with an air of certainty which has the rhetorical effect of convincing the reader of his accuracy and validity. Furthermore, while Loney never overtly calls for the overthrow of the Spanish by one of the Anglo-Saxon empires, his critique of them is consistent with later Manilaists who do call for it.

Correlative sentiments lurk behind the formal decisions other Victorian writers make about depicting the man-made and natural environments of Manila. If, as we saw in Chapter 1, Robert MacMicking and Charles Wilkes are despondent about the Spanish-constructed districts of Manila, they are cheerier when they gaze upon the natural beauty surrounding these places. In true romantic spirit, MacMicking's adjective-rich descriptions of the countryside bordering Manila ('fine river', 'ripe and yellow grain', 'splendid old trees')[29] and Wilkes's affection for the 'luxuriant scenery' around the buildings that bear 'evident marks of decay'[30] could have the ulterior motive of, as Barbara Korte has averred of Orientalist travel writing on other regions of the non-Western world, using 'landscape aesthetics [...] to veil the ambition to conquer the land'.[31] Other clues that steer us towards this inference include Wilkes's doubts, voiced later on in his short narrative, about 'how long it [Spanish rule] can continue'[32] and his assertion that English and Dutch tax procedures are preferable to Spain's. Similarly, at various points in his *Recollections*, MacMicking censures Spanish theocracy, metropolitan planning and commercial ineptness. By 1872 and the publication of the American seafarer and author William Henry Thomes's novel *Life in the East Indies*, this nature-culture binary has evolved into an affirmation of the improving potential of American technological knowhow and business acumen. Conforming to the directive of 'classic writing style' to place the most important idea at the end of a sentence or paragraph,[33] the vivid scene-setting of 'cocoa-nut trees, mango trees, and luxuriant vegetation'[34] at the start of *Life in the East Indies* concludes with the presence of 'the buzz of a thousand spindles, and the panting of a steam engine':[35] on first glance an anomalous phenomenon given Thomes's claim earlier about 'the Spaniard's aversion to [...] any innovation upon the forms of his ancestors'.[36] But the engine, we learn, drives a lucrative rope-making factory that 'was formed by American energy, carried through by American intelligence [...] entirely under American control, and owned entirely by American capitalists'.[37] Thomes's somewhat jingoistic preoccupation with this aspect of Manila's geography (soon after the quote he dedicates two pages to jubilant exposition of the origins and operations of the real-life Massachusetts company owning the factory) is arguably a product of both his personal interests in industrial development and his positioning within wider historical conditions. An obituary in the 7th March 1895 edition of the *San Francisco Chronicle* records Thomes's concerns about the inefficiency of a mule-powered flour mill he visited in Yerba Buena, California. The primary blame for the inefficiency lay with the mill being 'superintended by the laziest [Mexican] native he had ever seen'.[38] Thomes was making such observations during, as it were, the material 'prelude' to the American military assault on the Philippines two decades later: the increasing presence of US- and European-owned industrial sites in Manila. According to Renato Constantino, the liberalization of Philippine trade and industry in the late nineteenth century saw a marked increase in US and other foreign investment in cordage, cement and cigarette manufacture, among other sectors.[39]

The ideological disposition of these Manilaist authors is also apparent from their selection of specific words, phrases and ideas as well as topographical features. I have found it useful here to draw on Edward Said's concepts of 'excision' and 'reduction'[40] of foreign cultural phenomena. Said holds that the British Egyptologist Edward William Lane (a contemporary of many of the authors examined in this chapter) was so anxious about the reaction his Western readers would have to the radical otherness of Egyptian sexual mores that he, Said writes, consciously 'excised from [the Orient] what, in addition to his own human sympathies, might have ruffled the European sensibility'.[41] Another of Lane's signifying practices was to understate, argues Said, '[the Orient's] odd calendars, its exotic spatial configurations, its hopelessly strange languages, its seemingly perverse morality'. Such 'eccentricities of Oriental life' were 'reduced considerably when they appeared as a series of detailed items presented in a normative European prose style'.[42] According to Said, other Orientalists have applied the reduction strategy to non-Western political situations, as illustrated by the conservative historian Bernard Lewis's 'condescension' towards development in the Arab world: 'Revolution is excitement, sedition, setting up a petty sovereignty – nothing more; the best counsel (which presumably only a Western scholar and gentleman can give) is "wait until the excitement dies down".'[43]

Throughout MacMicking's *Recollections*, excision and reduction of Philippine politics operate in close symbiosis. For the sake of legitimizing the potential usurpation of Spain by another empire – ideally the one of which he is a subject – he must diminish Spain's record of governance (as we have seen earlier) while simultaneously downplaying or flatly ignoring nationalist militancy perhaps for fear it will dissuade Britain or the United States from deeper involvement in the archipelago. The nearest he gets to acknowledging such militancy is a peculiar anecdote about 'a party of young men' who would nightly sail a cargo boat into Manila's lagoon and fire guns at the buildings on the banks.[44] When MacMicking writes these sorties off as mindless acts of mischief by *tulisanes* (brigands) whose leader was 'one notorious for his love of fun, and what are called practical jokes',[45] he is at one with the official rhetoric of the Spanish colonial state of the time that regularly dismissed revolutionary activity as banditry.[46] MacMicking goes no further in evaluating these men's motives or demands, even though, given the political conditions of the 1850s, it is possible if not likely that they were anti-colonial resistors, if not necessarily well-organized ones. Laguna province had long been a hotbed of insurrection and, in 1840, just a few years before *Recollections* was published, its population had supported Hermano Pule's founding of the Cofradía de San José, the *indio* (indigenous)-only religious order that the Spanish saw as treasonous.[47] Given that Filipino historians such as Renato Constantino and Luis H. Francia have used voluminous primary sources to expose the full extent of anti-Spanish rebellion across the Philippines throughout this phase, we might conclude that MacMicking's omission is deliberate. But leaving aside the insights that intertextual confirmation can give us and casting a more formalistic eye over MacMicking's text, the internal contradictions of his account suggest that the actions of these 'robbers',[48] as he eventually deems them, are excessive if indeed they are mere robbers. Obtaining firearms, commandeering a boat and effectively declaring war on the state (and, MacMicking tells us, resulting in 'great efforts to put down the daring troop')[49] do not seem like the actions of petty or even organized criminals. Supposing we take MacMicking at his word, he does not go on to claim that these men have stolen or tried to steal anything from the neighbourhoods they have bombarded. Stranger still, they take great care 'not to do harm or to kill any one'[50] – behaviour more aligned, perhaps, to the freedom fighter's ethic of not hurting the very people he or she seeks to liberate.

Deviating slightly from MacMicking's line of enquiry, in his 1859 travelogue *A Visit to the Philippine Islands*, John Bowring, British governor of Hong Kong from 1854 to 1859, does mention at least a smattering of the copious uprisings by Chinese Filipinos and other subaltern groups throughout the history of the archipelago thus far. Be that as it may, he does not reflect on the nature of these groups' grievances against Spanish rule. Moreover, he claims, at the time of writing 'the public tranquillity of her [Spain's] island colonies was, on the whole, satisfactorily maintained, and interruptions to the ordinary march of affairs of short endurance'.[51] In the same mode, Charles Wilkes reports that 'Rebellions and revolts among the troops and tribes are not unfrequent in the provinces'[52] without elaborating on the aims or objectives of these rebellions and revolts.

Set during the first stage of the US appropriation of the Philippines, when the Americans were attempting to drive the Spanish out of Manila, Archibald Clavering Gunter's novel *Jack Curzon* (1898) is replete with the same kinds of reductions and for the same purposes. In one scene, the *méstiza* (mixed American-Filipina) character Maud Gordon breezily critiques anti-colonial aspirations when, during chatter with some US Navy officers at a Manila club, she refers to the political situation in Cuba (which, like the Philippines, the

United States has attacked under the pretext of aiding insurgent factions against the Spanish):

> 'Oh I believe there is a revolution or rebellion there or something of the kind,' replies the girl [Maud], and they all go into an Annapolis gossip as she tells them how Mrs. Rear-Admiral Dawson snubbed Mrs. Commodore Brown, and that Miss Sally Jenkins was the belle of the last graduation hop.[53]

Gunter relegates this seismic development in imperial geopolitics to an aside about local tittle-tattle. US involvement in it is excised. While Maud's political naivety could be read as a sine qua non of her gender – Gunter was a conservative Victorian patriarch who, elsewhere in the book, makes a number of essentialist and misogynistic claims about women as 'impulsive', 'vindictive' and 'fickle'[54] – his male characters, who ought to know something about international relations, are just as dismissive of or ignorant about the Cuban and Philippine struggles for self-determination. When the eponymous hero of the novel, a British shipping clerk, first learns of the rebels' siege of Manila, he nonchalantly states, 'Apparently something political and military is taking place even now.'[55]

Curzon's employment as a clerk is not just incidental, it makes him a protagonist who represents what Martin Green dubs the 'mercantile caste' (comparable characters propel the fictions of Daniel Defoe, Samuel Richardson and John Buchan)[56] in an archetypal 'capitalist adventure' story that expresses the importance of enterprise, industry, hard work and international 'luxury trade'[57] to the Western imperial programme. By the late 1800s, writes Green, luxury crops grown in the periphery such as 'coffee, tea' and 'tobacco'[58] were raising enormous profits on the metropolitan markets, and it is these commodities that feature prominently in both the real Manila of the 1890s and in the textual Manila of *Jack Curzon*. We learn early on that Maud's father is in trouble with the Spanish authorities for smuggling tobacco out of Manila, and Jack Curzon along with the other main characters of the piece such as the double-crossing German businessman Adolph Ludenbaum repeatedly glorify Manila as an axis of global exchange. These elements of the narrative gesture to the real-world economic determinants behind the United States' appetite for acquiring Manila and the Philippines.

Another manoeuvre typical of Manilaism's narrow purview is the application of the passive voice, a grammatical formulation that the socio-linguist Norman Fairclough holds is guided by 'ideological choices to [. . .] background agency' because 'action[s]' are described without 'responsible agents' or 'attributed state[s]'.⁵⁹ Although the passive voice was a more commonplace feature of literary style in Stratemeyer's time than it is today, partly because, as the linguist Geoffrey K. Pullum contends, '19th-century writers on grammar and usage explained the structure and function of passives without any negative spin',⁶⁰ MacMicking applies the mode more strategically. In the following passage, notice how a passive construction sweetens the pill of his suggestion for outside intervention in the southern Philippine islands (the italics are mine): 'There is little doubt that *were foreigners allowed* to settle at Zamboanga, Zooloo, Mindanao, and the entire southern coasts of the Philippines would be open to their enterprise, it would be productive of the most beneficial effects.'⁶¹ The use of the passive verb form 'were allowed' absolves MacMicking – ever the discreet Victorian gentleman – from revealing quite how foreigners would or could be allowed to settle in these regions. An obvious risk of occupying territories within Spain's jurisdiction would be military confrontation with the Spanish, but this is left unsaid. MacMicking then slyly transitions from mentioning 'foreigners' in the third person to discussing them in the first-person plural voice: 'our merchants and manufacturers', meaning those of his own country, even though he does not mention Britain or the British Empire by name. This is another, albeit terse and almost offhand example of excision.

After the Americans had beaten the Spanish and turned their sights on the Filipino liberation movement, Edward Stratemeyer's 'Old Glory' series (1898–1901) of 'boy's own' adventure novels deploy the passive voice to absolve the American troops of their active role in the aggression. In *The Campaign of the Jungle* (1900), the fourth book in the sequence that follows the fortunes of the Russell brothers serving under General Lawton, Stratemeyer writes, 'A howl arose on the night air, and one gun went off.'⁶² The reader cannot gauge from this sentence whether it was an American or a Filipino gun that was fired first. The following construction, while not passive in the formally linguistic sense, does not so much excise the agents of the hostilities as intimate that no one side is guilty for them, which in turn implies moral equivalence between a powerful imperial belligerent and its benighted victims, who are acting out of self-defence: 'At this time trouble began to break out between the United States and the insurgents who had been fighting the Spanish.'⁶³ To return to the Vietnam parallels, David Spurr highlights a 1961 *Newsweek* article that utilizes 'passive construction and a vocabulary which obscures the nature of concrete action'⁶⁴ to exculpate the role of the US armed forces in that conflict. 'The countryside,' Spurr continues '"has been pacified" and "brought under control". This leaves unnamed the agents and means of pacification and control.'⁶⁵

The diction of Stratemeyer's equivocating sentence is also significant, for the word 'trouble' is, in Fairclough's lexicon, a '*euphemism*' (Fairclough's emphasis) or 'word which is substituted for a more conventional or familiar one as a way of avoiding negative values'.[66] Just as Fairclough refers to a 1980s essay about British psychiatric practices that carefully substitutes the word 'seclusion' for 'solitary confinement' as a '[strategy] of avoidance with respect to the expressive values of words for relational reasons',[67] so Stratemeyer chooses the noun 'trouble', perhaps since its 'relational' synonyms ('stress', 'difficulty', 'nuisance', 'pickle') are not as redolent of 'negative values' – at least not for Stratemeyer's young, patriotic, late Victorian readership – as 'war', 'conflict' or 'bloodshed', let alone 'massacre', 'extermination' or 'genocide'. We see here then that the (conscious or unconscious) enterprise of deceiving the American public about both the nature and cause-and-effect of the US invasion was as much a question of the minute detail of individual words and phrases as it was a matter of broader-scale expurgations or de-emphases regarding the battlefield behaviour, political beliefs and military agency of the insurrectionists. Such a circumspect approach to language and its potential meanings was to become critical when the United States won the war and began consolidating the peace, as we will see in Chapter 3.

Preference for specific words is equally crucial to constructing, as Ashcroft, Griffiths and Tiffin write, 'statements that can be made about the world that involve certain assumptions [. . .] [and] become protected by the assertion of "truth"'.[68] Manilaists grappling with the Philippine–American War often attempt to reinforce the normativity of their propositions with a technique that Fairclough terms 'expressive modality': word choices and grammatical forms that reveal a 'speaker or writer's authority with respect to the truth or probability of a representation of reality'.[69] All of the Old Glory books pertaining to Manila feature pompous introductions that make obdurate promises of historical credibility. In *The Campaign of the Jungle*, Stratemeyer asserts that the story is based on real-life military reports and personnel testimonies: 'The author has endeavoured to be as accurate historically, as possible.'[70] In that quotation, the simple present-tense verb 'has' could have the modalizing effect of reassuring the reader of Stratemeyer's sincerity about the truth status of his story, for such words, according to Fairclough, are the 'conventions routinely drawn upon in discourse to embody ideological assumptions which come to be taken as mere "common sense", and which contribute to sustaining existing power relations'.[71] Another Stratemeyer potboiler, *Under Dewey at Manila, or the War Fortunes of a Castaway* (1898), which fictionalizes the Battle of Manila Bay when the advanced, steam-powered US Asiatic Squadron obliterated the Spanish fleet stationed in the Philippines, holds that 'What has been said [in the novel] concerning Cuba and the Philippines are simply matters of fact, known to all students of history'.[72] Moreover, it pledges to 'trace, incident by incident, just as they actually occurred'.[73] The intensifier 'actually' appears to endorse the authenticity of both Stratemeyer's statement and of the source material it is based on. Leaving aside these subtle modalities, the reader begins to doubt Stratemeyer's earlier assurance of impartiality when he descends into one-sided patriotism: 'the complete defeat upon one side was entirely outbalanced by almost total exemption from harm by the other'.[74] It is certainly verifiable from the historical evidence that the United States routed the Spanish in that skirmish, but the triumphalist adjectives and adverbs ('complete', 'entirely' and 'total') through which Stratemeyer conveys this fact betray his personal slant. In another ruse to wrap authorial opinion in the cloak of objective truth, *Under Dewey at Manila*'s expositional narration, which conveys the characters' thoughts and conversations, is frequently interrupted by an omniscient voice that makes value judgements replete with approving adjectives about the events recounted: 'the *wonderful* engagement of which I am about to relate'[75] (my emphasis). The device has become even more intrusive by the concluding chapters of the novel: 'That Larry was proud at having participated in the glorious conquest was but natural. What American boy would not have been proud?'[76] Neferti Xina M. Tadiar's research into the function of dream, desire and the social imagination in unequal Philippine–American interactions since 1898 provides further elucidation on why novels such as Stratemeyer's utilize expressive modality. Stratemeyer's convictions about the best intentions of the US invasion (its 'wonderful' and 'proud' aims) underwrite what Tadiar would dub a 'fantasy-production' of the Philippines that is persuasive precisely because it relies on emotional and subjective categories such as 'love', 'pride' and 'dignity'.[77] For Tadiar, who is here inspired by Slavoj Žižek's theories of mass-psychology and ideology, such categories cut deep into 'the symbolically structured meaning (the unconscious) that shapes and regulates our desires'.[78] They have become so politically and socially effectual in the Philippines because 'imagination [is . . .] a central force in the creation of social projects' and 'is an intrinsic, constitutive part of political economy'.[79]

In further efforts to sustain the myth of the noble American cause in the Philippines, *The Campaign of the Jungle* excises and reduces not only language but verifiable historical data. Besides bypassing the US atrocities alluded to at the start of this chapter, Stratemeyer frequently decries the abuses of the insurgents, including their 'terrible cruelty'[80] to prisoners and their penchant for arson attacks that imperil innocent civilians (when, as the historians Zinn, Francia and Constantino insist, arson was in actuality a far more common US tactic). Stratemeyer's approach here resembles Sigmund Freud's concept of 'projection' in which 'hostility [. . .] is ejected from internal perception into the external world, and thus detached from them [the mental patient] and pushed on to someone else'.[81] In colonial literary discourse, projection serves as a tool for mystifying the West's fears and desires relating to its unequal and exploitative interactions with the non-Western world. Robert J.C. Young holds that nineteenth-century English scientific and cultural texts imbued subaltern peoples and exotic landscapes with white male fantasies of interracial sex,[82] while Casey Blanton argues that Western authors with an interest in far-flung lands such as Graham Greene superimposed their traumatic childhood memories onto 'peculiar, haunted' landscapes 'that may or may not bear any resemblance to the place itself'.[83] That domestic critics of the Philippine–American War such as Mark Twain focused on the brutality of US troops may have aroused in supporters of the conflict strong enough insecurities about such transgressions that they were eager to re-imagine them as the fault of enemy combatants. Such insecurities are, in Alain Grosrichard's appraisal, fundamental to the West's vision of the Orient, for if the Orient 'seems to be politically insane, morally outrageous' and 'the very negative of our own society', at the same time 'it seems to lurk round the corner of our own homely world'.[84]

On the one occasion in the *The Campaign of the Jungle* when Stratemeyer shows a US soldier behaving unethically – he kidnaps a native woman and carries her on his back as a human shield before discarding her unceremoniously in a forest – the reader is invited to feel neither compassion for the woman nor disapproval of the soldier. Rather, it is a stroke of 'good luck' that the woman happens to be a 'close relative' of a rebel chief who will not fire on our escaping goodies lest he harm her.[85] Hence, in a bizarre process of moral alchemy, the wholly ruthless and self-serving behaviour of the soldier who risks the life of an innocent bystander is converted into a feat of heroic ingenuity because the soldier has God and righteousness on his side and the Filipinos are uncivilized subhumans whose lives are intrinsically cheaper than those of the Americans. The soldier's eccentric derring-do and utter insouciance towards the welfare of the lower orders are not the only reasons we might slot *The Campaign of the Jungle* into Green's 'aristocratic' sub-genre of colonial adventure. These narratives of the high capitalist-imperialist era, Green asserts, are possessed by a nostalgia for the dying aristocratic castes of Europe. Their protagonists 'belonged to old and honourable but impoverished families. And they used their rewards and their success to re-establish their families as noble.'[86] Often enough, these protagonists were 'good bad boy' types, starting their military careers as 'hyperactive', 'insubordinate' and 'rude' before achieving glorious feats on the battlefield, redeeming themselves and their family names.[87] These 'energizing myth[s] of adventure'[88] had the propaganda function of showing that service to the empire could mitigate the domestic social problems of youthful indirection and alienation.[89] (The British major-general and Raj executive Robert Clive 'of India' was the paradigmatic good bad boy of the aristocratic form, writes Green.) Although Stratemeyer's tales do not adhere to this trope exactly – there has of course never been a descendant aristocracy in the United States – nonetheless the Russell brothers are orphans from a broken home dictated over by a physically abusive and 'miserly' uncle, Job Dowling.[90] As a result of this troubled upbringing, the boys lack discipline and respect for authority when they enlist variously in the US Army and Navy for the Cuban and Philippine campaigns. Their participation in the vigorous and violent imposition of Western values on a hostile Oriental society soon bestows them with wealth, status, honour, knowledge and a new sense of well-being about themselves and their family background. In the closing pages of the final book in the sequence, *Under MacArthur at Luzon*, Ben Russell receives a letter from Uncle Job congratulating him on his exploits with Company D that have earned him $1,000 and will warrant 'a right royal send-off'[91] when he returns to his hometown of Buffalo, New York. 'Hurrah for Uncle Job!' cries his brother Larry, 'He isn't the crabbed old stick he used to be, but just the dearest old fellow ever was!'[92] and the boys are finally reconciled with their only older living relative. The omniscient narrator then intervenes to thank them on behalf of America – and, presumably, on behalf of the young readers of these romances who hope to emulate their deeds – for all they have done for empire: 'And here let us shake each of the Russell boys by the hand and bid them all good-by.'[93]

The lads' *Bildungsroman* arc is also compatible with what Green identifies as a more specifically American motif, that of the 'frontier' and its symbolic relationship to masculinity and the process of growing into manhood.[94] While the idea of the frontier was first assigned by European pioneers to the nascent United States itself, it was later appropriated by American adventure novelists like Stratemeyer and projected onto foreign territories that the United States coveted, Manila and the Philippines included. Just as the North American land mass had in the seventeenth and eighteenth centuries '[lured] [European] men outward, stirring them to mighty deeds, achievements and sacrifices',[95] Cuba, South America and the Philippines had the same appeal to American adventurers in the nineteenth and twentieth centuries; it is relevant that many of the US troops in Cuba and the Philippines, including General Henry Ware Lawton, were veterans of the US frontier wars with Native Americans. Indeed, Green's summary of the material attractions of the 'New World' to Europeans can be transposed easily to the material attractions of the Philippines to Americans: 'the frontier was [...] above all other things, a windfall of natural resources [...] [;] things that brought immediate profit or things into which little work had to be put.'[96] By the same token, as the Russell brothers would no doubt agree, the frontier 'set men free – made them rich – made them bold.'[97]

As we saw in the earlier parts of this chapter, the long-standing discursive blackout of the Philippine–American War started while the conflict was still going on, with the sentiments of most popular fiction, memoir, travel writing and journalism coterminous with the US military's attitude that the violent 'chastisement' of the archipelago 'was something best kept out of the public eye', Rockoff avers.[98] That said, there was no shortage of contemporaneous resistance to the campaign within the US political and business establishments; industrialist Andrew Carnegie, former US president Grover Cleveland and three-time Democrat Party presidential candidate William Jennings Bryan were all strongly opposed to America's new expansionist agenda. It logically follows, then, that some mainstream journalists of the period were prepared to disclose the true horrors of the Philippine battlefield. 'Our men have been relentless', wrote the *Philadelphia Ledger*'s Asian correspondent in November 1901, 'have killed to exterminate men, women, children, prisoners and captives, active insurgents and suspected people from lads of ten up, the idea prevailing that the Filipino as such was little better than a dog.'[99] Perhaps the most famous American writer of the turn of the twentieth century, Mark Twain, published caustic lampoons of the problematic mélange of religion, patriotism and militarism propelling the United States and other Western empires: 'I bring you the stately matron named Christendom, returning bedraggled, besmirched, and dishonored, from pirate raids in Kiaochow, Manchuria, South Africa, and the Philippines, with her soul full of meanness, her pocket full of boodle, and her mouth full of pious hypocrisies. Give her soap and towel, but hide the looking glass.'[100]

Valiant as they were, oppositional voices such as Twain's were, in the clamour to capture the hearts and minds of the American public, drowned out by the high-circulation, hawkish 'yellow' newspapers owned by Joseph Pulitzer and William Randolph Hearst, not to say the simplistic and tendentious – though widely read – fictions I analyzed earlier. Perhaps more importantly, though, the complaints of even influential figures such as Carnegie and Bryan were never likely to be heeded by the majority of politicians, tycoons, civil servants and diplomats, given the strategic and economic rewards offered by empire-building. As Theodore Roosevelt put it in 1899, 'The master of Manila can make terms with every power in the East, and those vast markets must be held open in the interest of our industry and our commerce.'[101] Through the manipulative and propagandistic employment of rhetorical conceits, Stratemeyer, King, Gunter and other authors were able to provide an ideological vindication for the manoeuvres by which the United States became 'master of Manila'. Like minds, working in fiction, print journalism, radio, television, film and the internet have been doing much the same ever since.

3

'The Pious New Name of the Musket'
Language, gender, race and benevolent assimilation

In July 1902, with most of the insurgent leaders dead or captured, the United States passed the Philippine Organic Act, which established in the new colony a bill of rights, an elected legislature with very limited powers and other political apparatuses informed by the new colonial ideology of 'benevolent assimilation'.[1] President McKinley had coined the term in 1899, holding that, once the US 'military administration' had achieved domination over the islands, it would guarantee 'the full measure of individual rights and liberties' to the people by 'sedulously maintain[ing] the strong arm of authority'.[2] With a more critical eye, historian Paul A. Kramer defines benevolent assimilation as bringing 'metaphors of family, evolution, and tutelary assimilation into a gradualist, indeed indefinite, trajectory of Filipino "progress" toward self-government'.[3] As is apparent from these quotations – one from a primary source espousing a hegemonic opinion on the matter, the other from a more sceptical secondary source long after the fact – glaring contradictions were inherent in the benevolent assimilation programme from its inception: political power-sharing with the Filipinos versus top-down control of them; the promise of liberal rights and freedoms versus censorship and coercion; free-market economic 'modernization' versus the prolongation of the Spanish-imposed feudal mode of agricultural production; a widely publicized aspiration towards Philippine independence versus the US desire to retain the territory as a subordinate protectorate. As briefly stated in Chapter 2, one of the few American commentators to properly critique these binary oppositions was the anti-imperialist Mark Twain, whose definition of benevolent assimilation as 'the pious new name of the musket'[4] vividly captures its problems.

As we have also seen, Twain belonged to a small minority of naysayers against the US imperial project in the Philippines. To vindicate that project, the overwhelming majority of American novelists and travel writers of the period aimed to bridge or excuse these contradictions using various formal devices, some of which bear likenesses to those I examined in Chapter 2. This timescale of literary history also saw the emergence of a new feature of the Manila textual space informed by a powerful metaphor that the Filipina cultural critic Vernadette Vicuña Gonzalez construes as a dominant male/submissive female relationship. As we will see, the Manilaist rhetoric of fraternity, guidance and mutual respect starts to make more sense when viewed from this gendered – and indeed racialized – paradigm. During this same, relatively short period, Manilaist hetero-stereotypes of Malay Filipinos altered radically and sometimes suddenly in accordance with the modulations of American strategic objectives in Philippines. However, it is crucial to appreciate that such discursive mutability is never the exclusive product of purely autonomous decisions made by colonizers who are oblivious to or insulated against the agency of their subjects. Rather, as Bart Moore-Gilbert contends of Orientalist formations more generally, 'a distinct flexibility in patterns of Orientalist representation corresponds to a recognition of the varying degrees and kinds of contestations of Western power by the colonized.'[5] It is these constructions that we will consider first, as they help to illustrate how the Manilaist consciousness prepared for the challenges of the US colonial era.

Prior to the outbreak of the Spanish–American War in 1898, Manilaist boilerplates of Malay Filipinos are founded on Victorian 'racial theory['s] insistence on the inferiority of non-Western peoples'.[6] The community is, so Charles Wilkes puts it, 'disposed to avoid all exertion',[7] a notion consistent with the Spanish Empire's perception of its foreign subjects elsewhere as 'lazy native[s]'.[8] This adumbration might also have emanated from Spain's triangulated colonial relationship with the Philippines and the 'New World'. Filipinos have resided in North America since 1769, when the Spanish first brought them to the continent as slaves, alongside Moluccans and Indians.[9] Most of the sailors on the ships that delivered them were Filipino or Chinese, and they were overworked, underpaid and underfed compared to their Spanish colleagues. Some froze to death due to inadequate clothing for the cold weather. After completing the first legs of these voyages, many of these Filipinos and Chinese deserted rather than risk their lives on the return trip to Manila.[10] The descendants of these slaves and press-ganged seamen in the nineteenth-century United States were unable to climb the social ladder very far; most were condemned to menial retail and agricultural jobs. By this juncture in history, received opinion characterized Filipino Americans – and Asian Americans more generally speaking – as weak, servile, pathetic beings,[11] and this perception is likely to have entered Manilaist awareness.

When the conflict with Spain had begun in 1898 and the United States had sided with the Filipino insurgents, the disparaging tone of Wilkes and other pre-war pundits vanishes from the Manilaist discourse. One of the American sailors in Edward Stratemeyer's *Under Dewey at Manila* describes 'the Tagals, a branch of the Malay race' in a more sympathetic light, as 'a good enough set if the Spanish would only treat 'em half decently'.[12] The 'good' natives are strategically signified as victims of the Spanish, whose comparative ruthlessness – earlier in the story, a petty officer declares that he would fare better as a prisoner under the Chinese or the Japanese than under the Spanish[13] – must be challenged by the Americans who *would*, it is suggested by the sailor, treat the Tagals at least half decently. Many US newspapers took the same line and the *New York Times* went further, paraphrasing with approval the US consul O.F. Williams's praise for the Filipino insurgent army's 'good state of discipline' and his expectation they will 'do good service for the Americans in attacking Manila'.[14]

However, once the Spanish–American War had been won and the Philippine–American War was looming, goodwill towards the Filipinos dwindled. Writing in January 1899, just a few weeks before the first shots were fired in Manila, an unnamed correspondent for the Associated Press quotes a Spanish priest named Diaz as saying, 'the Filipinos would not be now opposing the United States were it not for the Leaders spurring them on.' Whereas Stratemeyer had lamented the ordinary Filipino's exploitation by the evil Spanish, this priest – who supports the official US line – worries that the 'half breed' revolutionary vanguard who are '[working] solely for personal gain' have 'forced' the natives to 'take up arms' against the Americans.[15] The potentially disastrous consequences of the Filipinos switching their allegiance are laid bare in Charles King's novel *Ray's Daughter*, published in 1901 at the devastating nadir of the conflict. King's omniscient narrator frets over the 'vexing problem as to what Aguinaldo and his followers might do rather than see the great city given over to the Americans for law and order instead of to themselves for loot and rapine'.[16] Though largely forgotten today, King was a well-respected novelist in his time and literary journalists honoured the authenticity of his fiction, ascribing it to his distinguished service in the Philippines and other theatres as a brigadier-general in the United States Volunteers. 'Prominent in literary circles [...] [,]' states the Wisconsin newspaper *The Post-Crescent*, 'his histories, stories and sketches are all of military matters'.[17] 'Perhaps more than all others,' glows an unnamed reviewer for the *Indianapolis News*, '[King] has brought to the knowledge of the American readers the truth about social life in the American army.' Moreover, 'Contained in every chapter [of *Ray's Daughter*] are many things that readers of current events desire to know and cannot find in graver articles or letters.'[18] It is important to note, though, that such laurels were afforded to King by a popular media that largely concurred with his imperialist assumptions. Indeed, his critique of Aguinaldo's revolutionaries was not the first or last time a dedicated American empire-builder had posited the threat of native-orchestrated anarchy as a casus belli against a foreign foe. As the violence in the Philippines intensified and the casualties mounted, Manilaism started to demonize not just the mandarins steering the insurgency but their troops on the ground. We saw in the previous chapter how the juvenile romances of Stratemeyer and others used graphic set pieces and overplayed rhetoric to emphasize the violations of Filipino resistance fighters. In the same spirit, newspaper reports and editorials of the time augmented their descriptions of Filipino atrocities from crucifixion to 'burial alive' with adjectives such as 'savage', 'treacherous', 'cruel', 'brutal' and 'grisly'.[19] The major wave of Filipino immigration to the United States alluded to earlier began before the conclusion of the Philippine–American War in 1902, so it is not surprising that, according to the scholar of Asian American history Erika Lee, the US media rendered these new Filipinos in America in much the same way as Manilaists rendered Filipino insurgents, that is 'in racial terms as uncivilized savages, brutal rapists, and even dogs and monkeys'.[20] Crucially, though, despite the fury animating these stereotypes in both the United States and the Philippines, Lee observes that sometimes Filipinos were, 'at best [. . .] characterized as children in need of (U.S.) guidance'.[21] That word 'guidance' appears three times in a widely syndicated 1900 news article on the findings of a Congressional commission that the current bloodshed could have been avoided had Filipinos consented to 'an enlightened and liberal foreign power' providing them with the 'tutelage and guidance' necessary for 'self-government' based on 'intelligent public opinion'. That all of this must be underwritten by 'education [to elevate] the masses' to '[broaden] their intellectual horizon' and '[discipline] their faculty of judgement'[22] – which is perceptibly absent in a Philippine republic devoid of American leadership – suggests that Filipinos are currently in an infantile state of ignorance, unable to exercise agency or autonomy in their affairs of state. We might deduce from these comments that, however badly the Filipinos comport themselves in the plantations of California or on the battlefields of Luzon, they can find redemption if they accept their inferior position in American power structures, whether imposed at home or abroad.

Another notable facet of this new demonization is that, having previously been signified as the helpless prey of Spanish misrule, the Malay Filipinos are now deemed culpable for the Spaniards' faults due to the condition of 'going native' in which European settlers in Asia, Oceania and Africa were perceived to have 'wholly degenerated [. . .] from contact with other races'.[23] That the going native panic is a necessary adjunct to backward, oppressive political leadership (which US journals regularly accused Aguinaldo of) can be understood by reference to another colonial discourse, that of Grosrichard's Oriental despotism. Grosrichard has identified a tendency he calls the 'corruption of fear', a seemingly paradoxical – yet vital – instrument in the governance of Eastern societies.[24] While Asiatic slave-subjects remain loyal to their masters out of a visceral fear of death, often enough that fear of death is 'corrupted' into a 'fear of opinion – which assumes men led by self-esteem, not only self-love'.[25] This human-natural inclination to protect one's self-esteem entails an aversion to 'loss of liberty' that would explain instances of political revolt against despotic states when slaves have sacrificed their lives in the hope of freedom. This contradiction between fear of death – that obliges the ruled to obey their rulers – and yearning for liberty and self-esteem – that causes them to defy their rulers – would imply that despotism is an untenable form of government, destined to collapse at any moment or evolve into a better system that, at the very least, resembles European monarchy. As Grosrichard observes, Montesquieu's typically Eurocentric solution to this conundrum is that, in certain parts of the world, human nature – and its essential repugnance towards slavery – is in blunt antagonism with the 'physical nature'[26] of 'warm' climates and landscapes that render men lethargic, apathetic and 'excessively sensitive to the least threat of danger'.[27] Therefore, slaves may from time to time rise up against their autocratic viziers and sultans, but fundamental political changes to the 'timeless' despotic order are impossible – another familiar Orientalist canard – because slaves are at the mercy of the inhospitable topography they inhabit and of their irreconcilable attitudes: submissive terror versus thirst for emancipation. The decisive difference between Orientals and Europeans in this regard is that the former are closer to animals – and therefore less human, in the Enlightenment mind – in so far as they are forlorn victims of the vicissitudes of their natural environments, whereas the latter have realized 'the demands of human nature' by having mastered non-human nature, 'cancelling out even the empire of climate' through the application of the scientific method.[28]

In order to channel these ideas through the time and place concerning this chapter, it is worth turning our attention to the Irish Darwinian sociologist Benjamin Kidd, who achieved global fame with the publication of his 1894 study *Social Evolution*. Its ambiguous thesis divided critics, but pleased both reactionaries and progressives. On the one hand, Kidd railed against socialism and, unlike other Darwin-inspired theorists, promoted religion as a positive force for civilizational improvement. On the other hand, in utopian teleological mode he predicted that Western society would eventually become altruistic and classless.[29] In his 1898 essay, 'The Control of the Tropics', Kidd turned his attention to the subject of colonialism. The Spanish presence in the 'East Indies', he argued, typified a 'relationship existing between a civilized Power and a tropical possession'[30] that contaminated the physical health and moral integrity of those soldiers and officials serving the 'civilized Power': 'In climatic conditions which are a burden to him; in the midst of races in a different and lower stage of development; divorced from the influences which have produced him, from the moral and political environment from which he sprang, the white man [. . .] tends himself to sink slowly to the level around him.'[31] In a work of creative nonfiction for *McClure's Magazine* published a year later, the American physician Dr Henry C. Rowland blames the psychological deterioration of three US soldiers serving in the Philippine–American War on homesickness, alienation from a strange tropical ambience and encounters with 'furtive islanders, cold and stark'.[32] Spending too long among 'savages' has a mirror-like effect on a civilized white man's behaviour: 'Their [the soldiers'] lust of slaughter is reflected from the faces of those around them.'[33] If, in this particular version of going native, American infantrymen have caught the capacity to commit atrocities like an illness from a lower race (that, so Rowland states, is well-versed in committing atrocities itself) then the Americans cannot be morally culpable for their cruel actions any more than sufferers of disease can be blamed for their symptoms. As David Brody has found, US journalism of the early 1900s is replete with going native cautionary tales – often 'sensationalized' with medical figurations or literal references to hygiene and pathology – about American soldiers 'catch[ing] the bug of infidelity while in the Philippines', getting infected with leprosy from Filipino insurgents and losing their sanity from the severe climate.[34] Once again, this bodily infection metaphor may have originated in the sign-system of Oriental despotism for, as Grosrichard avers, the Oriental Vizier is 'an insatiable bloodsucker, compelling those to whom he transmits power to act like him'.[35]

We can contrast Rowland's narrative with Edward Stratemeyer's *Under MacArthur at Luzon*, which espouses less sympathy for a Spaniard who has gone native by defecting to the insurgents and adopting their bad habit of molesting captives: 'When we got ashore we found ourselves in the hands of a Spanish traitor who had joined the rebels some time before. He was very brutal, and handled us like dogs.'[36] Presumably, the double standard here rests on the Manilaist assumption that, as touched on in Chapter 1, the Spanish are not as civilized as the Anglo-Saxons, and thus no one should be shocked when they succumb to the horrors of going native. Note also how this particular manifestation of the trope betrays the true cynicism of Manilaist volte-faces about the relative worthiness of the Spanish and Malay Filipinos. Just a couple of years before, Stratemeyer had designated the Spanish oppressors of the 'decent' Malay Filipinos. But now he is hinting that Spanish oppressiveness is caused by exposure to the oppressive propensities of the Malay Filipinos.

When the United States was finally subduing the insurgency and trying to enact benevolent assimilation through its colonial state apparatuses, to some extent Manilaism reverts to its previous notion of Malay Filipinos as the 'right kind' of subalterns: child-like, 'contented'[37] and receptive to 'uplifting' by the white man.[38] However, the paradoxes of benevolent assimilation are apparent in several American commentators' descriptions of Malay Filipino lifestyles and attributes. In a 1902 anecdote-filleted polemic calling for the emigration of African Americans to the new Philippine colony, T.G. Steward writes that 'the Filipino [. . .] always has time for a fiesta' and 'enjoys a laugh as well as the negro',[39] which bespeaks hedonism and idleness. But, for Steward, Filipinos are also 'patient', 'their women are trained to work in the house and field and to business also' and they know how to extract profit from the timber and agriculture industries.[40] Writing in 1904, Senator George C. Perkins praises the Filipinos as both 'ambitious of becoming self-dependent' and 'capable of assimilating our own ideas'.[41] One gets the sense from these dissonant traits attributed to Filipinos that this momentous turning point in the history of Philippine–American relations has produced an imperative to portray the Malay Filipinos as at once obeisantly desiring of American supervision – so that the United States can reap the rewards of occupying a land mass in the Far East – and capable of organizing themselves politically and economically, thus heading off criticisms that the United States is acting like a coercive empire of the old-world European genus.

These contradictions between Filipinos' need for guidance and their hankering for liberty, as well as their dualistic penchants for violence (as depicted during the mal époque of the Philippine–American War) and submission (as depicted during peacetime) are apparent in the Social Darwinist classifications of American anthropologists of the early 1900s such as George Becker and Robert Bennett Bean. These pseudoscientists, observes David Brody, believed that '*Homo philippinensis*', the native Filipino, was 'uncivilized, devoid of modern man's refined sensibilities' and the 'missing link to man's current state'.[42] At the same time as *Homo philippinensis* could be measured, studied and incorporated into a 'place-image' that 'defined [the] boundaries of meaning that established the American colony in the Philippines', Becker's 'sensational' revelations that the Manobo tribe practised cannibalism 'must have been frightening to an American audience' and therefore a sobering reminder that *Homo philippinensis* was 'savage' and not easily known or tamed.[43]

Steward's construction of Malay Filipinos as, like African Americans, essentially 'country' people happy with the hot 'climate' and landscapes of 'rice, tobacco, cotton and corn'[44] coincides with the main line of employment of the first wave of Malay Filipino migrants to arrive in the United States and its other dependencies. They picked fruit in California or toiled in the sugar plantations of Hawai'i, tolerating unsanitary living conditions and twelve-hour working days.[45] Many who joined this exodus were farmers made jobless by the US colonial policy of reorganizing Philippine farmland into 'unsustainable plots', itself part of a broader strategy to prioritize the growing of cash crops to be sold abroad for vast profits accrued to American companies. As Lee asserts, the longer-term fallout of keeping 'the Philippines as an unindustrialized export economy' was disastrous; by the 1920s the archipelago 'could not feed itself' and was forced to import staples such as rice.[46]

While the Manilaist compulsion to deprecate the Spanish has dissipated now the Americans have achieved pre-eminence, Hispanophobic caricatures in Manilaist texts of this era serve the ideological purpose of, as per the city-as-hell device, showing the positive impact of American stewardship in antithesis to four centuries of inertia under the preceding regime. Hence, Walter Robb ruminates on an opulent palace that is the nefarious legacy of the 'tyrant' governor Fajarde who, not unlike Al Capone and other organized crime leaders in the United States of the time, built it with funds extorted from the public.[47] Gangster allusions are present too in an anecdote re-told by the American Methodist missionary Homer Clyde Stuntz about a sadistic friar who had a Katipunan (nationalist secret society that led the revolution against the Spanish) activist flogged and strung up by his thumbs.[48] 'The wonder is that he survived,'[49] adds Stuntz. 'The essentially vicious theory of colonial government'[50] that enabled such misdeeds is now, he assures us in grandiose parlance, being remedied by 'silently wafting the bloom of our civilization over the vast populations of the Orient, pollenizing them with ideals destined to bear fruit where despotism and ignorance and vice yield their apples of Sodom'.[51] The allusion to Sodom is instructive, for Stuntz's judgements conflate faith-based prejudice – 'typical Spanish Catholic intolerance'[52] – with disgust towards the Spanish friars' and colonial officials' land-snatching, 'stifling of all liberty of thought and freedom' and 'their insatiable greed for money'.[53] These comments should be considered against the historical backdrop of, as José S. Arcilla notes, 'the [Americans'] first open efforts to preach Protestant Christianity [. . .] in earnest'.[54] Reynaldo C. Ileto has acknowledged a comparable problem in the later American Orientalist historian Stanley Karnow's 'all too simplistic portrayal of the Spanish colonial phase as the "dark age" of the Philippine past supplanted in this century by an enlightened American "new age"'.[55] Stuntz's contemporaries utilize an emplotment device that I have coined 'the disparaging return' that customarily involves a character or narrator comparing a later stay in Manila with an earlier one, in order to highlight Spanish cunctation over developing the city. In *Under Dewey at Manila*, the US sailor Striker laments that Manila looks exactly as it did when 'I was here years ago'[56] while Frank G. Carpenter appends a paragraph of his *Through the Philippines and Hawaii* (1929) on the overcrowding, polluted canals and insalubrious accommodation he encountered in Manila in 1899 with a subsequent paragraph that fêtes the opulent hotels and efficient 'motor-car' taxis he enjoyed on his most recent stopover in 1928.[57] These sumptuous facilities are synecdoches for US colonialism's putative elevation of all aspects of Philippine life. Like almost all other triumphalist claims made by colonizers, these writers massively overstate the improvements their compatriots have made to Manila. The historical record shows, for example, that it was in fact the Spanish who introduced to the Philippines its first university,[58] lighthouse,[59] hotel[60] and electricity grid.[61] (While it does not negate my argument about American disdain for 'backward' Spanish colonialism, it is worth bearing in mind that Renato Constantino and other Philippine left nationalist historians have, in turn, challenged claims about the efficacy of the Spanish civilizing mission – or at least the notion that educational and scientific advancements in the archipelago would never have happened without the Spanish – by citing evidence of sophisticated pre-colonial societies in the region).

Assumptions about gender were as necessary to the Manilaist defence of benevolent assimilation as those behind the cultural and racial interpellation of Spaniards and Malay Filipinos. The protagonist of Archibald Clavering Gunter's *Jack Curzon* is motivated to travel to the Philippines by his love for Mazie Gordon, whose beautiful, mixed American-Filipina looks have 'captured the [hearts of the] United States Navy'.[62] Curzon's quest to win Mazie's affections runs parallel with the United States' deepening involvement in the revolutionary turmoil in Manila. In the dénouement of the novel, as the happy couple, Curzon and Mazie, are preparing to ride away in a carriage to a new life together, an Irish American soldier asks, 'Why are these beauteous brides loike these same blessed

Dewey Islands? [sic]'.⁶³ To which his senior officer replies, 'Because they'll be almighty ticklish critters to handle.' Mazie laughs at this, and the Irish American further compares Filipino women with American imperial ambitions by stating that 'the Germans wanted 'em and couldn't get 'em!'⁶⁴ After more laughter symbolizing concord between these characters – and the cultures and colonial-political interests they represent – Curzon 'step[s] into [his] carriage where a little fluttering beauty gathers in her gauzes to make room for Señor Jack Curzon'.⁶⁵ The scene would appear to reify Vernadette Vicuña Gonzalez's proposition that America's domination of the Philippines has historically been propelled by a male imperial fantasy of 'securing' a feminized, submissive periphery 'receptive to and in need of being claimed',⁶⁶ vindicated by 'deeply felt understandings of American rescue', 'liberation', 'benevolence', 'love' and 'allegiance'.⁶⁷ Such a fantasy is not exclusive to the Manila or Philippine colonial experience, as the scholarship of Martin Green demonstrates. Notable British historians of the nineteenth century, he notes, rendered the 'New World' of the sixteenth century as a 'feminine [character] unresistant succumbing to the conquistadors'.⁶⁸ For Gonzalez in the Philippine case, the fantasy has been sustained up to the present day not least because Filipino women themselves, from sex workers to domestic labourers, have internalized it due to indoctrination by myriad social, political and economic phenomena. Thus, Mazie's love for Curzon against all the odds, and her approving laughter at the overt analogies between native women and US geopolitical designs, can be seen as prototypical of the phenomenon Gonzalez identifies.

An abiding discursive fantasy such as benevolent assimilation is as much a matter of content as it is a matter of form, of how it is technically presented in language. Manilaists seeking to justify the American occupation knew this all too well. In his gazetteer-cum-travelogue, *United States Colonies and Dependencies Illustrated* (1914), William D. Boyce's dedication to the necessity of the American civilizing mission is evident from his surfeit of modalizing adjectives, intensifiers and exclamation marks. There is, he gushes, a 'really wonderful prison system'⁶⁹ and 'A good many Government officials live [in the Calle Escolta district], and army folks!'⁷⁰ Be that as it may, the almost histrionic tenor of Boyce's flourishes could be a type of apophasis, a device most famously illustrated by Shakespeare's telling line from *Hamlet*: 'The lady doth protest too much, methinks',⁷¹ whereby a speaker tries so assiduously to persuade the listener of their claim that the listener begins to distrust the veracity of that claim. If Queen Gertrude doubts the sincerity of the actress character in *Hamlet*'s play-within-a-play because she uses such extravagant rhetoric, we might respond to Boyce's text in the same way, given that elsewhere in his book he undermines his glowing hymns to Americanization by referring to unease within US officialdom about the efficacy of their task: 'The appointment of Mr. [Francis Burton] Harrison [as Governor-General of the Philippines]', he writes, 'has been to the detriment of our own just claims and anything but beneficial to the people of the Islands'.[72] Such modalities are as dubious as Boyce's easily verifiable excisions concerning the question of the new colonial order's moral authority. His belief that the unique experience of Americans having previously had 'every square foot' of their country dominated by foreign states has taught them to treat their own, present-day overseas possessions more altruistically and inclusively, as 'self-governing units of our great self-governing nation',[73] is countered by Ashcroft, Griffiths and Tiffin's assertion that, while 'new' imperial doctrines such as benevolent assimilation projected a rhetorical 'smokescreen of civilizing "task" and paternalistic "development" and "aid"', the material reality underneath involved the same old 'violent and unjust [colonial] processes'.[74] Furthermore, Boyce's sympathetic quoting of President McKinley – 'We are to take to [...] the Philippines the principles of liberty, of freedom of conscience, and of opportunity that are enjoyed by the people of the United States'[75] – is greatly at odds with Kramer's finding that Filipinos at that time did not in fact enjoy the same rights as their American counterparts; they had no guarantee of a jury trial and were not permitted to bear arms, for example.[76] Equally as tendentious is Boyce's claim that Filipinos are at liberty to 'criticize the rule of the Americans or talk about Philippine independence by the hour',[77] which conspicuously overlooks what was then the recent scandal over the Tagalog-language comic play *Kapahon, Ngayon at Bukas* (*Yesterday, Today and Tomorrow*). When the play premiered in 1903, a scene in which a character tramples upon a star-spangled banner was deemed seditious by the US authorities, who imprisoned its author, Aurelio Tolentino, for nine years. A signatory to the Philippine Declaration of Independence in 1898 which was drawn up when there was still hope that the United States would eventually allow national self-determination, Tolentino had grown disillusioned with the corruption of the US Insular Government of the Philippine Islands and American perfidy on the independence issue.[78] As a well-informed journalist and newspaper owner, Boyce would almost certainly have been aware of similar anomalies regarding the official interpellation of Filipino immigrants in his native United States. On the one hand, the new influx of 150,000 Filipino labourers during the early years of benevolent assimilation were formally classed as US nationals which meant they theoretically enjoyed better rights than other Asian nationals,[79] but on the other hand this, as Lee observes, 'translated into unequal treatment' because Filipinos encountered 'rampant prejudice and discrimination' at the hands of landlords, employment agencies and private individuals. Signs reading 'No Filipinos Allowed' or 'No Filipinos or Dogs Allowed' became commonplace in Californian towns.[80]

Frank G. Carpenter – whose widely read 'geographical readers' so closely accorded with US official thinking about the rest of the world that they were set texts in American schools for forty years[81] – indirectly cautions against Philippine nationalism by recourse to the type of false objectivity we saw in Stratemeyer's introductions to his novels in Chapter 2. Carpenter's plea for his personal neutrality – 'I have preferred to tell what I have seen, letting my readers judge of conditions for themselves'[82] – is a conceit to assure the reader that his observations thereafter will be received as fair, balanced and commonsensical. Carpenter then proceeds to cherry-pick some viewpoints 'expressed by men I have met in my travels who seem to me to be qualified to speak with authority on the subject [of the future of Philippine politics]',[83] all of whom just so happen to endorse the United States' continued presence in the archipelago. 'Possession of the Philippines is a vital necessity to the defence of the United States', one (perhaps conveniently) anonymous army officer tells him.[84] An American academic, also anonymous, 'contends that if independence should be granted, the Christian Filipinos are sure to set up a despotic rule'.[85] Carpenter's narrowing of the frame of the debate, which, as the media linguist Roger Fowler would put it, conveys 'a partial view of the world',[86] might have been motivated by either '[unconscious] ideas and beliefs'[87] or a conscious intention to parrot hegemonic political values. If the latter is true, Carpenter's entreaty about his own disinterest in the topic is arguably another case of apophasis.

In *Ray's Daughter*, Charles King imagines benevolent assimilation in spatial and geographic terms. He shows that the Americans will correct or at least improve Manila's status as a colonial city planned by the Spanish to segregate communities of natives from zones inhabited by the expatriate ruling class, or 'worlds cut in two', as Frantz Fanon has remarked of comparable colonial milieus, between the 'settler' and the 'Negro' (or indigenous equivalent) towns.[88] In King's starry-eyed vision, US sailors roam freely between the social, racial and cultural frontiers that the 'antiquated' Spanish had erected to divide and rule Manileños for centuries:

> All over the massive, antiquated fortifications of old Manila into the tortuous mazes of the northern districts through the crowded Chinese quarter, foul and ill savored, the teeming suburbs of the native Tagals, humble yet cleanly; along

the broad, shaded avenues, bordered by stately old Spanish mansions, many of them still occupied by their Castilian owners, the Yankee invaders wandered at will.[89]

King hints that Manila's heterogeneous populace will be unified by these sailors – and the colonial functionaries who will come after them – under a new cohesive identity defined by liberty, democracy and equality. Painting the American arrival in idyllic terms, he gleefully declares that the 'Yankee invaders' are 'brimful of curiosity and good nature [. . .] making themselves perfectly at home, filling [. . .] the natives with wonderment through their lavish, jovial and free and easy ways'.[90] (The phrase 'making themselves perfectly at home' is an intriguing choice given its relational function to the word 'assimilation'.) For King, benevolent assimilation is in the interests of both colonized and colonizer; the sailors who quickly get to know the city as well as 'the streets of their own home villages'[91] are assimilating into Manila life while Manileños appear happy to assimilate into the American way. However, with the benefit of historiographical hindsight, King's prescription seems impractical and idealistic even by the standards of gung-ho, jingoistic colonial fiction; the contemporary American historian Carl H. Nightingale argues that the US colonial state did little to rectify Spanish segregationism, instead extending and multiplying Manila's socio-geographical inequalities by converting the Escolta neighbourhood into a 'kind of American zone' and constructing the whites-only hill station of Baguio.[92] Looking at King's rendering of Manila in a different way, we might say he has in fact reinforced the city's spatial hierarchy of classes and ethnic groups (the Chinese quarter, the Tagalog suburbs and so forth) in a mode not unlike Archibald Clavering Gunter's delineation of a clear socio-geographical pecking order in *Jack Curzon*: 'More aristocratic San Miguel, the busy hives of enterprising foreign merchants, ingenuous Tagal artisans, crafty Chinese traders, and tireless sweating coolies'.[93] Gunter mentions the well-heeled suburbs and financial centre first, followed by Malay Filipino and Chinese Filipino professionals, and, at the foot of the ranks, the coolie menial labourers. However, he implies a certain equality – or at least unity of purpose – between these subcultures when he lauds their contribution to 'the modern Manila, that commercial emporium, which ships the immense produce of these islands to the utmost ends of the earth'.[94] Both his and King's employment of 'parataxis', defined by David Spurr as the tendency of the Orientalist gaze to '[place] things side by side'[95] in a hierarchy of value judgements, mirror one of the prime paradoxes of the American project in Manila: on the one hand, in order to cement its control the new colonial order needed to preserve three centuries-old power structures – often manifested in urban geographical divisions – while on the other, it wished from the outset to present itself as a more progressive administration that encouraged the social integration of Filipinos and their consent in their own governance.

Likewise, Carpenter's preference for elite ways of organizing data is reflected in his juxtaposition of the 'three Manilas', which exalts the contemporary, Westernized quarter of the city: 'the Spanish city within the walls; the native, more or less Malay, town of nipa palm shacks, carabaos and fishing boats; and the modern American Manila that is being developed according to plans that will some day make this one of the most beautiful cities of the East.'[96] It would be too chauvinistic for this disciple of benevolent assimilation to bluntly avow that American Manila is superior to the other two Manilas, so instead American Manila is presented as preferable by dint of its altruistic capacity to deliver advancement to the city as a whole. For Miller too, the 'Empirical democracy of America' exercises a benign authority over 'the social mosaic'.[97] Boyce expresses the same sentiment albeit through the more ostentatious metaphor of Manila as a 'layer cake': 'The caramel-coloured Malays form the bottom layer. The next filler is sixteenth-century Spanish. Then comes the blend of these, Spanish and Malay, with a strong dash of Chinese – the upper-class Filipino. The top layer, including the cream, is good old American.'[98] In reproducing the official American stance on urban demographics, Boyce trivializes the social and ethnic divisions in the city by invoking the playful, almost child-like image of the cake and likening its ingredients to skin colour.

As with other Western colony-making initiatives of the nineteenth and twentieth centuries, a key plank of benevolent assimilation was the implementation of a new education system that would inculcate Filipinos with American values.[99] The Pensionado Act of 1903 disseminated government grants for academically excellent students to travel to the United States for further study. The aim was, the historian Jonathan Lee avers, to 'Educate and bind current and future Filipino leaders to the American colonial administration'.[100] Most crucially, though, 'American education endowed the Philippines for the first time in its history with a lingua franca, English'[101] which, as Ashcroft, Griffiths and Tiffin argue, allows a colonial regime to assume a form of 'power which comes from the control of the language'.[102] More than that, an 'illusory standard of normative or "correct" usage'[103] regarding the lingua franca helps the colonizers to monopolize the 'means of communication'[104] in the peripheral space. William D. Boyce alludes to the linguistic ownership of the Philippines by observing that the Americans now spell the former designation with a 'Ph' rather than an 'F', as the Spanish had, and the latter with only one 'l' rather than two, as had been the habit previously.[105] In a similar vein, Mary H. Fee, a member of the Thomasite group of 500 American schoolteachers who were dispatched to the Philippines to set up new English language public schools, is pleased that the *cocheros* (coach drivers) of Manila now shout the English phrases 'Git up!' and 'Whoa boy!' at their steeds instead of Tagalog or Spanish equivalents.[106] Linguistic colonization is also reflected in certain of the authors mentioned earlier arrogating themselves the 'right . . . to speak for and represent [cultural] others'[107] – to invoke the literary critic Debbie Lisle's phrase – with little knowledge of or respect for either 'the specific terms that the culture uses'[108] or, as the anthropologist Massimo Canevacci terms them, the 'autonomous visions and reflections'[109] of individual members of that culture. Thus, many of those American writers who limn the Philippines at this time imbue their Filipino characters with vernaculars, cadences, prosodies and grammar patterns much more typical of Westerners. Rather unpersuasively, Gunter in *Jack Curzon* channels a decidedly Anglo-American, pre-First World War Teutophobia through the implausibly baroque dialogue of the bestial revolutionary leader Ata Tonga: 'When I catch the stink of the German, it is like the oily, fetid, sickening, pickle-flavor of the anaconda, who twines about, crushes, and then devours his prey.'[110] This depiction may be a concomitant of Gunter's assumption that dialogue between Westerner and Oriental, not to say between people of disparate national and ethnic heritages, is impractical and undesirable. The opinion is implied by his metaphorical deployment of a Manila crowd at a cockfight later in the narrative: 'These are all chattering and jabbering in as many lingos, dialects and mixed languages as were ever heard together upon this earth [. . .] their varying clatter runs into a kind of maddening symphony that would make the author of Volapük [the short-lived "international" language that was based upon English and German for, so it was argued, the sake of clarity and accuracy] cry: "I am outdone!"'[111] Ironically, perhaps, a contemporary reviewer of *Jack Curzon* applauded Gunter's deployment of 'local colour by the simple device of sprinkling the conversation of his personages with such exclamations as "Dios mio."'[112] However, for both Gunter and the reviewer, providing local colour is not the same as being sensitive to local culture; the latter writer goes on to discuss 'a savage of the Tagal race' and the 'rather funny conception' of a 'Europeanised Chinaman'.[113]

Much of this chapter has been preoccupied with showing the erratic and incoherent negotiations Manilaists undertook in order to sustain the reverie of benevolent assimilation. The following chapter explores how the hopeful, melioristic timbre of Boyce, King and others was supplanted by a more sceptical and sometimes mocking disposition towards Manila's development as a cynosure of 'Pepsicolonisation'.[114]

4

'She Can Take on American Ideas'

Desire, capital and flawed simulation in twentieth-century Manilaism

I now want to turn to several generations of British and American writers, from the 1910s up to the 1990s, who have employed certain representational techniques to at once highlight Manila's emergence as an advanced, state-of-the-art city under American auspices and to denigrate or lampoon precisely this same process as somehow second-rate or inadequate. The orbit of these strategies encompasses the phenomena of 'contact zones',[1] imitation and simulation. Predictably, Manilaists of this era do not envisage these phenomena as having the progressive or emancipatory potential that certain postcolonial theorists ascribe to them, mainly because these writers have little to no sympathy for the subaltern subjects who might have been able to appropriate these modes of subjectivity and expression in order to, in Partha Chatterjee's example, challenge Western colonialism through 'adopting [...] [the] modern attributes of Western culture' such as democracy, nationalism, justice, secularism and social equality.[2]

Some of the strategies considered in this chapter, such as the depiction of Manila as a flawed simulation of a happy, prosperous Global Northern city, would seem to run counter to other coterminous Western ways of seeing Manila such as city-as-hell, as outlined in Chapter 1. Often the discrepancy between the models is due to geographical emphasis. As we have seen, the city-as-hell proponents tend to fixate on those districts or landmarks in Manila which appear to instantiate their distaste for whatever social or moral ill they happen to be concerned about, be this the spooky Spanish keep of Intramuros or a begrimed shanty like Smoky Mountain. Often enough, these small, heterogeneous spaces are converted, in a sloppy, generalizing manner, into synecdoches for the city of Manila as a whole. In the same mode, the writers discussed later who trumpet the city's modernity – though not without telling qualifications – seldom gaze beyond the affluent, US-renovated enclaves such as Calle Escolta. In the works of Claire 'High Pockets' Phillips, DeLoris Stevenson, Maslyn Williams, James Fenton and James Hamilton-Paterson, there turns out, after all, to be not such a vast gulf in timbre between the city-as-hell and what superficially appear to be more optimistic and humorous symbolic modes informed by homage and copyism. Crucially, the latter three of these writers are somewhat mesmerized by the notion that the Philippine political elite – and much of the Philippine general public – have willingly bought into the fantasy of US popular acculturation. My analysis of this particular aspect of representational modelling is indebted to the work of Neferti X.M. Tadiar.

After crushing the Philippine insurrection and re-assuming control of Manila, the United States was then, according to Reynaldo Ileto, 'able to turn a situation of utter devastation and suffering, for which it was largely responsible, into a redemptive opportunity'.[3] Manilaists of this period tried to redeem Manila as a locus of Spanish political ataxia and ungrateful native unrest with the interlocking ideologies of Western democracy, urban progress and capital flow. The result was a Manila construed as a successful experiment in democracy, absorbing the best qualities of the Western metropolis replete with all the commodified pleasures a Westerner could want. Some writers were eager to plot this new imaginative geography before US empire-building had really begun in earnest. The American journalist William Gilbert Irwin and an unnamed 'Special Correspondent' published a feature article called 'Yankeefied Manila' in December 1898. This was several days before the Treaty of Paris that formalized US proprietorship of the Philippines and several years before the Americans had quelled the nationalist resistance. However, Irwin and his colleague write, 'marvelous change has been wrought in the few weeks that the city has been in our possession'. The main indicator that 'Manila is showing that she can take on American ideas' is greater accessibility to consumer goods. The United States has delivered 'great quantities of foodstuffs' to the city, and stores are now open 'all day' as would be expected of a modern, business-minded society.[4] Writing in 1914 when the United States had had more time to impose its values and policies on Manila, William D. Boyce lauds the Americanized district of Calle Escolta where 'You can find almost anything you ask for in the shops'.[5] The club life along the harbour, he points out, affords such all-American pursuits as cocktail drinking and movie watching.[6] Fifteen years later, Frank G. Carpenter celebrates the 'modern metropolis' populated by well-dressed and good-looking personages enjoying Euro-American music, food and leisure activities.[7] Such fancies conform to David Spurr's view that 'the West seeks its own identity in

Third World attempts at imitating it'.[8] But, in the Manila context at least, the operative word here is 'attempts', for the simulation is always flawed. Therefore, while Irwin and the 'Special Correspondent' appreciate the 'excellent brass band here in Manila made up entirely of natives', it 'seems odd to hear them play our national airs and later tunes'.[9] For Boyce, while the US-built Manila Hotel is as luxurious and comfortable as any American could desire, it falls short of delivering 'bread and pie "like mother used to make"'.[10] Although she is generally upbeat about the quality of accommodation and hospitality in Manila, the colonial educator Mary H. Fee objects to the 'cheap, unattractive-looking European wares'[11] of the shops and the canned food available in her guesthouse; her insinuation is that goods and services in Manila are shoddy parodies of those available at home. Such anxieties about the simulation may derive from Homi K. Bhabha's notion of 'ambivalence' wherein a colonial order is never wholly committed to projecting its values onto its subjects for fear they will come to identify too closely with those values and demand more rights and privileges from their masters.[12]

In Chapter 1, I cited several narratives that present Manila during the Second World War as an infernal site of air raids and explosions, with the Japanese positioned as the evil antagonists because they have temporarily displaced US paramountcy over the city. *Manila Espionage* (1947), the memoir of Claire 'High Pockets' Phillips, who came to the Philippines as a singer and later became a spy on behalf of anti-Japanese guerrillas, contains mutually reinforcing images of both Manila-as-hell and Manila-as-simulation, yet with fewer flaws in the latter image than Carpenter's or Fee's constructions. Phillips's oscillation between these negative and positive impressions can be explained by a number of factors – including temporal moment and geographical location – that are in turn connected to postulations about the United States' historic duty in the Philippines and around the world. After alighting from the S.S. *Annie Johnson* in Manila just two months before the Japanese were to attack, Phillips scoffs at her émigré friend's concerns that 'there may be a war'.[13] As a good patriot, Phillips asserts that the Japanese would be 'crazy'[14] to fight the United States. While what she almost certainly means by this is that the Japanese would be crazy to go up against such great military odds, we might also infer that the Japanese would be crazy to destroy all the Western-style improvements the United States has made to the city's architecture, commerce and social life, given her enthusiasm for the 'romantic setting' of the 'ultra-modernistic Alcazar Club', the 'most attractive residential' area of 'Ermeta' [*sic*][15] and a 'gay party' that is a 'sight for the gods'.[16] Taken together, these landmarks and social events constitute a hypnagogic world of endless hedonism where 'cocktails or champagne would appear as if by magic'.[17] In true Hollywood romance style, Phillips quickly falls in love with and marries a handsome American sergeant of the Thirty First Infantry, with whom she can chat wistfully about 'far-off California' and 'the cattle-ranches back in the Midwest'.[18] That being said, this charmed quasi-American life – enjoyed inside the chic nightclubs and apartments of the well-to-do districts – is interspersed joltingly with the distressing conditions out on the streets that symbolize challenges, past and present, to the spatial inscription of Manila as a protégé of American meliorism, an ideology that Phillips subscribes to. When '[speeding] through the ancient city' – an allusion to the remnants of the old Spanish capital – Phillips is 'acutely aware' of abhorrent hangovers from the Hispanic era such as 'carromata' horse-and-carts 'drawn by diminutive flea-bitten nags'.[19] A much more urgent threat to the stability of the simulation soon comes in the shape of 'practice black-outs' that augur the impending Japanese invasion.[20] When she first arrives in Manila, Phillips views the black-outs with a gung-ho dauntlessness: 'I hope they will have one soon.' But one night when she is singing at the Alcazar Club, the noise of sirens and aircraft accompanying the black-out forces her and the orchestra to quit their performance.[21] The nightmare of the coming Japanese occupation is now impinging upon the dream of Americanization.

After the Second World War, Manila returned to the orbit of American power by assuming a subordinate role in the international system of 'dollar imperialism' that meant 'much of the world suffered from a degree of dependence on trade with the dollar area'.[22] A string of Manilaist authors of the 1950s and 1960s perceive the city as a blemished imitation of American popular culture rather than as a potential utopia as Phillips does. At the same time, these writers replicate Phillips's blended Manila-as-hell/Manila-as-simulation formula by alluding to aspects of the city that lag behind Western 'norms' of security, justice and prosperity. A 1957 feature article in the American *Catholic Advance* newspaper captures the dichotomy thusly: 'Manila [. . .] is something less than a tropical paradise.'[23] We saw earlier in this study how DeLoris Stevenson's *Land of the Morning* (1956) limns parts of Manila as infernally ravaged by warfare. In the same book, though, Stevenson extols other districts of the city for looking 'like the United States in the Far East',[24] albeit facets of that resemblance are kitschly parodic of rather than tastefully faithful to the original: 'You'd laugh to see the "jeepneys" – corrected American jeeps – used as buses at 10 centavos a ride.'[25] It is not only the price that is cheap about this tacky appropriation of an iconic American vehicle; Stevenson's remark that the simulation currently has deformities is necessary for her concluding proposition that 'the Philippines is truly a land of tomorrow' because, while at this point in time the country may be falling short of Western ideals, this 'daughter of the American republic' will surely grow up into a closer likeness to her father.[26]

Such optimism vanishes from Manilaism during the Marcos dictatorship when the Philippines was even further away from a model of Western liberal democracy than it was in Stevenson's time of writing. Manilaists remain fascinated by Manila as a Western simulation but are compelled by grim material realities to extend the boundaries of the textual space to incorporate threats to the validity of that simulation. Hence Australian author Maslyn Williams contrasts his meeting with Ferdinand and Imelda Marcos and the positive 'image they project [which] is as stimulating as that presented in the US at the beginning of the 60s by the Kennedys'[27] with his later encounter with 'relatives of a woman who has recently been reduced to a heap of neuroses' from being tortured by state enforcers.[28] An October 1966 *Journal Herald* (of Dayton, Ohio) report on US president Lyndon B. Johnson's visit to Manila maps these contradictions spatially and thematically onto the Manila Hotel, erected in 1909 by the US colonialists as a symbol of America's 'civilizing mission' in the Philippines. The unnamed correspondent mentions that the Manila Hotel has recently hosted the Beatles, which could reflect a certain amount of Filipino understanding of and affection for Western culture. This must be good news for American geopolitical interests given that President Johnson has come to Manila to strengthen his alliance with Marcos against Vietnamese communism. On the downside, though, there are protestors currently picketing the same hotel waving placards that accuse Johnson of being a 'modern Hitler'.[29] The protest rather takes the shine off an otherwise effective ritual of Philippine-US conviviality. According to the Manilaist psyche, when the Manila Hotel was created it was supposed to be the defining landmark of a future Manila of Americanized consumer capitalism. From the semiotics of the *Journal Herald* piece, though, we can deduce that such a future will never be realized while leftist malcontents are prepared to besiege the hotel and therefore resist the Philippines' continued vassalage to American money, power and violence.

Another, more potent image from that same news story introduces a representational trope that becomes significant to Marcos-era Manilaism. The writer describes a motorcycle policeman called Lt. Jose who wears a 'red cowboy hat' while escorting President Johnson and his entourage.[30] There is of course a note of crass sycophancy about this mimicry that conforms to the broad mechanic of flawed simulation, but more importantly Lt. Jose is presented as enjoying *literally* disguising himself as an American. Williams, Hamilton-Paterson and other Manilaists of the 1970s and 1980s are equally keen to demonstrate the consent of Filipinos in their constructions of Manila as a place of imperfect Western copyism. As Tadiar explains, 'while the West owns the codes of fantasy, the non-West is no less an active and willing participant in the hegemonic modes of imaginary production that are predicated on these codes'.[31] While Tadiar adroitly debates how, why and to what extent Filipinos have internalized these fantasy codes, I am more interested in how, why and to what extent late-twentieth-century Manilaists *assume* the Filipinos they write about to have internalized Manilaism's codes of imitation and flawed simulation. Often enough, the rhetorical objective for Manilaists here is to dodge allegations of inaccuracy or ethnocentrism by asserting that their adumbrations are supported and corroborated by Manileños themselves. Sometimes this is achieved through awareness – conscious or otherwise – that, to borrow from Tadiar again, 'the postcolonial nation-states of the non-West demonstrate that they have acquired a certain fluency in these codes of fantasy of the West, making full use of them in the pursuit of their elites' desires'.[32] The key phrase here, in my view, is 'the pursuit of their elites' desires' because, all too often, the writers I am scrutinizing are only able to vindicate their constructions of Manila through canvassing the opinions of those *comprador* Filipinos whose power and status depend on Western financial, martial and political patronage, or those lower-class Filipinos who have been indoctrinated by *comprador* hegemony to desire Western commodities, copy Western lifestyles and seek out migratory opportunities in Europe and the United States. This problem of preferential selection is crystallized by the postcolonial theorist Benedict Anderson when he castigates James Fenton's 1986 reportage on the fall of the Marcoses for its over-reliance on the opinions of upper-class Filipino officials and privileged Western habitués; 'He [. . .] misses the opportunity to see a single Muslim' and talks with 'the owner of a vast banana plantation (but not with any of his 6,000 labourers)'.[33] Had Fenton consulted a socially wider range of sources, it may have invalidated his construction of a Manila that, while not exactly a simulation of a Western city, is nonetheless a site of commercialized thrill-seeking that Fenton, writes Anderson, '[transforms] into advertisable commodities' for a Western readership.[34]

At the other extremity of the social spectrum, the dream of most provincial Filipinos of low or medium income is to relocate to the 'Fantasyland' or 'Las Vegas' of Manila, James Hamilton-Paterson informs us in his memoir-travelogue *Playing with Water* (1987). 'There in the distance,' he writes, 'beckons baroque structures of vice' and 'Disney-esque set-pieces of outlandish appetites'.[35] If the hopeful refugee can travel as far as the simulation then they may be lucky enough to graduate to the real thing, for Manila is seen as 'a necessary first step to emigration' to a Western country, although 'America remains the Promised Land'.[36] While Hamilton-Paterson perceptively elucidates the psychological allure of these fantasies to ordinary Filipinos, he does not entertain other sources that are particularly critical of the false consciousness around emigration. However, to his credit – and unlike any of his contemporaries – he does reflect on the link between Manila's function as a preparatory experience for relocation to the West with the economic necessity of overseas remittances to the degraded Philippine economy and the labour demands of foreign capital. We will examine this theme in more detail in Chapter 7's discussion of 'anti-Manilaist' texts.

Across Philippine history it is the Marcoses who epitomize an elite – if eccentric – fantasy-production of Manila as a city enjoying its ersatz Americanization. Williams is clear that the Marcoses' identification with the Kennedys is a myth of their own making,[37] and Hamilton-Paterson eloquently summarizes the couple's careful and conscious propagation of 'myths and fragments of myths, ranging from the conquering hero to Cinderella, from cosmogony to Camelot, [. . .] snippets of Abe Lincoln' and a 'Disneyfied version of handsome princes and happy endings'.[38] By the same logic, when such imitations fail – as they invariably do – the blame lies with the Marcoses for being the architects of the chimera or with ordinary Filipinos for being gullible enough to fall for it. While Fenton, Williams and Hamilton-Paterson are fairly critical of American political and military sponsorship of the autocracy, other Manilaists shy away from indicting Western-influenced underdevelopment or penetration of Philippine markets, as we saw with the third world blues device in Chapter 1. Ian Buruma goes even further than exculpating the West by dismissing those Filipinos who wish to hold the West to account for its corrosive impacts on the Philippines. He attacks the socialist historian Renato Constantino's thesis that 'Washington, through the CIA and multilateral lending agencies, has deliberately kept the Philippines in a state of colonial dependence' because it is 'uncomfortably close to anti-Semitic nightmares of an international Jewish conspiracy of bankers and politicians to dominate the world'.[39] Buruma's analogy is intellectually slovenly given that neo-colonial injustices in the 1980s Philippines have nothing to do with anti-Semitism in 1930s Europe, historically, ideologically or geographically, or in terms of common victims and/or perpetrators. The puzzling incoherence of Buruma's point – not to say its tone of emotional agitation – betrays an unease within the Manilaist discourse when it is forced to confront an argument that contradicts its proposition that the failings of flawed simulations occur in a national vacuum and cannot be imputed to world-historical factors.

For Buruma and his contemporaries, repressing counter-hegemonic perspectives such as Constantino's is as much a part of the discursive strategy as recuperating such voices or citing previous Western visitors to Manila to vindicate their own prejudices via a technique Debbie Lisle calls 'shadowing', wherein a Western travel writer explicitly alludes to another Western travel writer from an earlier period who limned the same geographical site(s).[40] For Lisle, the device often bolsters a reactionary nostalgia within the later writer because 'to mimic the adventures of great colonial explorers' is 'part of the attraction of reviving colonialism and patriarchy'.[41] Like so, we find Buruma indulging in a form of simulation or mimicry himself by composing 'in the shadow' of the American Second World War General Douglas MacArthur to support his opinion that, long after achieving independence, Filipinos remain infatuated with a Western personage who once played a significant role in their governance: 'There is something extraordinary about a colonised country receiving the general of the colonial power back as a savior.'[42] Occasionally, Manilaists will shadow Filipino writers and intellectuals, but usually only to substantiate ethnocentric prejudices. We saw in Chapter 1 Buruma's misappropriation of the radical scholar Reynaldo C. Ileto to make the case that the contemporary Philippine political malaise derives from archaic mystical beliefs.[43] In a similar spirit, while Hamilton-Paterson commends the renowned Filipino author Nick Joaquin for his capacity to 'glimpse the palimpsest beneath'[44] the 'shapeless, confused and unrelievedly twentieth century mess'[45] of Manila's streets, ultimately what Hamilton-Paterson finds in Joaquin's shadow amounts to yet another glum Manilaist banality: 'A pleasurable sense of history is hard won in Manila.'[46]

It was during Ferdinand and Imelda's 'conjugal dictatorship'[47] that Tadiar's conception of the Philippines as 'a country dominated by misplaced dreams' was properly established. 'It is a place of ironic contrasts and tragic contradictions,' she continues, 'where politics is a star-studded spectacle set amid the gritty third world realities of hunger and squalor. A third world place in first world drag.'[48] Tadiar's 'ironic contrast' bears parallels with the dissonance between the Manila-as-flawed-simulation and the Manila-as-hell modes as Manilaists apply them to the Marcos context. In that period, the Manilaist representation of both the city's replicas of Global Northern metropolitan urbanism and its crime-addled, Global Southern poverty zones is partly a response to, as Tadiar notes, government 'strategies for the containment of [. . .] [Manila's] contradictory and antagonistic elements'[49] including inequality, overcrowding, pollution, inadequate housing and political protest. Thus, the Marcoses committed themselves to 'erecting walls to hide slums, relocating squatters, and imprisoning and torturing members of urban resistance movements (including squatter organizations)'.⁵⁰ The scheme was prototypical, with succeeding initiatives to 'beautify' Manila addressing new crises that 'have necessitated a makeover of capital's infrastructure for greater and more efficient accumulation.'⁵¹ In the 1990s, the administration of Mayor Alfredo Lim embarked on a programme of slum demolitions and zero-tolerance towards crime in the service of stimulating investment and raising productivity. This tension between social ills and the efforts to mitigate or conceal them is apparent in the Manila-esque city of Gobernador de Leon of the British Chinese writer Timothy Mo's novel *Brownout on Breadfruit Boulevard* (1999). Here, 'democracy and prosperity are not bedfellows'⁵² because the economic progress symbolized by new investment opportunities and construction projects – 'space-age 2001 slaps of the New Asia',⁵³ as Mo describes them – is being undermined by widespread corruption, political chicanery and an official cover-up of a foreign mining company's malpractice.⁵⁴ The city's Cultural Centre (perhaps modelled on the Manila Film Center, Imelda Marcos's real-life pet boondoggle from the 1970s) is an impressively large venue that is ultimately unpopular and under-attended.⁵⁵ Similarly, the 'snowily dressed cashiers looking like starlets on $2 a day'⁵⁶ and other poorer Filipinos with access to the gamesome codes of Western style and consumerism are heavily outnumbered by petty-minded gangsters, contriving politicians and sexual perverts. Much the same is true of the British novelist Alex Garland's *The Tesseract* (1998), wherein Manila is a frightening abyss of murder, intimidation and vendetta occasionally brightened by the gaudy, playful semiosis of Western materialism: McDonald's, trashy American film and television and so forth. By the late 2010s and President Rodrigo Duterte's 'war on drugs' – a far bloodier and more ambitious programme than Lim's – the flawed simulation tool has gone astray from the Manilaist kit. Towards the end of this book I show how, for myriad ideological and geopolitical reasons, writers such as Jonathan Miller and, once again, James Fenton damn Manila as an abominable quasi-warzone that can no longer be redeemed either by elite efforts to spruce it up or by the *jouissance* of Western apery.

It was also in the 1990s when the gaze of other Manilaist writers was re-calibrated by what Graham Huggan has called the 'domestication' and 'global marketing' of postcolonial societies by Western tourism and culture industries.⁵⁷ The material backdrop to this was that by 1986 – incidentally the year the bloodless People Power Revolution toppled the Marcoses – tourist arrivals in the Asia Pacific region were increasing by 10 per cent a year,⁵⁸ and the globalization of the world economy was boosting Western exports of consumer goods to the Philippines and other parts of the developing world.⁵⁹ Thus Manila simulations come to be dominated by fantasies of play, pleasure, desire and consumption of metropolitan goods and services that have been transplanted to the periphery – though, of course, imperfectly. The geographer John Connell has detected a coincident process in the regeneration of parts of Manila in the 1980s and 1990s, when new neighbourhoods with titles like 'Little Italy' would be 'designed and marketed as fragments of Europe in a global era'.[60] Similarly, Hamilton-Paterson sums up post-Marcos Manila as an 'Asian re-creation of an American garrison town'[61] catering for the peccadilloes of comparatively wealthy foreigners, while Pico Iyer's *Video Night in Kathmandu* (1988) posits Manila's identity as determined by the most vulgar aspects of Western popular culture; a textual space crowded by European pornography, indigenous sex workers dressed like their American counterparts, rock bars where Filipinas sing songs by Madonna and Cyndi Lauper, and steak houses evocative of 'New England' serve food tasting of 'cardboard'.[62] The artifice of it all is underlined by Iyer's wry allusion to black-and-white minstrels: 'Master of every American gesture, conversant with every Western song [. . .] the Filipino plays minstrel to the entire continent.'[63]

It is not just Iyer's simulation that is furnished with sexual licentiousness. The late 1980s/early 1990s saw a profusion of Western media reporting on the new phenomenon of British and American men obtaining Filipina 'mail order brides' or 'video brides' from the Philippines. In her 1988 dispatch from Manila, Sara Barrett of the British *Daily Mail* newspaper stretches Iyer's metaphor over a Manila that, somewhat more than a counterfeit of the West, is a space onto which Western men project their fantasies of sexual domination. In an authorial voice that is, to borrow a phrase from another *Mail* article on the same subject three years later, 'a mix of fascination and revulsion',[64] Barrett visits a queue of 'beautiful' Filipinas waiting to be filmed by an agency that will match them with 'old men who looked like Peter Cushing in the Hammer Horror films, gaunt-faced, bald-pated'.[65] This conjuring of Manila as a hedonistic sexual playground has survived into more recent Western narratives, such as Rafe Bartholomew's sports memoir *Pacific Rims* (2010), in which a US marine boasts to the author that 'he'd parlayed a hot hand at a craps table into an "eight-some"' and advises that 'I shouldn't board my Manila-bound flight without first packing a suitcase full of rubbers'.[66] However, Bartholomew's liberal cosmopolitanism obliges him to critique such macho posturing, unlike Barrett the reactionary hack who objectifies and dehumanizes the Filipinas she meets, reducing them to a cluster of basic physical functions sure to entice a self-serving, misogynistic Western man. These women are, writes Barrett, eager to perform maid duties and 'provide sex'.[67] Interviewee Gloria Camit, twenty-eight, with her 'neat little face'[68] and 'chocolate eyes',[69] wants as soon as possible to have a baby with whoever her future groom will be.[70] Disturbingly, Barrett reveals, some British men have sexually abused or forced their Filipina wives into prostitution. While Barrett does not herself condone these violations, it is significant that she quotes without judgement Gloria's declaration, 'I am not afraid of a man trying to make me a slave'.[71] A potential predator reading that in 1988 might have been tempted to use the same match-making service if he thought it would give him access to a 'slave' who would acquiesce to his mistreatment of them.

Westerners born long before Barrett – and who were far more accomplished writers than her – have similarly placed docile, unfeeling brown-skinned women centre stage in their Orientalist mise-en-scènes. In the nineteenth century, the French novelist Gustav Flaubert, shocked by what he believed to be a shortage of chastity and fidelity in the Middle East, wrote, 'the oriental woman is no more than a machine: she makes no distinction between one man and another'.[72] In our contemporary age of Western sex tourism facilitated by inexpensive travel, accommodation and other goods and services, this 'machine' metaphor has come to stand for poverty-stricken Filipinas as just another product for sale – either legally through services like the one in Barrett's article or semi-legally via prostitution or pornography – on the international market of jaded male desire. According to Tadiar, 'Produced as physical commodities, they [Filipinas] cease to be treated as humans. To their consumer-clients, they are indeed what they are advertised (on t-shirts around the US bases) to be: "little brown fucking machines powered by rice."'[73]

These submissive female bodies, Tadiar avers, are a constituent feature of a larger-scale imaginative geography – and geopolitics – of the 'Philippines [as] an exploitable body', 'the "prostitute" of "America" who caters to the latter's demands (ostensibly demands of global production and consumption)'.[74] When Tadiar argues that US-established 'free trade zones' are yet another sexually and economically exploitative feature of the 'body/land of the Philippines',[75] it is hard not to think in the same terms about Barrett's imbuing of the physical topography of Manila with the typology of paedophilia, the most egregious sub-genre of Western sexual proclivities brought to bear on the Philippines: 'All the way past the Hyatt hotel in Manila, where the palm trees with white painted trunks look like schoolgirls in bobbysocks.'[76]

If we agglomerate the observations of all the writers in this chapter, we find ourselves imagining a profoundly strange, surrealistic, patchwork Manila made of scraps of Florida theme park, Tinsel Town studio, Upper East Side club, Las Vegas casino and Texas whorehouse. It is populated by, among others, Filipino Elvis impersonators, Californian lounge singers, politicians aspiring to cinematic heroism, nubile native beauties and perverted British retirees. While this unflattering textual-civic identity has followed the protean fads of Western popular culture (itself, of course, shaped by wider geopolitical economy), it is, in Orientalist terms, traditional, conventional and no more than the updating of an attitude long held by Western intellectuals that Eastern cultures are, as Edward Said avers, 'repetitious pseudo-incarnations of some great original (Christ, Europe, the West)'.[77]

5

The making of a supranational stereotype
Western constructions of the Chinese in Manila and Beyond

The momentous origin story of the Chinese in the Philippines has much commonality with those of other diasporas around the world. It is a narrative of adaptation and reinvention, negotiation and integration; and, more disturbingly, of the community's ridicule, ruthless interpellation and frequently lethal oppression at the hands of the 'host' regime. Chinese emigration to the Philippines dates back to at least the tenth century AD when merchants from Fujian and neighbouring regions flocked to the archipelago to trade cotton, textiles and other profitable commodities.[1] When the Spanish established their colonial government in Manila in 1571, they were keenly aware of the economic value of the capital city's *sangley* – as the Spanish now dubbed the Chinese – traders, craftspeople, artisans and goldsmiths. To ensure the loyalty of their new subjects, the Spanish launched a campaign of religious conversions and encouraged intermarriage with *indios* (Christianized native Malay Filipinos). Those who complied were placed into the ghetto of Binondo, which is now thought to be the oldest 'Chinatown' district of any city in the world. Those who did not comply were semi-imprisoned in a worse ghetto called Parián, where they had to observe strict curfews and could not leave without formal permission from the Spanish.[2]

Throughout the seventeenth century, the mistreatment of the Chinese along with further 'Chinese immigration would periodically contribute to rising tensions between the Spanish settlers and the growing numbers of Chinese labourers and artisans,' argues Luis H. Francia.[3] In 1603, 1639 and 1662, these tensions led to Spanish massacres of over 50,000 Chinese in total.[4] As is conventional of racist violence in other historical contexts, these atrocities were justified ideologically by slandering and stereotyping the victims. Under the Spanish colonial gaze, the Chinese were variously but often concurrently homosexual,[5] disease-carrying, unhygienic, untrustworthy, seditious, parochial, irreligious and – most significantly for the focus of this chapter – economically successful enough to destabilize the status quo. As with other cultural and racial stereotypes, these can be contested and deconstructed using notions around hypocrisy and victim-blaming. For instance, the homosexuality sleight was borne from Spanish suspicions about the predominance of male *sangleys* in Parián, as, due to a policy authored by the Spanish, few Chinese women settled in the Philippines at that time.[6] As J. Neil Garcia avers, this particular moral panic was fuelled by 'the damning attitude of the Catholic Church in the Philippines toward homosexuality [. . .] conflated with (xenophobic) issues of race'.[7]

While the Western literary texts on the Philippines that I consider in this chapter do not repeat this particular slur, they nonetheless appropriate other Spanish anxieties about Chinese Filipino professional activities and class positionality. In addition, these Western constructions are inflected to different degrees by Western metropolitan concerns about the Chinese in China, and their presence in other parts of Asia and in Western societies themselves. The result is a supranational stereotype of the Chinese patterned by Western assumptions about the characteristics of Chinese populations in at least three continents. (By the late nineteenth century, argues the historian Richard T. Chu, this supranational framing of the Chinese was beginning to ideologically influence the Malay-origin majority in the Philippines because the Western 'discourse on the Chinese in other parts of the world no doubt affected the views of those in the Philippines').[8] As is the wont of classic Orientalist generalization and homogenization, the stereotype therefore is not especially alert to the unique traits of the Chinese in Manila.

A brief passage from Daniel Defoe's fictionalized travelogue *A New Voyage Round the World by a Course Never Sailed Before* (1725) inaugurates the main coordinates of this supranational stereotype that will beget later Manilalist writing on the Philippines:

> Our ship was now an open fair; for, two or three days after, came the vessel back which went away in the night, and with them a Chinese junk, and seven or eight Chinese or Japanners; strange, ugly, ill-looking fellows they were, but brought a Spaniard to be their interpreter, and they came to trade also, bringing with them seventy great chests of China ware exceeding fine, twelve chests of China silks of several sorts, and some lackered cabinets, very fine. We dealt with them for all those, for our supercargo left nothing, he took everything they brought. Our traders were more difficult to please than we: for as for baize and druggets, and

such goods, they would not meddle with them; but our fine cloths and some bales of linen they bought very freely. So we unloaded their vessel and put our goods on board. We took a good sum of money of them besides; but whither they went we knew not, for they both came and went in the night too, as the other did.[9]

These merchants are Chinese nationals encountered off the coast of Luzon and not residents of Manila, but this does not matter to the supranational stereotype Defoe is helping to hatch. The merchants are, writes Defoe, clearly good at their jobs for their wares are 'very fine', although they have a fastidious, 'difficult to please' business mindset. Such emphasis on 'the Chinese [. . .] association with money' has, since Defoe, become a 'pervasive truism' in Philippines-related discourses, according to the Chinese Filipina literary historian Caroline S. Hau.[10] For Defoe, these men are inscrutable (are they in fact Chinese 'or Japanners'?) and unpredictable creatures of the night whose onward destination is an enigma. This 'othering' of the Chinese as estranged and displaced would have concurred with official Spanish attitudes of the era, given that the colonial state decreed in 1686 the mass exile of the Chinese and would do so again in 1744.[11] As far as Defoe is concerned, the mysterious actions of these seaborne Chinese fit with their 'strange' appearances. As we will see, later Manilaists will go further and reduce Chinese conduct, customs and habits to biological attributes, conforming to the classic racist world view in which 'group differences in physical traits are considered a determinant of social behaviour and moral or intellectual qualities'.[12]

Problematic as it is, Defoe's portrait of the Chinese is more lenient than those of succeeding Manilaists; more Sino-suspicious than Sinophobic, as it were. We might impute this to the fact that, while the 'Yellow Peril' bogeyman of China as a territorial and civilizational threat to the 'Occident' had been a staple of Western European political rhetoric since the reign of Genghis Khan,[13] by Defoe's time the 'First British Empire' was not yet in competition with China, and British public sentiments towards the Chinese were generally favourable.[14] But around the same time *A New Voyage* was published, European settlers in North America were seized by a 'Chinamania' for imported Chinese tea, porcelain and fabrics; a societal craze that solidified the notion in the fledgling United States that the Chinese were shrewd entrepreneurs.[15] After the Declaration of Independence in 1776, American businessmen were eager to compete with Europe for gainful Chinese trade, a venture that began in November 1783 when the first ever US cargo ship (filled with ginseng) set sail for Beijing.[16]

In the mid to late nineteenth century, Euro-American political elites changed their stance to one of fear about Chinese encroachment into the Dutch colony in

Java and the prospect of a Chinese invasion of Australia as serious challenges to Western hegemony in the region.[17] While such apprehension certainly instructed Manilaism, its imaging of the Chinese was motivated more by anxieties about a double Chinese threat to capitalism in the Philippines and in the West. In both locations, Chinese entrepreneurs were allegedly siphoning business opportunities away from other ethnic communities while lower-level Chinese workers were seen to be obtaining jobs that rightfully belonged to 'native' groups. In the case of the Philippines, after the Spanish relaxed immigration laws in the early 1800s and the Chinese population mushroomed from 8,000 to 100,000,[18] Chinese Filipino business clans came to dominate the country's lucrative cash crop industries (the products of which were often processed in and always exported from Manila), to the detriment of foreign companies' profits.[19] At the same time, there was a sharp increase in the number of Chinese employed in more proletarian retail and 'coolie' roles,[20] which chipped away at *méstizo* and Filipino dominance of 'urban provision', among other sectors.[21] In the case of the West – or more specifically the United States – there was establishmentarian envy towards Chinese ownership of laundry, horticulture, retail and catering operations thought to require 'enterprising acumen',[22] while the big American labour unions, purporting to defend the interests of the white proletariat, blamed poorer Chinese labourers for '[driving] down wages, [taking] away jobs' and supinely volunteering to become 'pawns of factory owners and greedy capitalists'.[23] The doubleness of this monetary-based alarm about the Chinese in both the East and West is captured in numerous Manilaist comments of the period. Robert MacMicking states, 'These China shopkeepers have nearly driven all competition, except with each other out of the market, – very few Mestizos or Spaniards being able to live on the small profits which the competition among themselves has reduced them to.'[24] Meanwhile, for Charles Wilkes, 'the Chinese [. . .] have almost monopolized all the lucrative employments among the lower orders.'[25] But this note of caution in Wilkes's account is mitigated by his praise for the Chinese as 'all activity'[26] thanks to their enthusiasm for trade. This further double, even contradictory gaze was echoed in a late Victorian edition of the London *Times* which intersowed warnings about the influx of Chinese jobseekers to England with admiration for their 'hard-working, patient and economical' disposition.[27] Indeed, in the 1840s and 1850s, the stance of US newspapers on Chinese miners in the American West alternated between admiration for their work ethic and disdain of their 'servile', 'clannish, deceitful' ways.[28]

It is probable that Manilaist Sinophobia was also determined by formal and informal restrictions placed on the types of work Chinese could carry out in both the United States and in the Philippines. In the United States, out of fear of competition for their livelihoods, Irish and French immigrant miners – and, later, American trades unionists – physically intimidated many Chinese migrants into taking up alternative employment in the laundry, restaurant and other sectors stated earlier. In the Philippines, the existence of a Chinese bourgeoisie in the nineteenth century was partly the long-term consequence of an early Spanish colonial policy of prohibiting the Chinese from farming, leaving them little choice but to indulge in mercantile activities. Therefore, the complaints Wilkes, MacMicking and others make about Chinese over-representation in certain economic areas lack historical understanding and constitute another form of victim-blaming in which the Chinese are to be held accountable for conditions not of their own making.

Such victim-blaming along the lines of labour and capital bears a close parallel with European anti-Semitism which, according to David Nirenberg, grew out of medieval laws '[barring] Jews from many economic activities' that '[channelled] Jews into specific financial institutions such as money lending and tax collecting'.[29] Coterminous with Victorian/Edwardian Manilaist unease about lower- and upper-class Chinese, British novelists from Benjamin Disraeli to G.K. Chesterton to Hilaire Belloc variously sketched Jews as 'skilful accumulators of property';[30] poor, insular and submissive;[31] and guilty of financial crimes such as the 1912 Marconi insider trading scandal.[32] Of course, the Jewish and Chinese diasporas are not the only subaltern ethnic groups ever to have been vilified as economic parasites, but the comparison seems appropriate to the time and place under scrutiny here. As Chu observes, 'Spanish historical experiences with non-Christians such as the Jews and the Muslims may have influenced Spanish policy toward the Chinese' in the early colonial epoch discussed earlier, when Spanish endeavours to either Christianize the Chinese or ban them from the Philippines replicated Spain's campaign a century earlier to convert the Jewish population of Iberia on pain of expulsion.[33] By the nineteenth century these aggressive policies were no more, but conflations between the Spanish maltreatment of the Jews in Iberia and the Chinese in Manila survived in residual hegemonic attitudes towards the Chinese as a 'national minority'[34] and as 'economic scapegoats' for an array of capitalist crises in the colony.[35] As learned men who diligently researched the destinations they wrote about Wilkes and MacMicking would probably have been aware of such Spanish anti-Sinicism, if not its exact affiliations with Spanish anti-Semitism.

A good proportion of the British novels cited earlier, along with much visual media of the same period, feature the stereotypical physiognomy of the

Jew, the most infamous aspect of which is an exaggeratedly large nose. As Sara Lipton argues, this characteristic probably originated in mid-medieval art as a derogatory emblem of the Jews' 'misdirected gaze'[36] away from Christ, implying a heretical 'materialism' inimical to Christian spiritualism. Later, the proboscal trope came to symbolize a form of 'materialism' that is much closer to our modern understanding of the word: when money lending had become a leading enterprise in Europe, Jewish '"worldliness" and "fleshiness" was underscored by luxurious clothing and exaggerated facial features, especially large, hooked noses'.[37] Although redrawn slightly by subsequent incidents of economic scapegoating such as the 'Jewish banking conspiracy' peddled by fascists and some leftists in the 1930s and 1940s, the stereotype has survived more or less intact to the present day.[38] (The modelling of the Jews as a global clique somewhat immune to local peculiarities is an additional congruity with the supranational stereotype of the Chinese in or around Manila.)

Similarly, in the second half of the nineteenth century when social Darwinism was á la mode and the United States was enacting a series of eugenic laws that effectively banned Chinese immigration, Manilaist authors present certain biological attributes as the outward expression of their Chinese characters' mean, parsimonious and/or enterprising dispositions. As with the most prominent Western supporters of eugenics in the nineteenth and twentieth centuries (including economist John Maynard Keynes, writer H.G. Wells and intellectual Sidney Webb), these Manilaists were politically liberal or leftist, at least by the standards of their time. During his governorship of Hong Kong in the mid to late 1850s, John Bowring was known as a progressive reformist who increased native representation in the colony's legislative council and lifted the embargo on Hongkongers from serving as jurors and lawyers.[39] But making such concessions to the Chinese did not dampen Bowring's attitude of racial essentialism, as is apparent from the claims he makes in his 1859 travelogue *A Visit to the Philippine Islands*. 'The Chinese physiognomy,' he writes, 'and the Chinese character, had left their unmistakable traces in the whole population' of a district of Panay Island, south of Manila.[40] He goes on to append a description of 'The slanting position of the [Chinese men's] eyes, forming an angle over the nose, the beardless chin, the long and delicate fingers' with the claim, 'the Indians [Malay Filipinos] [. . .] believe them [the Chinese] to be masters of the art of money-getting.'[41] Implicit in Bowring's almost abutting juxtapositions of Chinese facial lineaments and personality traits is the close association between the two phenomena. But to understand the full implications of those menacing 'slanting eyes' and 'delicate fingers' for the unpleasant demeanour of the Chinese, we must read on fifty or so pages: 'the Chinaman makes his profit, buying the labour of the indebted and extorting its maximum with coarse and often cruel tyranny. The Chinese have a proverb that the Indian must be led with rice in the left hand of his master and a bamboo in the right.'[42] Gait and posture could also be signifiers of a penny-pinching world view, as in the case of William Henry Thomes's novel *Life in the East Indies* (1875) which depicts an 'awkward China man [. . .] appearing courteous to all, while in his heart he despises the throng for its waste of money in riding in carriages as long as feet are able to support the body'.[43] The Victorian Manilaist preoccupation with the semiotics of the Chinese body may have originated from the case of Afong Moy who, in 1834, was the first recorded Chinese woman to immigrate to the United States. The Carne Brothers impresarios took her to New York City and placed her on public display in a 'Chinese Saloon' simulation replete with red lanterns, satin curtains and Chinese objets d'art.[44] In Lee's view, 'Afong Moy's exhibit sent out a clear message: China and the Chinese were exotic, different, and as Moy's bound feet further illustrated, degraded and inferior. By relegating her to an exotic curiosity, the Carne Brothers and all who came to gawk at her reaffirmed the West's superiority as well as the great differences between the United States and China.'[45]

Manilaist constructions of Chinese Manileños took a different tack during the political upheavals of the 1890s. The new, rising bourgeoisie of Chinese *méstizos* would have provoked a mixed reaction among outsiders with a political and commercial stake in Manila. While Western firms required the goodwill of the Chinese *méstizos* because they dominated the domestic cash crop trade, the centrality of the group to the burgeoning independence movement – not to say its vital intellectual role in defining Filipino national identity – would have caused Western imperialists to label them as subversive.[46] The character of Ah Khy in Archibald Clavering Gunter's novel *Jack Curzon* (1898) illuminates this dialectical positioning of the Chinese in the racial-social-political configuration of Manila. This 'Chinese dandy', as Gunter describes him, has benefited from contact with Western civilization, having studied at Yale University, learned upper-crust American slang and assumed a dapper, metropolitan style of dress.[47] On the boat trip from Hong Kong to Manila, Ah Khy impresses the hero of the novel Jack Curzon as a member of a pan-Asian dominant caste because his father owns a multinational shipping company. While Ah Khy's wealth and high breeding allows Curzon to accept him as a gentleman and near-equal, the Briton has misgivings about the hybridity of the 'Chinaman's' Oriental physiognomy and the authenticity of his 'Fifth Avenue swell'.[48] Moreover, when Ah Khy invites

Curzon to conspire with him against the shady German arms dealer Adolph Ludenbaum, Curzon inwardly reflects, 'Ah Khy is by no means a safe partner in anything that may bring us under the suspicion of the Spanish Government.'[49] Curzon then urges Ah Khy to avoid entanglement in 'the insurgent business', for the Spanish are now shooting Chinese dissenters on the street, at which point Khy turns pale.[50] Despite his commendable Western airs, Khy is a coward and cannot be trusted; now Chinese like him are enemies of the state. Indeed, a reviewer of *Jack Curzon* for the Glasgow *Herald* shortly after the book was published hints at these alarmingly contradictory aims and motives when he refers to a 'rather funny conception' of Ah Khy as a 'Europeanised Chinaman'.[51] The word 'funny' in this context has a 'relational value' closer to words such as 'strange', 'eerie' or 'disturbing' rather than 'droll' or 'amusing'.

The Philippine–American War did nothing to alter the fetish of the Chinese as '[artful] salesmen',[52] as H. Irving Hancock put it in his 1912 adventure yarn *Uncle Sam's Boys in the Philippines*. But, in this same story, Hancock, who had reported from the Philippines during the Spanish–American War of 1898 and afterwards made a remunerative career out of writing pro-imperialist 'dime' novels,[53] uses one such salesman to make an ideological point about the correctness of American expansionism in the Philippines and how this is to be negotiated with subject populations. A conspicuously soigné Malay Filipino man follows Sergeant Hal Overton of the Thirty-fourth United States Infantry into a Chinese-owned shop on the Escolta filled with beautiful but expensive goods. When the 'smiling yellow heathen'[54] of a proprietor tries to cheat Hal over the price of a teak and sandalwood chest, the Malay Filipino intervenes and offers to pay for it himself. 'I have been permitted to do a courtesy to an Americano,' he glows. 'I am not a poor man,' he continues, 'not since the Americanos came to these islands and gave us the blessings of liberty and just government'.[55] When the Malay Filipino informs Hal that he is a 'silent partner'[56] of the Chinese shopkeeper, Hal nobly refuses the gift and the dispute is settled. This scene could be read as a colonial allegory: any threats that Chinese prosperity may pose to US authority in Manila can be delicately mollified by the comprador class of Malay Filipinos – 'little brown brothers', as the discourse of benevolent assimilation had it – and the Chinese will accept their proper place within the new social order. However, this process of interpellation may not be as straightforward as all that because, soon enough, the Malay Filipino, whose name we learn is Vicente Tomba, becomes a 'little brown monster'[57] when he and his insurgent comrades abduct Hal as part of a 'plot against the American Government'.[58] When Hal's unit is dispatched out of peaceful, Americanized Manila to crush the last of the

Moro Muslim rebels in Mindanao in the southern Philippines, Tomba reappears in this theatre of war as 'right-hand man to the datto [enemy chieftain]';[59] a metaphorical reminder that, even by 1912, a decade after the official end of the Philippine–American War, US control over the territory and its social/ethnic groups had not yet been cemented and the Chinese population were not to be trusted for at least two reasons. According to Chu, the Chinese Filipinos took a pragmatic, 'wait-and-see attitude' to the Spanish–American and Philippine–American wars that presaged the US occupation and were willing to cooperate for the sake of self-survival with both the 'local rebels and the imperial powers'.[60] (In Hancock's narrative, the shopkeeper's sneaky compact with Tomba makes sense in these terms.) Neither these acts nor the Chinese Filipinos' attempts to petition mainland China for protection during the hostilities[61] would have inspired American confidence in Chinese loyalty to the new colonial set-up.

After the conflict, Manilaists came to see the Chinese in increasingly gendered and sexualized terms. Again, this perception was as likely shaped by public affairs in the West as in the East. As alluded to earlier, labour legislation in the United States had, in the latter 1800s, compelled Chinese men to take up work that was traditionally the preserve of American women such as washing, cleaning and cooking. By the 1910s, Hollywood films were stocked with effeminate Chinese caricatures engaged in these activities.[62] Although the Chinese in Manila were not in reality subject to the same divisions of labour, it is telling that the Manilaist gaze at this time rests upon a 'waiter, pigtail flying',[63] a dry goods (foodstuffs and sewing equipment) trader[64] and other Chinese employed in servile and arguably feminine lines of work. If the Chinese were belittled for being domesticated like Western women, they were also accused of being a threat to Western women. Perhaps mindful of the mass-popular Fu Manchu novels by Sax Rohmer, whose eponymous antagonist abducted and mesmerized respectable Caucasian ladies[65] and of the American eugenics lobby's moral panic over the Chinese influx weakening the white race through miscegenation,[66] the American Associated Press foreign correspondent Walter Robb reports on a Manileño Chinese dry goods trader who victimizes white females specifically: 'every American woman who comes to Manila gets cheated in her first encounter with the wily heathen.'[67] In an unusually caustic – even for that time – feature article in the *Atlanta Constitution* newspaper, journalist Muriel Bailey is more explicit about the sexual menace of Chinese Filipinos. That these men have a monopoly over Manila's 'places of vice' and 'their own women are not allowed in the country' suggests that they are prone to promiscuity and miscegenation.[68] Indeed, the warning sign for Bailey is that many Chinese have already married into and dominated the 'lower class of native women [who] prefer them as lords and masters to their own countrymen'.⁶⁹ If Bailey is disturbed that 'traces of Chinese blood are very noticeable in the general population',⁷⁰ we can only imagine how she might feel about Chinese pollution of the white, Anglo-Saxon race that is now settling in the archipelago. Intriguingly, Bailey also openly admits the supranational frame of her dislike of the Chinese 'plague' that 'can live anywhere' and whose faults – moral, sexual or otherwise – are congenital to a Chinese man wherever he may be on the planet because 'He is rarely troubled by conscientious scruples either in these islands or in his own country'.⁷¹

Nor are Robb's and Bailey's adumbrations sui generis to Chinese Filipinos in other important ways, as students of racist depictions of African American or Afro-Caribbean men will be aware. Frantz Fanon's seminal problematizing of interracial relationships in *Black Skin, White Masks* (1952) can, in a broad sense, shed more light on this iteration of anti-Sinicism. According to Fanon – by way of a quotation from the French novelist René Maran – when a black man realizes his 'desire for that white flesh that has been forbidden to us Negroes as long as white men have ruled the world',⁷² it is a subversive political act that blurs a racial binary dependent on assumptions about the superiority of whites and the inferiority of blacks. When a black man marries a white woman, avers Fanon, he '[marries] white culture' and his 'restless hands [grasp] white civilization and dignity and make them [his]'.⁷³ Moreover, he is able to 'prove to the others [white people] that he is a man, their equal'.⁷⁴ Whether in Fanon's post-war Francophone world or in Bailey's American colonial Manila, white supremacist (and indeed patriarchal) regimes cannot tolerate such transgressions for they may persuade subaltern subjects that they ought to be treated with a measure of humanity, respect and, as Fanon puts it, the feeling that 'I am worthy of white love'.⁷⁵

It is worth noting that, like the liberal eugenicists earlier, Robb's racist demonization of the Chinese predator coexists with a relatively progressive – though hardly anti-colonial – critique later in his book of the American political class's tendentious rhetoric about the Philippines being 'a United States possession, colony or what not' when in fact 'these islands are territory of the United States'.⁷⁶ William D. Boyce was another American liberal – again, by the criteria of his day – commentator on Philippine matters, who opposed media monopolization⁷⁷ and supported labour unions while proprietor of a newspaper publishing company.⁷⁸ Boyce's liberalism is less blatantly derogatory to Chinese Filipinos than Robb's, although it remains beholden to the same imperialist, racial-reductionist ideology. Interbreeding between Chinese and

Malay Filipinos, he writes as if assaying the relative merits of horses, is not only acceptable but welcome for it yields 'the best native type, more intelligent than the Malay, stronger physically than the Chinese'.[79] Whereas for Gunter and Manilaists of the 1890s such hybridity was a cause for US concern because many of the *illustrado* revolutionaries were Chinese *méstizos*, by 1914 these same men are now 'foremost Filipinos',[80] to use Boyce's terminology, and include Emilio Aguinaldo, once the head of the revolution but now a sworn ally of the Americans.

After the Philippines attained limited independence from the United States in 1946, Manilaist Sinophobia came to echo the anxieties of Filipino nationalist discourses. Caroline S. Hau holds that these discourses situated the Chinese as 'objects of distrust and censure' because they '[hitched] their desire to acquire citizenship to their desire to protect or enhance their business interests'.[81] The anxiety about Chinese wealth accumulation was borne from a double standard: the 'nationalization' laws of the 1950s and 1960s restricted Chinese involvement in retail and other industries while '[extending] equal treatment to American investors in all areas of the economy'.[82] The discrepancy is replicated in texts such as Raymond Nelson's narrative-discursive nonfiction *The Philippines* (1968) which, largely myopic about the enormous scale of US economic involvement in the Philippines, casts vague aspersions about the prosperity, insularity and cronyism of 'the Chinese minority [. . .] [that] remains loyal to its cultural heritage'.[83] Also noteworthy about Nelson is that his depiction of the Chinese as a disquietingly discrete community marks a departure from the often individualized, sometimes biologized ad hominems of previous Manilaists. Put in another way, Nelson is a product of Western hegemonic discourse's turn away from race-based value judgements to those of a 'culturalist' tenor, as Tzvetan Todorov regards it.[84] 'What will remain unchanged' between racism and culturalism, Todorov continues, 'is the rigidity of determinism (cultural rather than physical now) and the discontinuity of humanity, compartmentalised into cultures that cannot and must not communicate with one another effectively'. Furthermore, '"Culturalism" [. . .] replaces physical race with linguistic, historical or psychological race.'[85] While Timothy Mo's culturalism is understated in his 2000 novel *Renegade or Halo²* (a minor character Danton has a 'positively Chinese talent' for the property acquisition board game Monopoly),[86] it is emphatic in an interview Mo gave to the British *Independent* newspaper:

> It seems to me absolutely demonstrable that cultures are different. [. . .] And if they're different, they will by definition be unequal. [. . .] A society where you're

taken off in the middle of the night for torture, or your kids fail an exam at school because you don't pay a bribe to the teacher: they are inferior societies.[87]

While Mo is himself a member of the British Chinese diaspora and has won critical accolades for addressing the intricacies of cultural identity, in the final analysis he is a démodé essentialist: in *Renegade or Halo²* he writes of 'The immutability of our natures'[88] and elsewhere in that *Independent* interview claims, 'Stereotype has got a negative connotation, in ordinary life and for a novelist. But I've never found it a bad word. [. . .] Stereotypes are more likely to be correct than anything else.'[89] As we can see, while Sinophobia hinging on 'economic function'[90] was articulated more subtly than before in Manilaist texts, relevant paratexts (such as Mo's interview) reveal the same old crudely homogenizing stances towards race and ethnicity.

Another material development that may have patterned these attitudes was the Manila kidnapping 'crisis'[91] of the 1990s, during which at least $11 million was paid in ransoms.[92] As the business scholar Mark Turner explains, the families of Chinese Filipinos, as well as mainland Chinese and Taiwanese, were disproportionately targeted because they were 'widely perceived to be successful in business'.[93] Turner further asserts that these crimes incited public and official concern about the security of the Philippine economy, given the risks of 'loss of investment opportunities and the withdrawal of funds' to 'safer locations'.[94] This is a central theme of Seth Mydans's 1996 *New York Times* feature, which paraphrases with approval then-President Ramos's warning that 'the current wave of kidnappings has begun to have a dampening effect on the overseas Chinese investment that has been an important part of the country's recent growth'.[95] There is arguably a very subtle form of victim-blaming at play here, since the implication is that foreign-based Chinese withdrawal from business activities in Manila – an understandably self-preservational response to the threat of kidnapping – is making them a liability to continued Philippine prosperity. This perception takes on a supranational dimension when we consider that, coincident with fears of non-Filipino Chinese capital flight was a relaxation of Philippine nationalization laws that prompted 'the rise of large-scale retailing [. . .] concentrated in the hands of a small group of upper-stratum "Chinese Filipino" individuals'.[96] Additionally, commentators such as Mydans might have been party to a popular sentiment in the United States at the time that American 'national identity' was being eroded by Chinese 'direct foreign investment' in New York City.[97]

The latest incarnation of Manilaist Sinophobia stems from a momentous change in China itself rather than any events in the United States, United

Kingdom or the Philippines. Deng Xiaoping's market reforms beginning in 1979 triggered a period of extraordinary growth and production which was to culminate in China becoming the second largest economy in the world in 2011, a position that it has retained ever since. Over this period, Western media significations of China went through several stages, avers Zengjun Peng, beginning with optimism about the country's embrace of capitalist policies. But after the Tiananmen Square massacre of 1989, the media focused on China's authoritarian politics and internal repression. In the 1990s and early 2000s, the picture became more nuanced, with China 'regarded both as a strategic partner and a potential rival' given the strengthening economic bonds between the United States and China.[98] By the 2010s, the *New York Times*, the leading establishmentarian US newspaper, was deprecating 'vulgar displays of newfound [Chinese] wealth'[99] and other hegemonic media were expressing a 'concern' about 'China's economic achievements'.[100] The Scotland-born, Australia-based nurse and memoirist Duncan Alexander McKenzie's narrative-discursive book *The Unlucky Country* (2012) emerged from this ideological climate even if its hetero-stereotypes are so retrograde they could have been lifted from the pages of a Manilaist text published a hundred years before. McKenzie animalizes Filipinos ('innocently sensual creatures'),[101] condemns their culture as so much 'nonsensical superficiality' that 'offers no future for the Philippine nation'[102] and accuses them of preferring 'sociability as opposed to a strong work ethic'.[103] McKenzie's construction of Filipinos as unsophisticated and lackadaisical is perhaps a corollary to his warning that, in this new millennial world of Western decline and Eastern growth, the Philippines is lagging behind its neighbours economically, and this could have gloomy consequences for Western regional hegemony and the Philippines' supporting role in it: 'Look to the Chinese and the Taiwanese and the populace of Hong Kong. They have a life-long drive to academic achievement and economic success, and that is why they will rule the region, and perhaps the world.'[104] There is a note of lament for the old days of Western regnance in McKenzie's bogus distinction between the Philippines' current 'problematic' dealings with China and its historically 'straightforward and uncomplicated' relationship with the United States.[105] Moreover, McKenzie cautions melodramatically, 'China is a tiger, and it is hungrily pacing back and forth eying its prey. It is unashamedly hegemonistic. Nothing will shake its resolve.'[106] In his restricted view, such errant aggression contrasts negatively with 'the friendly big brother, the good old US of A',[107] a description which, coming from a more historically literate author, would surely be ironic. Rather, what is blindingly evident here is that the myth of US magnanimity towards the Philippines continues to thrive in Manilaism, despite having been long discredited by more reliable analyses.

Since President Rodrigo Duterte's 'pivoting' towards Beijing which began in 2016, Western liberal commentators have been more assertive than McKenzie in their animus towards China. Tom Smith, the *Guardian* pundit and academic with the Royal Air Force College in Cranwell, UK, laments that surging Chinese investment in the Philippines and an apparent climbdown by Duterte in a dispute with Beijing over territories in the South China Sea is tantamount to a 'surrender of the US alliance . . . [not] in the better interests of the Filipino people'.[108] But his case is far from watertight. While it is true that Beijing has pledged to invest $24 billion in the Philippine infrastructure, this does not mean Duterte has turned his back on the United States, however anti-American his rhetoric can be. The United States is erecting new military facilities in the archipelago[109] and is the Philippines' chief trading partner with regard to 'countries that imported the most Filipino shipments by dollar value during 2019' (China is third on this list).[110] Further to this, in June 2020 Duterte suspended his signature anti-Americanist policy of cancelling the Visiting Forces Agreement that allows US forces to be stationed in the country.[111] At any rate, Duterte is not the first Philippine president to play a 'cat-and-mouse game'[112] of maintaining good relations with the United States while improving relations with China. In 1975, Ferdinand Marcos signed a joint agreement with the People's Republic of China which included the statement 'there is but one China and that Taiwan is an integral part of Chinese territory'.[113] In 1997, Gloria Macapagal Arroyo allowed a Chinese naval ship to enter Manila in a gesture of solidarity with Beijing.[114] Even supposing Western fears about realignment with China are well founded, they are nevertheless predicated on a hypocritical assumption that China is a singular threat to Asian peace. In his book *Duterte Harry: Fire and Fury in the Philippines*, the *Channel 4 News* (UK) correspondent Jonathan Miller makes much of 'Beijing's remorseless militarisation of the South China Sea'[115] while staying silent on the far larger and more provocative cordon of 400 American bases in countries surrounding China, some equipped with long-range missile capabilities.[116] More to the point, unlike China, US armed forces are currently operating in seventeen Asian countries including the Philippines. While the official justification for this is the so-called War on Terror,[117] Tadiar perceives the real agenda as the 'imposition of global martial law' to ensure the obedience of 'crony states' like the Philippines to 'US hegemony'.[118] Furthermore, as M.G.E Kelly avers, while we should be suspicious of Chinese pledges not to 'interfere in the internal affairs of other countries,' by contrast the United States 'arrogates a right to global interference in almost everything'.[119] If we compare the two powers' track records as imperialists in Asia since the Second World War, China invaded Tibet in 1950 and continues to viciously repress separatist movements there and in other regions such as Xinjiang Uyghur,[120] while America has fought devastating wars of aggression in the Korean and Indochinese peninsulars, Afghanistan, Kuwait and Iraq, and pursued lethal covert operations in China (on behalf of the anti-communist Guomindang nationalists in the late 1940s), the Philippines, Iran, Lebanon, Syria and Yemen. Apparently, it is not militarization of Southeast Asia per se that bothers Smith, Miller et al., just the Chinese militarization of Southeast Asia. There are economic as well as geopolitical reasons to doubt that the new 'Yellow Peril' has the strength, resources or inclination to rampage across the Philippines and Southeast Asia. 'Far from being an imperialist power,' Kelly writes, 'China remains, in effect, a victim of imperialism (particularly in the form of unequal exchange)'. On pitiful wages and in perilous conditions, Chinese workers make cheap goods for Western consumption, and most of the profits generated in China from trade with the West end up being reinvested in the West.[121]

The new continental military- and economics-based Sinophobia has redrawn the textual map of Manila. A May 2018 *Bloomberg News* article offers a snapshot of the daily realities of Duterte's Faustian pact with China. 'Restaurants serving Chinese hotpots and dumplings' and 'Mandarin broadcasts at the Mall of Asia' are catering for 100,000 recent Chinese immigrants, whose arrival in Manila has profited several local corporations.[122] However, in keeping with the hoary old cliché about Chinese avarice, this human 'deluge' has also contributed to soaring house prices which is a source of worry for one Filipino resident, at least. 'I hope they become an asset to the community,' he says, 'and not just out to make money'.[123] The unnamed writer's framing of the Chinese as at once useful to and alien to Manila society is consonant with Caroline S. Hau's claim that Philippine nationalism has construed the Chinese Filipinos as 'a foreign presence, but they are a familiar foreign presence'.[124] 'Nationalist thinking about money,' she continues, 'was articulated with the idea of the "foreigner"',[125] despite a grudging acceptance of the Chinese Filipinos' 'contribution to national development'.[126] In a further signifier of problematic cupidity, the *Bloomberg* piece states that dozens of Chinese gambling companies are setting up shop in the city, producing a boom that '[won't] last forever'.[127] It is instructive to compare this foreboding coverage of Chinese investment with the celebratory tone of a 2013 BBC report on how 'innovative technology'[128] is driving Manila's 'amazing'[129] (so the Filipino head of the Contact Centre of the Philippines puts it) call centres and BPOs

(Business Process Outsourcing concerns) that are contracted to British and American corporations. Rather than, as per the *Bloomberg* story highlighting the risks of this burgeoning sector, call centres are presented as an unalloyed 'success' that are fully sustainable thanks to government 'tax breaks, fast-tracked permits and other perks'.[130] Whereas *Bloomberg* paints the expatriate Chinese workers and businesspeople as a 'deluge'[131] that is culturally reshaping Manila and stoking anxiety among its indigenes, no such concerns are raised by several recent media accounts of Western retail chains opening branches in Manila, for example.[132] This 'one rule for the West, another rule for China' discrepancy is conspicuous in Jonathan Miller's work too. Swift to admonish Duterte's spending programme for leaving the Philippines in 'Debt bondage to China',[133] Miller has nothing to say about how, in the 1980s and 1990s, Western-led international financial organizations beggared the Philippine economy with crippling loans and destructive free-market 'reforms'.[134] Ironically – or perhaps appropriately – a legacy of these policies was the popular discontent that swept Duterte – whom Miller accuses of bringing unprecedented 'chaos and disequilibrium to the Philippines'[135] – to power in 2016, as the next chapter of this book investigates in greater depth.

In the era of Duterte's 'drug war' – in truth a campaign of extrajudicial killings (EJKs) of drug dealers and abusers – Triad gangsters and other Chinese involved in the narcotics trade are a malevolent presence in Manilaist narratives. Unsurprisingly, this presence is not immune to the now age-old suspicions of greed, criminality, otherness and foreignness. According to a 2016 work of investigative journalism by John Chalmers, an illicit Chinese facility north of Manila is capable of producing a stunning $24 million worth of methamphetamine per day.[136] The 'Chinese-looking men',[137] as locals identify them, who run the operation are a synecdoche for the disproportionally high representation of Chinese nationals in the Philippine drugs trade. The trope of yet another malignant Chinese infiltration of Philippine society is reinforced by Chalmers's claim that the 'cooks' and 'chemists'[138] needed for such labs are flown in from mainland China and are liable for a national 'problem' that is 'made in China'.[139] In Jonathan Miller's book there is also a going native-style theme of Filipinos being morally compromised after they have been bodily besmirched by unscrupulous Chinese. In an echo of the Filipino villains forcing 'the indelible mark of the Katipunan' secret society[140] on the British lead character of Archibald Clavering Gunter's 1899 novel *Jack Curzon*, Miller recounts the now-infamous anecdote of Duterte's son Paolo who refused to remove his clothes and show a Senate inquiry a Triad tattoo he was alleged to possess.[141]

At first glance, whereas previous Manilaist models of the Chinese rested on shaky empirical foundations – Rupert Hodder has identified long-standing epistemological obstacles to ascertaining the 'degrees of Chineseness' within a historically hybrid Chinese Filipino population and therefore the true ethnic composition of Philippine business ownership[142] – the contemporary Manilaist focus on Chinese traffickers would appear to be more firmly grounded in objective truth. After all, China is 'the biggest source of the meth and of the precursor chemicals used to produce the synthetic drug that are being smuggled into the Philippines,' reports Chalmers.[143] Moreover, between January 2015 and August 2016, 'Of 77 foreign nationals arrested for meth-related drug offenses [...] 49 were Chinese [...], Taiwanese or Hong Kong residents.'[144] However, while these facts are indisputable, the ideological slant of the writers who deploy them is betrayed by the omission of other relevant facts that cast doubt on the notion of Chinese omnipotence in the narcotics realm. In just one month, July–August 2016, reports the Philippine news website Rappler, '12,923 individuals [were] arrested and 626,556 voluntarily surrendered',[145] which somewhat dwarves the figure of 49 arrests of Chinese over the much longer nineteen-month period Chalmers cites. As the social psychologists Bordalo, Coffman, Gennaioli and Shleifer have found, 'stereotypes are often inaccurate. The vast majority of Florida residents are not elderly, the vast majority of the Irish are not red-headed, and flying is really pretty safe.'[146] But this does not stop 'Social groups that have been historically mistreated' falling prey to 'bad stereotyping, perhaps because the groups in power want to perpetuate false beliefs about them'.[147] According to this theory, Manilaist 'false beliefs' about Chinese crime have more to do with pre-existing anti-Chinese sentiment than with real contemporary statistics. And, as we have seen many times in this book, the singling out of one group for ills that other groups also bear responsibility for is as ethically odious as it is intellectually sloppy. It is therefore worth noting Philippine Drug Enforcement Agency spokesman Derrick Carreon's assertion that it is not just Chinese crime syndicates that are responsible for methamphetamine supply to the Philippines; gangs from Mexico and several African nations are complicit too.[148] Would that all Manilaist writers were as judicious as Mr Carreon in their analyses of the Chinese Filipinos throughout the ages.

For the sake of clarity, it is important to assert that criticisms made earlier of Western media and literary distortions of current Chinese–Philippines relations do not and should not produce a contraposition that in any way exonerates Chinese state-corporate exploitation of the Philippines. While there is some truth to Western commentators' allegations that Duterte has 'sold out' his country to

Chinese interests, the validity of such allegations is somewhat undermined by their selective excision of other factors that point to Western evasions about, or even complicity in, the current problems. We should not be unduly surprised about such selectivity given that it is a sine qua non of regressive cultural stereotypes more generally. As the psychoanalyst Willem Kooman has revealed, 'It is generally accepted that in processing information people are guided by relevant cognitive representations or schemas [supporting perceptions of "outgroup" stereotypes]. There is also agreement that information relevant to an activated schema is preferentially encoded, whereas irrelevant information is more or less neglected.'[149] To be sure, the making of the supranational Chinese stereotype over the last four centuries has involved a good deal of such 'selective processing', to borrow further from Kooman's lexicon, about the Chinese in Manila, China, the United States and Europe. The supranationality of this symbolic order means that it necessarily resonates with a broader debate about the representation of new economic and diplomatic hostilities between China and the Atlanticist West. I examine this topic in greater detail in the conclusion to this book.

6

Call of Duterte

Cacique despotism and Western (neo)liberal crisis

In June 2016, Rodrigo Duterte won a convincing victory in the Philippine presidential elections. Part of his appeal to alienated, working-class voters was his ebullient reputation as a provincial mayor who had overseen the extrajudicial killings (EJKs) of drug dealers and petty criminals in Davao, the southern Philippines. As president, he duly extended this de facto war to the rest of the archipelago and Metro Manila became its key battlefield. In just one night in 2017, a police sting operation left thirty-two suspected drug dealers dead in Bulacan, north of the city.[1] The national body count at the time of writing is estimated to have exceeded 20,000, 'the largest loss of civilian lives in Southeast Asia since Pol Pot took Cambodia back to Year Zero,' as Jonathan Miller points out.[2] Understandably, Miller and other Western authors of the Duterte era have foregrounded this genocide-in-progress in their work and, in some cases, tried commendably to educate a largely *blasé* Western reading public about its true horrors. However, in doing so, these writers have often reached for some of the more moth-eaten clichés of Manilaism, wider Orientalism and Western mass-culture. This is most visible in their constructions of Duterte as a monstrous neo-*cacique* whose laddish charisma belies a demonic intent to destroy the fabric of Philippine society and the tenets of international law. As Reynaldo C. Ileto asserts, 'Images of the Filipino elite (oppressive caciques, bosses, patrons) and masses (blindly loyal and manipulated *táo*, clients of the bosses [. . .] reappear in modern journalistic garb.'[3] Furthermore, these writers have been less than scrupulously balanced in their diagnoses of how 'Murderous Manila'[4] came to be, and absent from their register are terms such as 'neoliberalism', 'US imperialism' and 'Western propaganda biases towards the non-Western world'. Ultimately, they are symptomatic of a neoliberal world view in crisis; while they castigate the Duterte regime for its aberrant brutality, they do not admit any Western responsibility for this totalitarian drift in Philippine politics, and nor do they accept that their own ideology, despite its ostensible support of human rights and 'rules-based' international relations, has, asserts Pankaj Mishra, been an 'incubator' for 'authoritarianisms' and an apology for 'the occupation and subjugation of other people's territory and culture [as] a wonderful instrument of civilization'.[5]

Duterte Harry (2018), Jonathan Miller's blend of biography and reportage, is an intensively researched and multi-fronted critique of Duterte's gruesome necropolitics and sociopathic personality. Miller interviews an ex-hitman in hiding, relatives of EJK victims and political figures who have taken extraordinary personal risks in opposing the regime. Intended for a Western market, *Duterte Harry* has something of the structure, style and tone of a British or American crime thriller and makes various allusions to Hollywood culture, although such features are probably not postmodernist gestures à la Alex Garland or Timothy Mo. The title of the book is an obvious pun on the 1971 action movie *Dirty Harry* and one chapter on Duterte's sexual improprieties is named 'Duterte Harvey', presumably after the Tinseltown predator Harvey Weinstein. Other chapters end on cliffhangers that promise more gunplay, gossip or depravity if we read on.[6] The American cinematic frame of reference extends across the entire narrative from the 'mobster moustache' of ex-Manila mayor Joseph 'Erap' Estrada[7] to the climactic scene where Miller watches Duterte, 'his Dirty Harry face on',[8] publicly confessing to the EJKs at a Philippine National Police (PNP) event. Miller's investigation of Duterte's son Paolo and his alleged drug connections falters due to the classic McGuffins of '[opaque] allegations, key evidence missing, witnesses not forthcoming'.[9] Although not as redolent of the potboiler genre as Miller, James Fenton's 2017 reporting for the *New York Review of Books* has a kindred tone and atmosphere. In one scene, Fenton is, Philip Marlowe-like, 'standing in heavy rain, under an umbrella, in a dark Manila alleyway, outside a house known to be a drug den'.[10] The landmarks of Miller's discursive map of Manila include the River Styx-like 'liquid grime'[11] and 'claustrophobic, muddy passageways strewn with rubbish'[12] of third-world-bluesy slums, one of which has been colonized by the Western kitsch of Queen's 'Bohemian Rhapsody' playing on a 'giant speaker'. When Miller notes that 'Freddie [Mercury] crooningly asks whether this is real life or just fantasy',[13] he is almost certainly not making a metatextual statement about his own mimeses of Manila. Nonetheless, it might provoke the curious reader to think about the ambiguous relationship between Miller's factual source material and the fictive conventions he articulates it through. The same could be said of his comment that a 'special report' on the EJKs 'read[s] like something from a convoluted thriller'.[14] There is an equivalent lack of self-awareness in

Miller's proposition that, during Duterte's wayward youth, 'He became the pastiche of a Hollywood tough-guy',[15] given that Miller neglects to recognize that Western writers like him incessantly limning Duterte as a Hollywood tough-guy might have contributed to such an image.

Apart from calling on the codes of modern Western popular culture, Miller draws deep from mainsprings of Orientalist signification that predate Clint Eastwood by centuries. Miller's Duterte Harry is the apotheosis of the Philippine *cacique* stereotype as defined by Reynaldo Ileto (see Chapter 1). Ever since US intellectuals and policy-makers framed the Philippine–American War as 'a time not of continued resistance to foreign occupation, but as one of banditry, religious fanaticism, disorder and dislocation,' the pre-eminent Western view of the Philippines has emphasized its chaotic, tribal, violent, 'pre-political' character.[16] As one would expect, the Philippines is not the only non-Western society to be characterized this way by Western power-knowledge systems. As Tamara Pearson explains,

> [Western] News discourse is based on the assumption that the only way to do democracy, elections, and economics is the highly dysfunctional two-party neoliberalism of the US and Europe. If countries stray from the West's way of doing politics, or from 'free' trade and privatization, they are labelled as tyrannies, dictatorships, regimes, and more. Though the news claims to be unbiased, there is a stark inconsistency in the terminology used for the West and for poor countries.[17]

A society where the rule of law and democratic institutions – as narrowly defined by Western hegemony – are in short supply will, so the '*cacique* democracy' discourse has it, necessarily produce draconian, autocratic leaders. Perhaps the gravest symptom of such a political malaise is, Ileto writes, 'repressive, manipulative' governance.[18] Aside from drawing attention to the drug war's affrontery of human rights and judicial due process, Miller summarizes Duterte's assaults on press freedom,[19] his arbitrary arrests of opponents[20] and his supporters' mobilization of 'fake news' to mislead the voting public.[21] Ileto's labels of 'clientilism' and 'factionalism' can also be pinned firmly on Miller's Duterte Harry, given his preferential treatment of alleged high-level drug pushers once he forms a personal attachment to them[22] and the palpable 'cronyism' that fuelled his ascendance in provincial politics.[23]

Many of these traits also accord with the even older European invention of Oriental despotism. According to Alain Grosrichard, Rousseau, Voltaire and other Enlightenment French men of letters portray Asian rulers who 'upon a whim [. . .] elevate this or that subject, who for a moment before was nothing, to the highest office'.[24] Had these eighteenth-century critics been reincarnated in our time they may have written much the same as Miller about Duterte's nepotism and arbitrary exercise of power. Just as, according to Grosrichard, 'the despotic economy [. . .] leads to the widespread impoverishment of all and the exclusive enrichment of a single man',[25] Duterte's 'personal slush fund' amounting to $260 million is corruption of epic proportions, avers Miller.[26] 'It is in his [the despot's] power to watch anyone anywhere,' writes Grosrichard, 'for example, by assuming the guise of anonymous passer-by in a Constantinople street'.[27] According to Miller, Duterte lurks incognito around his home turf of Davao, warning panoptically, 'I have this city covered. Even if you fart, I will know you've farted.'[28] As with other repertories of cultural stereotypes, Grosrichard claims, Oriental despotism often 'appears in two opposing – not to say contradictory – guises'.[29] The sultan or vizier is simultaneously all-powerful and a mere 'manikin, and usually the most cowardly and womanish in the nation [. . .] he is a totally spent force'.[30] Intriguingly, Miller uses that exact same phrase to describe Duterte: for all his machismo, he is a 'spent force' whose ruthless efficiency at slaying suspects is inversely proportional to his incompetent, indecisive management of Philippine economics, foreign policy and much else.[31] Grosrichard's French thinkers 'observed [the] effectiveness' of unfree Eastern polities, 'an effectiveness all the more surprising for its apparent dependence upon extremely fragile – not to say non-existent foundations'.[32] In Miller's final analysis, there are bizarre absences and anomalies at the heart of Duterte's rule over the Philippines: the president himself 'has had very little to do with Dutertenomics [his administration's fiscal programme] personally';[33] he is capable of both 'murderous threats on live TV' and 'Mafiosi subtlety';[34] and his 'populist knack of making everybody feel he is "their guy"' succeeds precisely because he 'remains beholden to absolutely no one'.[35] These denotations of Duterte the Orientalist despot are open to the charge of what Stuart Hall dubs 'having-it-both-ways', where 'other' or 'different' people 'seem to be represented [in discourses] through sharply opposed, polarized, binary extremes [. . .] and they are often required to be both things at the same time!'[36]

One explanation for this 'having-it-both-ways' representation of incompatible opposites is the timeworn assumption that Western modes of logical thought cannot be transposed to the non-Western world. And why would they be when, as Grosrichard's Gallic writers contend, Orientals are more likely to act on their raw emotions than on their faculties of reason no thanks to various racial, social and climactic factors? The crucial question, then, of how, as Grosrichard puts it, 'a people bends to the absolute authority of one man'[37] can be explained by a phenomenon that '[European] political theory has rejected, refused to think of as political, which might well be something stronger than strength, more seductive than ideology, more enticing than gain – the very source of political power: love'.[38] Thus for Miller, Duterte's electioneering 'inflamed fierce loyalty'[39] and, after a year in power, he 'could do no wrong'[40] in the eyes of 78 per cent of Filipinos, despite his epic miscalculations and controversies. As the newspaper editor Stella Estremera tells Miller, 'You don't talk with that man – you listen to him,'[41] which further implies that the bedrock of Duterte's success is blind, irrational devotion to a domineering father figure whose actions must never be questioned. (In this same sequence, Miller makes a bizarre and culturally insensitive comparison between Estremera, a Filipina journalist, and Mr Kurtz, the white, self-deified master of the African natives in Joseph Conrad's 1899 colonial novel *Heart of Darkness*.)

'That such a monster [despotism] should be a viable one in Asia,' writes Grosrichard, 'assumes the monstrousness of men themselves in their love of servitude in that part of the world.'[42] While Miller does not go quite this far in his assessment of Duterte's allure, his choice of the title 'Slaves and Tyrants' for the book's final chapter is telling, as is his litany of claims that portray Filipinos as passive actors and overly vulnerable to Duterte's deceitful bluster. Before the 2016 election, a homogenous 'disappointed country' was 'ready for another strong man'[43] and when Duterte 'assured' the people that the drug problem 'threatened national security', they duly 'believed him'.[44] Just as the slave subjects of Grosrichard's Arab tyrannies were interpellated through emotional manipulation rather than appeals to rationality, so Filipino citizens are prone to Duterte's evidence-free scaremongering about crime, online 'cyber-babble' that lacks all substantiation and an esoteric theory that Duterte is a new 'messiah'[45] peddled by an 'evangelical cult'.[46] But according to Grosrichard, Oriental despotism requires from its subjects something more than love, obedience and fear. In Chapter 3 we examined Grosrichard's concept of the 'corruption of fear' in which brusque tropical conditions prohibit the aspiration for lasting social progress in the Orient. However, Grosrichard proposes another manifestation of the 'corruption of fear' in the belittling gazes of Ricaut and Montesquieu: 'among the peoples of Asia the fear of death is replaced by a kind of joy in, or even frenzied passion for, suffering or dying.'[47] Long before Duterte's presidency, Nicholas Loney and George A. Miller had taken a Pecksniffian line on what they regarded as Philippine Roman Catholicism's perverse infatuation with pain and death, as we saw in Chapter 1. More recently, in his 2008 autobiography, the

British socialite Sebastian Horsley fetishizes – and personally participates in – a mock crucifixion ceremony in San Fernando near Manila. 'As a dandy I was excited about the project,'[48] writes Horsley. He is spellbound by this 'freak show' involving 'mostly young Filipino men' who 'believe that through pain they may reach more closely to the divine'.[49] Again, Duterte-preoccupied Manilaists are subtler than that and substitute a Filipino's passion for his or her own suffering and death with a passion for other people – drug users and pushers – to suffer and die. Michael Peel, foreign correspondent for the *Financial Times*, quotes a 'a Duterte loyalist' as exclaiming, 'Whenever you feel that your life's threatened, fight it out and kill your enemy.'[50] In addition to the electorate projecting a bloody 'revenge fantasy' on to Duterte, Miller asserts that, during the presidential election campaign, the denizens of 'crime-infested shanties' were seduced by his 'take-no-prisoners' style.[51] The more vicious his rhetoric against criminals, other politicians, the West and organized religion, the 'more media attention he won, and the more his growing army of supporters laughed and loved him'.[52] Alternatively, in James Fenton's Manila there has been such an excess of death and destruction that passionate frenzy is no longer an appropriate habit of mind. Instead a film *noir* fatalism is preferable. Fenton recounts attending the scene of an EJK in the casual, world-weary voice of a veteran reporter who, having grown used to man's inhumanity to man, is not only morally equanimous about it but possibly even bored by it now. 'There wasn't much to it,' he writes of the quadruple murder of marijuana smokers. One can almost hear the tired sigh as he summarizes the investigative procedure: 'Now the police were examining the upstairs room, while we examined the alleyway. [. . .] There was an established routine in these matters.'[53] Whether it exhibits itself in a morbid bloodlust as per Miller or in an apathy about wickedness as per Fenton, the corruption of fear is a dysfunctional social phenomenon that, for the Manilaist, is typical of – or at least acceptable in – the Philippines, but would be decidedly out of place in the more sane, ordered and enlightened West.

Indeed, these Manilaist writers' tacit allegiance to Western exceptionalism is a necessary adjunct to their limited constructions of late 2010s Manila. One such limitation is a certain monomania in their analyses of Duterte's power base. While Miller acknowledges that poverty and inequality contributed to the popular disaffection that won Duterte the 2016 election, Miller's preference for a 'global trade' system that disproportionately benefits Western economies (indeed he warns that Duterte challenges the 'stability' of that system)[54] may explain why he does not address a key material cause of *Dutertismo*. The Filipino global development expert Walden Bello asserts that, in the 1980s and 1990s, the US-dominated World Bank and IMF plunged the Philippines into extreme debt and 'massive poverty' by imposing free-market trade, industry, land and spending 'reforms'.[55] Over subsequent decades, this 'neoliberal disarmament' caused the Philippines to lag behind most of its neighbours in terms of poverty reduction and annual average growth rate.[56] The mushrooming debt burden resulted in acute under-investment in infrastructure and human services.[57] Alienated from this economic and political order, millions of Filipinos voted for Duterte's heady populism.[58] Manilaism's excision of this vital detail would also invest a certain amount of hypocrisy in its withering portrayal of Duterte as the alien, aberrant bogeyman. As Tadiar cogently observes, it was precisely the unintended consequences of self-interested Western policy towards the Third World in the late twentieth century that laid the groundwork for Filipino politicians of Duterte's strain: 'The rise of a "strong-man" regime was a World Bank-endorsed response to the growing and intensifying crises felt in the nation as a result of the political and economic system installed by US colonization being pushed to its limits by the acceleration of global capital.'[59]

Western-centric hypocrisy also distorts the moral calculus Miller and company apply to Duterte's atrocities, encapsulated in Noam Chomsky's aphorism: 'When they do it, it's a crime. When we do it, it's not.'[60] Writing in *The Guardian* in 2016, the academic and journalist Tom Smith makes the highly tendentious point that Duterte is 'more of a threat to the world' then-President Donald Trump. While Duterte has slaughtered 20,000 Filipinos, he is incapable of attacking people beyond his own borders, whereas US military actions have killed up to 4 million in the Middle East alone since 1990. These actions have included – and continue to include – the legally controversial drone strike campaigns in Asia and North Africa, and the wars on Iraq and Afghanistan that breached international legal treaties and normalized torture and kidnapping. While Michael Peel argues that another reason for Duterte's ascent is his 'mining of a seam of anti-US sentiment', Peel only briefly – and uncritically – mentions acts of American imperialism.[61] Similarly, Miller remarks on a 'rich vein of unresolved colonial angst'[62] in Philippine society, but does not elaborate on the potential rationales for this angst. 'The Philippines was the Americans' first overseas colony,' he writes, 'acquired from the Spanish after a short war in 1898 for US$20 million.'[63] The employment of the euphemism 'acquired' would lead the less informed reader to believe that the US conquest of the Philippines did not require the grisly racist genocide of the Philippine–American War. Indeed, Miller's only reference to that genocide is a disturbingly trivial one: while it was raging, US troops imported '*bundok*', the Tagalog word for 'province', into the English language.[64] The Filipino historian

E. San Juan, Jr. has pinpointed continuities between these US aggressions of the late 1800s/early 1900s and its present-day 'counter-insurgency maneuvers' against both Islamist and Maoist rebels in the outer provinces of the archipelago. 'US troops are "recolonizing" the Philippines,' writes San Juan, Jr., to 'preserve its eroded world hegemony' post-Cold War and post-9/11.[65] Unfortunately, Miller is as ignorant of these latest abuses by the American Empire as he is of those from 1898 to 1903. 'US forces were operating [. . .] in Mindanao,' he writes, 'in support of Philippine army operations against the jihadist Abu Sayyaf group.'[66] His assessment is typical of commentators bedazzled by the rhetoric of the 'romantic' relationship – to use Tadiar's metaphor – between the United States and the Philippines. American military 'support' for the Philippine state against a common enemy implies 'Equal, democratic partnership,'[67] as Tadiar puts it, but San Juan Jr.'s description is more accurate: the Philippines is yet another 'sovereign nation'[68] that the United States is exploiting as a 'battlefront' in the so-called War on Terror, and the ruling classes of both states are collaborating against 'Muslim separatists born from the Cold War and the seasoned combatants of a revitalized popular democratic, socialist revolution'.[69]

Given such indifference to the historical record, it is not surprising that Miller reduces Filipino anti-American sentiment to either petty vanity or conspiracy theory lunacy. He psychologizes Duterte's hatred of the United States away by proposing it is motivated by his 'perceived rejection'[70] when he tried unsuccessfully to obtain a visa to travel there. When interviewed by Miller, Duterte's 'increasingly irate' sister Eleanor rants about Zionist as well as Atlanticist plots against the postcolonial world while 'leaning forward, jabbing her finger at me'.[71] In the same chapter as this encounter with Eleanor, Miller shares the cloak-and-dagger tale of Michael Meiring, an alleged CIA agent who blew himself up with an explosive device in a Davao hotel in 2002, while Duterte was serving as mayor of the city. Miller claims that Duterte pounced upon 'conspiracy theories surrounding this not-so-quiet American' to whip up populist ire against US operatives acting 'as if they own the place [Davao City]'.[72] Deluded or not, members of the Duterte family are probably not the most articulate or principled theorists of US imperialism. Miller's failure to talk to Filipino scholars such as Tadiar and Dylan Rodriguez – who are much more persuasive than the Dutertes about how a century of American state violence, exploitation and 'global white supremacy'[73] has shaped modern Philippine attitudes – amounts to an insinuation that only vindictiveness, paranoia or cynicism could possibly explain antipathy towards a binational connection that, states Miller, is held in 'high regard' by Filipinos.[74]

At any rate, neither this assertion about 'high regard' nor his claim that 'millions of Filipinos [...] love America more than many Americans themselves' are on evidential terra firma because they rely on recent opinion polls apparently showing that most Filipinos are 'pro-American'.[75] Miller does not pause to consider that these responses may have been conditioned by decades of indoctrination through the ideological state apparatuses (the establishmentarian media, organized religion, the education system and so forth) largely controlled by the upper stratum of society whose hegemony depends upon a 'fraternal' illusion of Philippine–American ties. Miller also cites the legions of Filipinos who have, since the turn of the twentieth century, migrated to the United States for work as proof of the society's Americophilia.[76] This is, however, a dubiously monocausal analysis that excises the true plurality of reasons why Filipinos relocate abroad. According to the migration scholar Mirca Madianou, these include 'fulfilling one's family obligations',[77] improved healthcare, better education and escape from 'domestic violence'.[78]

The only time Miller does allude to the spectre of imperialism and the 'troubled colonial past',[79] he somehow exonerates the Americans from such charges, but not the Spanish, even though they were overthrown in 1898 and have had no political or economic influence over the Philippines ever since. He favourably cites Jose Rizal's fictional critique of Spanish rule, *El filibusterismo* (*The Reign of Greed*) (1896), contending that its warning 'What use is independence if the slaves of today will be the tyrants of tomorrow?'[80] has come to pass in the Duterte era of *cacique* despotism and political retardation. In a sense, then, we have come full-circle back to the villainous governors and Mephistophelian dictators of nineteenth- and twentieth-century Manilaism, these images themselves informed by the American historiographers identified by Ileto, as examined in Chapter 1 of this book.

When Duterte lambastes Western interventions in Libya, Panama and Iraq, and US police shootings of innocent African Americans,[81] Miller, *The Atlantic*'s Jonathan M. Katz and other Western liberal literati have rightly called Duterte out for 'whataboutism', or what is more formally termed the '*tu quoque* fallacy' in which 'An argument [...] consists in retorting a charge upon one's accuser'.[82] Duterte's ham-fisted strategy here is to cynically rebuff scrutiny of his own atrocities by appealing to vulgar nationalism and anti-Americanism, as if the fact that Americans killing poor, non-white people in the developing world somehow justifies him killing poor, non-white people in his own country. But coming from Western liberals, the 'whataboutism' charge can, as it were, be reversed due to these pundits' almost pathological inability to recognize that, as shown earlier, the European and American empires themselves have much longer and more egregious records of committing state-sponsored slaughter. As the philosopher Andrew Spear avers, '*tu quoque* can be used legitimately to question whether a particular moral principle is in fact one we endorse and, if so, whether everyone is consistently following it.'[83]

Another issue on which Duterte has played the *tu quoque* card is the International Criminal Court's (ICC) investigation into his transgressions, which began in February 2018.[84] While we should, again, seriously doubt the sincerity of his complaint, it does nonetheless speak to a pressing practical problem: how can Duterte be brought to justice when UN delegates,[85] legal experts and academic commentators[86] have repeatedly excoriated the ICC's erratic treatment of Global Northern and Global Southern state crimes? In 2009, Jean Ping, president of the African Union Commission, said, '[the] ICC always targets [. . .] Africans. Does it mean that you have nothing on Gaza? Does it mean you have nothing [on the] Caucasus? Does it mean that you have nothing on the militants in Colombia? There is nothing on Iraq? We are raising this type of question because we don't want a double standard.'[87] After examining the West's lack of liability for its crimes in Vietnam, among other 'colonial wars', and stating that Western 'corporate impunity remains rife', the secretary-general of the European Centre for Constitutional and Human Rights, Wolfgang Kaleck, concludes that 'The practice of double standards will have to be addressed to protect this project [the ICC] against erosion of legitimacy and global endorsement'.[88] Suffice to say, there is no consideration of the uneven moral landscape of international law in Miller's half-page disquisition on the ICC, nor in any of the dozens of reports on the topic by other Western journalists. It is not in their interests to raise the subject, for they would have to admit that the case against Duterte is in part driven by a conception of human rights as, so the Filipino historian Vicente Rafael holds, 'essentially [. . .] a form of imperialism: the West dictating to the non-West the norms of proper conduct'.[89] These norms are particularly 'problematic', continues Rafael, because the 'UN rapporteurs [are] lecturing the Philippine president-elect about human rights from a location that is historically responsible for their daily violation in its complicity with the "war on terror", neoliberalism, and drone warfare, to give a few examples'.[90]

These discordant ethical principles are imposed not only on the Duterte/West binary but on comparisons between Duterte's reign of terror and those of other non-Western world leaders. As the political analyst Richard Seymour points out, the United States and British media have repeatedly criticized Duterte while turning a blind eye to the crimes of another Asian 'quasi-fascist', prime minister of India Narendra Modi.[91] In 2014, while serving as governor of Gujarat state, the Hindu fundamentalist Modi helped to instigate a massacre of 1,000–2,000 Muslim civilians. But instead of casting doubts on Modi's fitness to lead his country, the Western press – as well as Western politicians from Barack Obama to Theresa May – have been highly complimentary to the point of being 'mythopoeic' about his 'business-friendly' economic strategy.[92] The discrepancy between the coverage of Modi and Duterte, Seymour argues, is a twofold matter: Duterte 'does not present himself as an economic liberal' while Modi clearly does, and 'Modi aligns to the US' whereas 'Duterte has undertaken a "pivot" to China'.[93] Although I challenged the conventional definition of this pivot in chapter 5, it is worth noting at this point that, not for the first time in the annals of Orientalism, cynical realpolitik trumps moral objectivity when it comes to assessing the relative failings of Global Southern regimes. Although no Manilaist author specifically likens Duterte to Modi, Miller does try to recruit Duterte into the evil pantheon of 'populist [authoritarian]'[94] world premiers of which Modi is also apparently a member. This is as much a logical category error as it is an illustration of moral disparity. While Miller and his ideological confederates penning op-eds in *Time*, the *Guardian* and the *Independent* group these 'strongmen' together according to their shared animus towards liberal values, they have little else in common with each other. That Duterte, who has promised to 'destroy' Islamic jihadism in the Philippines,[95] can be equated with the Islamist firebrand Recep Tayyip Erdoğan of Turkey[96] or that Duterte's self-professed socialism – whether we take his word for it or not – can be slotted in neatly next to Central European demagogues with their 'roots in Nazism'[97] is perhaps a function of Manilaism's/Orientalism's impulse to haphazardly homogenize anything it deems to be 'other'.

The economic liberalism which Seymour references is, I think, vital to fathoming the disjointed, Janus-faced and denialist perspectives of contemporary Manilaism. As I hope to have shown earlier, these writers cannot stomach the possibility that the (neo)liberal policies and practices they endorse may have been among the foundational causes of the Duterte nightmare. Nor can they accept that their own countries of origin – the so-called liberal democracies – are themselves deeply culpable for larger-scale unjust war and multiple homicides beyond due process. Nor do they give anything more than cursory thought to an older version of Western liberalism that, Mishra writes, 'did not seem particularly liberal to the peoples subjugated by British, French and American imperialism in the 18th and 19th centuries'[98] and that inclined many Filipino voters to Duterte's anti-Americanism, however coarse and self-serving it may be. On the Philippine domestic front, Manilaist writers gloss over the illiberal misdemeanours of Duterte's predecessors – just as long as they were nominally economically and politically liberal – as in Tom Smith's baffling proposition that Gloria Macapagal Arroyo (president of the Philippines 2001–10) is a 'good role model' for the progressive resistance to Duterte.[99] The conclusion depends on historical amnesia, given that Arroyo's administration heavily censored the press, imposed a 'state of emergency' (a limited form of martial law) and was ultimately responsible for at least '1,093 victims of extrajudicial killings, 209 victims of enforced disappearances, and more than a thousand victims of torture'.[100] Furthermore, Smith's inclusion of Arroyo, along with the (admittedly more honourable) current vice president, Leni Robredo, in a clique of 'strong' elite Filipina politicians whom he hopes will 'combat the macho autocrat' Duterte smacks of a problematic identity politics that is just another symptom of the (neo)liberal malaise. Societies that have been so badly broken by the global and local historical forces explained earlier cannot be quick-fixed by placing a few more women into positions of leadership, especially if these women's political assumptions deviate only superficially from those of the men presently in charge. But to labour under the illusion that such reforms will rescue the day excuses Smith et al. from, once again, admitting that the deeper causes of the crisis are closely connected to their own ideological dictates.

Modern-day Manilaists go to such Herculean lengths to disavow the role of (neo)liberalism in the 'Duterte Problem'[101] that they can only retreat to the rusty platitudes of by-now-classic Manilaism: Filipinos are easily led, irrational and so forth ad nauseum. Ironically, though, some of these writers' reliance on narrative forms (police procedural, Hollywood motion picture etc.) that are the quintessential products of the Western globalized culture industry, is the nearest they get to admitting any kind of Western collusion in causing the dire straits that Manila – and the Philippines – are in today.

7

Towards an anti-Manilaism

The literary scholars Justin D. Edwards and Rune Graulund are surely right to argue that the Western 'writing of travel' is dominated by texts that 'perpetuate Empire'.[1] Certainly, all Manilaist travelogues – as well as novels, memoirs and other narrative works – sit somewhere on that scale, whether they make clarion calls for civilizing missions, apologia for the Philippines' debased position within global capitalism or ethnocentric slurs against Manileños. However, it would be inaccurate – as well as unnecessarily pessimistic – to therefore claim that it is impossible to write about Manila or other parts of the non-Western world without recourse to Orientalist structures. Indeed, early on in *Orientalism* Edward Said writes, 'Perhaps the most important task of all would be to undertake studies in contemporary alternatives to Orientalism'.[2] Another book that has been crucial to my thesis, Martin Green's *Dreams of Adventure, Deeds of Empire* may be primarily concerned with the reactionary adventure story idiom, but it also includes cogent chapters on Leo Tolstoy, Mark Twain and Mahatma Gandhi, whose work vigorously contested the orthodoxies of Russian, American and British imperialism respectively. Edwards and Graulund themselves have identified an oppositional trajectory of letters that posits an antidote to Orientalist bigotry. What they dub 'innovative travel writing'[3] can 'reveal' a 'progressive politics [. . .] wherein the travel writer is self-reflexive about the genre (and his or her participation in it)'.[4] Furthermore, they aver, the innovative form is 'polyphonic' given that it absorbs 'diverse narrative voices'[5] and is 'sensitive to multiple points of view' because it 'recognize[s] the power relations – the political agendas – that are often concealed behind the force of knowledge'.[6] According to another literary critic, Debbie Lisle, 'In order for travel writers to accept the discursive construction of their destinations, they would have to engage in another meta-conversation – this time about fundamental spatial categories underscoring the genre of travel writing as a whole'.[7] In addition, Lisle regrets the 'unwillingness of travel writers to address the difficulties of representing others'.[8]

I now want to explain how the recommendations made and challenges posed by Edwards, Graulund, Lisle and a host of other scholars with postcolonialist affiliations can shed light on a counter-hegemonic canon of narrative writing – not just the travel form that these critics focus on – that interprets Manila in ways that repudiate Manilaist representations. What I want to term 'anti-Manilaism' dates back to at least the 1930s and includes Filipinos (such as the novelist Jessica Hagedorn and the essayist Luis H. Francia) and non-Filipinos (including the Australian aid worker/travel writer Tom Bamforth and the American historical novelist John Sayles). This chapter is not in any way intended to be a comprehensive survey of the rich, fecund and innovative traditions of Philippine literature in English, which, for priorities more cultural and political than aesthetic, has not yet received the international critical attention it so deserves.[9] My aim instead is to focus on a relatively tiny number of these texts and how they break with Manilaist dogma. While critiquing the non-Filipino writers who appear in this chapter, I have kept in mind two of Edward Said's most instructive observations: the first is his call to 'study other cultures and peoples from a libertarian, or a nonrepressive and nonmanipulative, perspective'[10] and the second is, 'I certainly do not believe the limited proposition that only a black can write about blacks, a Muslim about Muslims, and so forth'.[11] In the mode Said is alluding to, I have tried to demonstrate that several Western outsiders have effectively represented the voices of marginalized and subaltern Filipinos in a more sensitive and less manipulative fashion than have their Manilaist counterparts. In speaking *about* Filipinos and allowing Filipinos to speak for themselves rather than speaking *for* Filipinos in this manner, these writers adhere to Massimo Canevacci's (from whom Edwards and Graulund may have loaned the term 'polyphony') assertion that 'nobody wants to delegate to another professional the right to represent him/herself'. Empirical researchers, then, must appreciate that their human subjects of study are engaged in 'self-representation [. . .] understandable only through their autonomous visions and reflections'.[12]

Unlike the previous chapters, which were structured by literary trope or literary-historical epoch, this chapter organizes its considerations of narrative strategies, linguistic devices and research approaches into themed sections. In the first section, entitled Self-Reflexivity, I argue that certain authors' awareness of their own assumptions, research ethics and, in some instances, status as Western professional writers operating in a postcolonial site produces a counterweight to Manilaism's arrogant trust in the infallibility of its own gaze. In the next section,

Polyphonic Agendas, I hold that particular texts promote multiple points of view for the purpose of exposing harmful power relations and political agendas. They achieve this using several methods including parody, irony and writing in the 'shadow'[13] of Filipino rather than Western authors who reduce or excise those aspects of the city they find distasteful. In Challenging Spatial Assumptions, I focus on authors who have answered Lisle's call for travel writers to '[identify] the formations of power that make distinctions between here and there seem natural' and to 'stop conceiving of the world in terms of the static geographies of Empire'.[14] Broadly speaking, this is done through interrogating the ontological grounds of Manilaist constructions of urban geography and rescuing positive value from an often degraded and embattled cityscape. Finally, the section titled Representing Others outlines the formal techniques used to overcome 'the difficulties of representing others' such as by illuminating the social, economic and political forces that shape jaundiced Manilaist perspectives of individuals and social groups.

Self-reflexivity

As we have seen throughout this study, Manilaists from Nicholas Loney in the nineteenth century to Jonathan Miller in the twenty-first century have imposed a 'commanding view' on Manila that suggests they have done little to no critical thinking about the accuracy or reliability of their adumbrations. Alternatively, in the spirit of Edwards and Graulund's assertion that 'the innovative travel writer does not position himself or herself as the primary source of authority',[15] Maslyn Williams, who in Chapter 1 I argued both conformed to and kicked against the Manila-as-hell construct, is generally more interested in posing questions to himself about 1970s Manila than rushing to judgements about it. After meeting Ferdinand and Imelda Marcos, he even-handedly '[wonders] what place there will be for them in history' and whether they will '[steer] the Filipino Ship of State between the Scylla of communism and the Charybdis of foreign economic domination'. Furthermore, does the Marcos' 'promise of opportunity and justice for everyone seem real to the young and poor?' and can this gesture towards greater egalitarianism supplant the 'enslaved degradation' of previous colonial and neo-colonial administrations?[16] Williams is self-conscious about the limitations of his outlook because he is open to having his preconceptions challenged by the Filipinos he encounters. After agreeing with a former medical student that communism and democracy both involve 'masters and slaves' and that, when either system 'enters into a conflict situation it [becomes] [. . .] tyrannical, ruthless and cruel', Williams's interviewee loses his temper and starts railing against the hypocrisy of Westerners condemning the Philippines' human rights record while 'their own countrymen run the biggest, most corrupt and insidious armaments business in history'.[17] Although fazed by this 'excessively overemotional' tirade, Williams admits that it is 'shot through with truth' and is persuaded enough by its logic that he concludes his trip to Manila on this thought: 'Our pretences and our hypocrisies are part of its [the Philippines'] history – the hard part – during which it has been subjugated, cheated, betrayed and treated as third rate.'[18]

Going further than Williams in his rejection of Manilaist authorial sureness, is the Filipino memoirist Luis H. Francia. In the introduction to his *Eye of the Fish* (2001), a compilation of personal essays, Francia writes that his status as an expatriate Filipino who has been re-visiting Manila over the last two decades has compelled him to meditate on his own identity and subjectivity as a writer. 'Where was the "I" in all this,' he writes, 'where the "we"? [. . .] home had changed. And so had I. How then to measure each other?'[19] According to Celia Hunt and Fiona Sampson, such 'reflexivity'[20] is an integral component of thoughtful memoir and autobiography writing, in which 'the author or at least narrator' locates him or herself in the '"present day" in relation to (another) narrative time.'[21] 'Autobiography says both "I am here" and "I was there". Its temporally bifurcated narrator stabilises him or herself by "having a foot in" both these moments of narrative time.'[22] Ultimately, Hunt and Sampson argue, when writers are prepared to map their 'self-in-process'[23] in this way they gain the 'opportunity of making [their] [. . .] own unique contribution' and are able to establish their own 'particular ways of speaking to others via the page'.[24] While Francia's self-in-process has been – and continues to be – shaped by the complicated condition of being both an insider and outsider in Manila, the advantage for him is that he can mitigate the material problems of the contemporary city – the poverty, sexual criminality and corruption – with happier memories of 'my childhood' for the sake of construing a 'Manila [. . .] of the imagination' that is 'forever sacred' and 'immune from the mutability of time and even place'.[25] If Manilaism can conjure a mythical Manila hampered by a refusal to self-examine (particularly when it comes to prejudices towards the Other), then it is feasible, we see with Francia, to conjure another mythical Manila that embraces the intricate fluidities of subjectivity and identity. Francia's psychogeography is one of the most eloquent expressions of a tendency within Filipino writers of recent years to seize back control from the Manilaists – and their comprador allies – over how the city is imagined and to what ends. In Chapter 5, I examined several Manilaists from the 1960s to the 1980s who implied that Filipinos had, to loan another of Tadiar's formulations, 'been collectively dreaming the dreams of others [Westerners]' and internalized 'the rote mythographies of their given identities'.[26] According to Tadiar, these Manilaist portrayals have some empirical truth to them because Filipinos themselves – whether film stars such as Nora Aunor or political families from the Marcoses to the Aquinos – embody fantasies about mimicry, submission and the postcolonial nation. But what has been made can be unmade, because, as Tadiar goes on to write, 'now that globalization has arrived, and (some) people have immediate access to other lived imaginaries through new telecommunicational technologies and increased labour migration, we are all of a sudden imagining for ourselves, creatively dreaming beyond our nation-bound imaginations (if not re-inventing them) and exerting that dreaming on the world in ways that we had never done before.'[27]

An awareness of one's subjectivity as a writer in the world is also a matter of acknowledging the ethical and epistemological obstacles that can arise during the research process, and integrating them into the fabric of the narrative composed.[28] For Rosalind Coward, this is one of the 'techniques of classic reportage', as exemplified by the nineteenth-century British journalist Henry Mayhew, who 'foregrounds how he constructed his research' by candidly recounting the problems he faced gathering data from a "costermongers" girl who is reluctant to be interviewed', in addition to other members of the Victorian London poor.[29] Traditionally, Philippine literature in English has been defined by a 'didacticism'[30] seeking to educate Filipinos about their political responsibilities and instil in them a 'national consciousness', argues novelist Miguel Syjuco.[31] Since a writer who wants to overtly persuade a reader of a political perspective needs to project an air of authority and self-assuredness, there is not a very rich seam of Filipinos writing about Manila with the same candour about their epistemological mishaps as Mayhew. However, the Philippines' status for some years now as one of the most dangerous places in the world for journalists[32] has produced a lineage of Philippine investigative reporting that necessarily places the frustrations and perils of knowledge-gathering at the forefront of its narratives. Unlike Manilaist correspondents who, as previously illustrated, tend to admit fear, confusion or uncertainty only when it suits an agenda of cultural disdain informed by 'the priorities and fashions of established power', as John Pilger terms it, their Philippine counterparts tend to admit the same when fulfilling what Pilger sees as the correct function of journalists, to evince 'scepticism' towards 'higher authority and deference to "experts"'.[33] In *Altar of Secrets*, a 2013 exposé of sexual and financial impropriety in the powerful Philippine Roman Catholic Church, the late, acclaimed Filipino reporter Aries C. Rufo recounts his troublesome interactions with a crucial source called Christine Rances, whose claim that she has fathered the 'love child' of Bishop Crisostomo Yalung is about to ignite a national scandal. First, Rances agrees to be interviewed several times, 'only to back out later'.[34] When she does eventually talk to Rufo, she says that hospital staff have doubted the 'authenticity' of Yalung's signature on the birth documents of the love child, yet after the meeting finishes, Rufo receives an anonymous text message that casts doubts on Rances's own authenticity, warning 'that she was capable of mischief'.[35] Later, when it appears Rances will not receive child support from either Yalung or a religious charity, she is 'encouraged [. . .] to be creative in making money' by baptizing her second illicit child with Yalung 'not once but several times'.[36] Although many of her allegations can be cross-verified, Rances's mercurial behaviour and the counter-claims against her impede Ares's endeavour to construct a watertight journalistic case against Yalung's misconduct. Furthermore, while Rufo has, by the end of his research, gleaned enough piquant data for a reasonably revelatory story, he is denied proper closure by Yalung's refusal to answer questions from his place of exile in Sacramento, California.[37]

Polyphonic agendas

The Manilaist authorial certainty that anti-Manilaist self-reflexivity dissents from is often sustained by the excision – or 'reactionary forgetting'[38] – of cultural, social, political or historiographical data that might undermine the clichés and stereotypes Manilaism deals in. In addition to foregrounding hitherto neglected data, F. Sionil José's novel *Dusk* (1998) problematizes the conditions that result in historical events – particularly the American conquest of the Philippines that, as Chapter 2 elucidates, is something of a Manilaist taboo – being not only expurgated from the Manilaist canon but under-discussed in contemporary media and political discourses. A nationalist allegory of sorts, *Dusk* charts the fortunes of a family of Filipino serfs in the 1880s who, after their patriarch murders a callous Spanish *padré*, are forced to flee into a wilderness that José frames as a revivifying sanctuary untouchable by the Spanish diadem. For one of the young men of the family, the aspirant rebel intellectual Istak, Manila is a symmetrically seductive proposition, a 'dream, [. . .] another world, unreachable' that is a storeroom of the cosmopolitan 'wisdom', 'goodwill' and 'knowledge' necessary for political emancipation.³⁹ These lived experiences and aspirant imaginings radicalize the protagonists against first Spanish and then American imperial aggression. When the latter has supplanted the former as the *bête-noire* of the Philippine Revolution, José renders the marauding American soldiers as 'a ruthless enemy who defiled women and bayoneted children'⁴⁰ and makes a meta-textual nod to how the full gruesome facts of the conflict will never be properly comprehended in the real world beyond the fictional milieu of the novel: 'Yes, Eustaquio – there is so much the world does not know, how the Americans have tortured our people, committed the most brutal crimes against humanity.'⁴¹ John Sayles's *A Moment in the Sun* (2011), the most astute, I think, historical fiction penned by a Westerner about roughly the same period that José covers, vividly dramatizes the discursive censorship of the American conquest that has led to the kind of near-universal ignorance José decries. Sayles offers us access to the inner life of a minor character only ever referred to as 'the Cartoonist', who wilfully distorts photographic evidence of the war for a jingoistic American newspaper. When drawing a native *kris* sword jutting from the back of a US infantryman, the Cartoonist thinks it appropriate to add 'a few extra serpentine curves' to the weapon 'for effect'.⁴² However, depicting 'the wily Filipino is a bit of a problem' because the 'peon's rags' in the photo he is working from too closely resemble those worn by previous colonial nemeses of the United States such as Cubans and Mexicans (whom his editor 'hates so much').⁴³ To distinguish the Filipino insurgents from these other villains and to emphasize the new threat they pose to the United States, the Cartoonist makes 'a slight exaggeration' to an image of rebel chief Emilio Aguinaldo by giving his physiognomy 'the cunning stamp of the Jap'.⁴⁴ Sayles's reconstructions of such 'yellow' journalistic skulduggery help us to understand the motives behind Manilaism's endorsement of early US imperialism that I delved into in Chapter 2.

As we saw in Chapter 4, a technique akin to excision is 'shadowing', wherein a Manilaist only references texts that support rather than test his or her preconceptions. In contrary mode, another of the Philippines' most celebrated authors, Nick Joaquin (using the pseudonym Quijano de Manila) published *Language of the Street* (1980), a collection of lyrical essays on Manila which proceeds in the shadow of other writers who defy that tendency within Manilaism to diminish the city's cultural and aesthetic value. In a cool, reflective tone that is antithetical to both the portentousness of the Manila-as-hell exponents and the serio-comic contempt of the flawed simulation enthusiasts, Joaquin cites an impressive array of sources – from Ernest Hemingway to esoteric theology to the anti-imperialist intellectuals José Rizal and Claro M. Recto – to construct a palimpsest of Manila whose hybrid architecture, cuisine, fashion, art, literature, educational institutions and religious festivals bear the hallmarks of US, Latin American, Chinese and European cultural influence. But the fact that, as he writes, 'Manila has been a Malay city, a Spanish city, an American city, and is now a Filipino city'[45] does not mean Manila is confused or uncertain about its identity; rather this dynamic cultural blend is precisely a precondition for the city's uniqueness and a valid reason for 'civicism':[46] 'When a Manileño speaks, he speaks – whether he knows it or not – with all his past behind him, which is why his voice rings with such authority and pride.'[47] Another virtue of Joaquin's Manila is that it does not succumb to the temptation, as many postcolonial counter-discourses do, of proposing an essentializing nativism that glorifies 'pre-colonial, indigenous ways' and makes debatable claims about a pure, unadulterated national or local identity.[48] In addition to proposing alternative shadows to productively inhabit, it is possible to immanently critique the shadows of Manilaist writers. Jessica Hagedorn's *Dogeaters* (1991), an intertextual, temporally disjointed, post-modern novel that charts the fortunes of a well-connected Manila family from the 1950s to the 1990s, is intercut with excerpts from nineteenth-century Western texts whose turgid rhetoric ironically counterpoints the gritty, sordid realities of late twentieth-century Manila. For instance, an 1898 address by President McKinley to Methodist clergy in which he promises 'by God's grace [. . .] to uplift and civilize and Christianize [. . .] Manila; then Luzon; then other islands'[49] prefaces a chapter in the book about an American tourist drunkenly harassing a Filipino male sex worker in a dingy 1980s Manila nightclub.[50]

Another way of looking at Hagedorn's intervention is through the lens of parody, which, as Tadiar argues, can repurpose the vulgar copyism that captivates Manilaists for oppositional ends (see Chapter 4). 'Beyond the one-sided story of global "Americanization",' she writes, 'within which Filipino "mimicry" could only be a sign of domination, there is the much more complex story of global cultural flows and exchanges, within which such imitative renditions can also be seen as a form of agency, perhaps even resistance.'[51] One of the discourses subverted in Filipina novelist Gina Apostol's vivaciously inventive, multi-layered mise an abyme, *Insurrecto* (2018) is that of a fictional 'cultural curiosities' website called 'praxino.org' which depicts Manila and the Philippines as a flawed simulation, although not at all in the mode of Manilaists from Mary H. Fee to Pico Iyer. The website presents Philippine society as obsessed with gossip about British and American celebrities, listing sightings of Tom Cruise, Sandra Bullock, Madonna and Eric Clapton. But this reverie of Western glamour is tarnished by these celebrities' tactless or manipulative attempts at cultural appropriation – the opposite process, one could say, to the ungainly endeavours of Manileños to impersonate Westerners à la the flawed simulation conceit. Thus, Tom Cruise's wearing of Asian-style flip-flops betrays an 'ugly ingrown toenail' and Sandra Bullock 'did not buy her black baby in an area near the old US Air Force base'.[52] Although it may not be parody in the strict formal sense, a 1970 piece of reportage by Filipino journalist Jose F. Lacaba fits Simon Dentith's definition of the genre as one that 'typically attacks the official word, mocks the pretensions of authoritative discourse'.[53] The first three quarters of Lacaba's narrative comprise an eyewitness account of a pro-democracy student uprising in Manila against the Marcos dictatorship that strikingly captures the brutality of the police shooting and injuring protestors.[54] Lacaba ironically post-scripts these images with quotes from 'the official word' of warped government propaganda that departs drastically from what Lacaba has seen with his own eyes. The Marcos PR machine ascribes to the demonstrators an 'evil purpose'[55] and casts the state as the guarantor of 'peace and order'[56] that is being undermined by an extremist menace. Given that Marcos was to declare Martial Law just two years later, there is also a measure of dramatic irony in Lacaba's inclusion of the president's promise that 'In the matter of the preparation of the plans of reaction against any attempt to take over this government [. . .] [,] there will be no attempt to curtail constitutional freedom'.[57] The cagey, cautious tone of voice and verbose, euphemistic diction of these remarks brings to mind numerous Manilaists over the years, which is appropriate enough given the time-honoured collaboration between US imperialism and national bourgeois leaders such as Marcos. Hence, Lacaba's decision to juxtapose such a myopic discourse with his own precise, matter-of-fact depictions of, for example, an injured student with his 'fingers dangling like dead worms attached to his wrist only by a few threads of broken bones',[58] constitutes a rejection of the partial, self-serving conception of history and reality that the powerful (which includes Manilaism and its native sympathizers) cleave to.

Earlier Filipino fictions of a Marxist disposition address the problem of the national bourgeoisie that was to lead to the Marcos catastrophe. In doing so, they offer a corrective to the brands of Manilaism that either ignore the harmful consequences of Philippine elite collusion with US power or that try to justify Manilaist fantasy-productions by alleging Filipino complicity in them (see Chapter 4). This is often achieved by invoking the epistemology of the 'history from below' movement pioneered by Eric Hobsbawm, E.P. Thompson and Thorold Rogers. The objective of the movement is to revise our understanding of historical change by giving attention to the perspectives of '"real people" [. . .] whose lived experiences was thought by scholars to be of no interest', and in so doing challenge 'a lofty nineteenth century vision of the great deeds of ruling elites'.⁵⁹ In Manuel Arguilla's short story 'The Socialists' (1930), a well-to-do Manileño socialist attends a meeting of peasant radicals and feels increasingly alienated from their cause. The major insight of the story is that upper-class *mestizos* who claim to have a social conscience can never sincerely join the struggle against American imperial capitalism for fear of losing all the privileges they have accumulated under the status quo. Akin to this, Maximo Kalaw's 1929 novel *The Filipino Rebel* simultaneously 'addresses the passivity and self-interest of the Philippine political classes under compadre colonialism',⁶⁰ as Rajiv S. Patke and Philip Holden put it, while fêting proletarian resistance to the Americans during the 1899–1902 war.

Challenging spatial assumptions

Lisle acknowledges two main deficiencies in the contemporary travel genre's construction of foreign spaces in its bid to uphold 'discursive hegemonies':⁶¹ some texts '[resuscitate] outdated tropes of Empire and colonialism' while others 'promote a version of cosmopolitanism saturated with privilege'.⁶² The city-as-hell and third world blues tropes (Chapter 1) could conceivably belong to the first category while the flawed simulation (Chapter 4) could belong to the second. I want to show that all three modes can be challenged by now examining sequences in anti-Manilaist texts that accentuate the culturally and socially affirmative features of daily urban existence, opening up spaces in which intercultural dialogue can occur. At the same time, we must be mindful of the risks of overstating Manila's assets to the detriment of recognizing its problems in their proper social contexts. *Traveler's Choice: North to South* (1994), a collection of short chronicles by the Filipino travel writer Madis Ma. Guerrero, goes some way to remedying the Manilaist habit of modelling Manila as an inexorably depraved, corrupt and crime-blighted metropolis by emphasizing the city's street-level atmosphere of joy, warmth and gusto which somehow flourishes amid unpromising conditions. Guerrero's nostalgic disquisition on the 'group singalongs' in the 'beer houses, pub houses and the folk- and rockhouses'⁶³ during the dark days of Martial Law (1972–81) conveys the carnivalesque character of working-class Manila life. The reader is left with an impression of solidarity through hedonistic sociality. Something of this spirit makes it into the American sports journalist Rafe Bartholomew's *Pacific Rims*, with its affectionate rendition of the passion ordinary Filipinos have for basketball, from marginalized individuals like 'Elmer Gonzalez, the Cebuano midget who buffed his playing sneakers like they were his most prized possession' to lower-class 'beauty queens crowned on their barangay [neighbourhood] basketball courts'.[64] But bearing in mind Edwards's and Graulund's remark that, in innovative travel writing, 'the narrating subject is [. . .] determined by identificatory markers (nationality, ethnicity, race, gender, class, economic status, religion etc)',[65] it is obvious that Bartholomew's ruminations as a foreigner from a very different socio-cultural background to that of a Filipino can never be equivalent to Guerrero's intimate reminiscences about his youth from the subject position of a native Manileño. While Bartholomew and others cannot claim anywhere like the same degree of authority as Guerrero, and nor are they capable of speaking for Manileños of his generation as he does, I would suggest that there is at least some virtue in outsiders highlighting the more positive features of Manila that have escaped the gaze of others working in the Manilaist rubric.

'What right do travel writers have to speak for and represent others?'[66] Debbie Lisle asks suggestively. When we pose that question to Manilaism we could reasonably answer 'not much'. Nonetheless, Lisle asserts that, while Western travel writers will always be strangers looking in to a non-Western site, opportunities for 'cross-cultural communication' can arise when such writers constructively engage with an aspect of an unfamiliar culture with an open and empathetic mind.[67] As we saw in Chapter 3, Archibald Clavering Gunter and other early- to mid-Manilaist anxieties are pessimistic about the prospects of such accommodations. To prove Gunter wrong and Lisle right, we should return to *Pacific Rims* and consider how basketball functions in it as a common language between the American Bartholomew and the Filipinos he encounters. Before he drills down into the details of this phenomenon, Bartholomew is notably more candid than other Westerners about the dark history of US colonization of which sport is an undeniable component. After discussing the 'brutal conflict to suppress the Filipino independence movement' and the American Empire's need for a 'commercial foothold' in the archipelago, he explains that the US educational programme to 'indoctrinate Filipinos' included teaching schoolgirls basketball.[68] However, basketball was soon appropriated by Filipinos themselves and the Catholic Church (which predated the Americans' arrival) had a 'zeal for teaching [its] values through [the] sport'.[69] Bartholomew goes on to acknowledge other local 'factors' that helped to, as it were, 'Philippinize' basketball such as paucity of space and equipment.[70] Despite this happy hybridity, Bartholomew has a 'discomforting picture of my future home'[71] in his head before he moves out from his native United States to the Philippines due to the Manilaist-like scaremongering of the patrons of a New York City bar he tends. Upon arrival, he makes friends easily due to a shared, almost religious devotion to basketball, but he is at first bashful about being a 'particularly novel hanger-on – tall, foreign, always scrawling in a spiral notebook' that 'spectators were curious about'.[72] Near the end of his trip, this barrier to being accepted by Filipinos lifts when the laundryman of the Aces basketball team anoints him their 'lucky charm' and the chef at a Quezon City restaurant merrily recognizes him for this 'association' with the team. Thus, bi-directional intelligibility has been achieved in the teeth of cultural difference: 'They came from the disparate nooks of Philippine society; I came from thousands of miles away. Yet I understood their passion as well and as deeply as anything I'd ever know. [. . .] The food and the footwear were different here, but the soul of the game was the same.'[73]

While Guerrero's and Bartholomew's positivity about Manila is a refreshing alternative to Manilaist contempt or indifference, it would be as disingenuous for writers to fix solely on Manila's assets as it has been for Manilaists through the ages to report exclusively on the city's defects. To overcome third world blues by simply ignoring or whitewashing Manila's problems risks establishing an alternative – yet equally problematic – repertoire of fallacies based upon the lionization of localities and the suppression of their less desirable traits, as Patrick Holland and Graham Huggan remind us with their exegesis of the 'neofeudal fiction' of the British author Peter Mayle. His writings on the Luberon region of southern France betray a 'nostalgic appreciation for a regional way of life [. . .] characterized by the apparent absence of class conflict, by the happy coexistence of the local peasantry with the landowning bourgeoisie'.[74] A comparable text in the Manilaist canon is *Two for the Road* (1998) by Anita Feleo and David Sheniak, a lowbrow fusion of tourist itinerary and unreflective life writing that rests on superficial lists of trivia and innumerable clichés ('living history', 'to walk in his footsteps' etc).[75] While *Two for the Road* lauds the touristic value of Manila's topography, there is political pusillanimity towards neoliberal economic development. Amid the bland praise for the 'well done' trompe l'oeil paintings found in Intramuros is a swift mention of the 'squatters' (a Newspeak term used in the Philippines to describe poor, homeless people) who were driven out of the district by gentrification. But the authors do not care enough to investigate what happened to the squatters after their eviction.[76] If we recall Benedict Anderson's excoriation of James Fenton as a 'political tourist', this is surely worse: a political tourism with next to no politics. Feleo and Sheniak's critique of pernicious

US influence goes no further than a terse summary of the American treasure hunter Charles MacDougal's unintentional destruction of antique buildings while excavating for wartime Japanese gold.[77] *Two for the Road* represents one of the perils of confronting centuries of Orientalist *idées fixes* about the worst of urban Manila with an equivalently dogmatic triumphalism that concentrates only on the city's positive attributes, at least as they are defined by elite political and commercial criteria (it is telling that Feleo and Sheniak habitually recycle Department of Tourism public relations copy).[78]

Avoiding the representational hazards of both third world blues and third world idealization is a cluster of anti-Manilaist writers who delve into poverty, corruption, conflict and sexual exploitation while grasping these phenomena in their proper material contexts. Crucially, these authors also draw attention to the abetment of the powerful – both inside and outside Manila – in their propagation. If the garbage dumps, whorehouses and polluted rivers of late Manilaist textual spaces such as P.J. O'Rourke's are presented as steadfast fixtures that cannot be imputed to social-systemic flaws, counter-hegemonic renderings of Manila often gesture towards the bellicose role of globalized capital in the making of these gloomy loci. While Luis H. Francia deprecates contemporary Manila as 'a city of bad dreams',[79] he attributes the city's decline to a 'mass-market capitalism' serving the rapacious demands of foreign corporations, tourists and paedophiles.[80] We saw earlier in this study how Manilaists from various epochs tried to indict religion and superstition for Manila's social and political predicaments while having little to say about the damage done by Western cultural beliefs and (neo-)colonial practices. Maslyn Williams turns this formula on its head when he criticizes the West's failure to live up to its own religious ideals: 'We are excellent pretenders. We pretend to believe in a Christian style of democracy to feel for the underprivileged.'[81] He is just as caustic about the West's conduct on the world stage that is a factor in the sustenation of cities-as-hell like Manila: 'I am also aware that the West is in large part responsible for the fact that countries like the Philippines are going through a time of internal political conflict, and that our economic policies are aggravating the poverty and inequality that create these conflict situations.'[82]

Correspondingly, in *Deep Field: Dispatches from the Front Line of Aid Relief* (2014), the Australian humanitarian coordinator Tom Bamforth learns of the complicity of Western-led capitalism in the impoverishment, atomization and alienation of Filipinos. When he travels to Manila's financial district to solicit donations for the victims of a typhoon in the southern Philippines he is spurned by Western businesspeople whose definition of aid, informed by 'Bush-era prejudices,'[83] amounts to exploiting recruitment opportunities which, as Bamforth learns, perpetuates the 'physical, sexual and economic abuse' of migrant workers and increases the 'vulnerability of children and families left behind'.[84] Although a realist novel rather than a nonfiction travelogue like Bamforth's, *Soledad's Sister* (2007) by José Y. Dalisay nonetheless follows a convention of modernist travel writing where 'landscape [...do[es] the work of symbol and myth'[85] by mobilizing the grimly nondescript site of Ninoy Aquino International Airport (NAIA) in Manila as a cipher of the mistreatment of OFWs (Overseas Filipino Workers). The novel opens with a description of the dehumanizing process by which the corpse of 'Cabahug, Aurora V.' arrives at NAIA in crates, is stamped by apathetic officials and then left to be claimed by relatives.[86] The body, we later learn, has been misidentified and in fact belongs to Soledad, Aurora's sister, who is just one of approximately 600 deceased OFWs per year shipped back to the airport from abroad. Unlike the unexamined voyeurism of similarly foreboding scenes in Garland or Mo, the fate of Aurora is synecdochal of Filipinas who become second-class citizens when they migrate to the rich world, vulnerable to neglect, derision and molestation. They belong to Tadiar's category of the 'feminization of exploited labour',[87] a relatively new theme in the long, tragic story of foreign extraction of Filipino human resources that has produced a new caste of dehumanized victims: overwhelmingly female domestic staff, sex workers and healthcare employees. In *Soledad's Sister*, there is barely any recognition that Aurora ever existed at all as a human being with rights, freedoms and an individual identity. Her remains have come from Saudi Arabia with 'no police report, no autopsy' and no passport, 'which was customarily confiscated from foreign workers by their employers'.[88] Later on, we discover that Aurora, in her quest for a better life, had left behind a 'son many thousands of miles away' in Manila.[89] Bamforth's and Dalisay's exposés of the injuries done by emigration to communities and environments in Manila and abroad are substantiated by M.G.E. Kelly's thesis that the Global North's 'biopolitical' care of its citizens – which includes giving them access to free or affordable education and healthcare – relies upon the exploitation of human resources in the Global South, and that such a 'parasitical' arrangement contributes to the 'pitiful conditions'[90] of many non-Western locations blighted by hunger, 'environmental devastation'[91] and 'inadequate medical and educational systems'.[92]

Representing others

In *Reel Bad Arabs* (2001), his study of the representation of Middle Eastern people in American cinema, Jack Shaheen holds that prevailing discourses use cultural and racial stereotypes to 'dehumanize' a 'people',[93] and to crudely reduce human beings to 'barrages of uncontested slurs' such as Arabs are 'the villain'.[94] We have seen how pulp-textured Manilaist fictions from Archibald Clavering Gunter to Timothy Mo relegate Manileños to sly, amoral and/or mendacious terrorists, fanatics, molls, hired guns and gangland bosses. 'Even-handed'[95] writers and filmmakers have, Shaheen writes, 'contested' such stereotypes by presenting foreign characters as 'human' and as 'regular person[s]'.[96] In an insightful, anecdote-laden 1996 op-ed for the *Honolulu Star-Bulletin*, the Filipina expatriate writer and ethnic studies scholar Linda A. Revilla resists certain stereotypes of Filipinos based in Hawai'i that intersect with Manilaist stereotypes of Filipinos in Manila (which were, at any rate, often informed by prejudices towards Filipinos in North America). Using interviews with and anecdotes relating to young Filipino diasporans, their older relatives, newer migrants and academics with expertise in the area, Revilla refutes notions such as the Filipino 'accent'[97] being the butt of 'jokes',[98] when 'Of course, there is nothing wrong with having an accent, but the stereotype makes it seem there is'.[99] If these enduring boilerplates can be dismantled, she asserts, then 'our youth' will gain a 'sense of belonging' and 'be proud of being Filipino'.[100]

Evidently, Revilla takes a much more compassionate and refined view of Filipinos than Manilaism's character assassinations, and, I think, for two interconnected reasons. First, she possesses the subject position of a loyal member of the Filipino community in Hawai'i, and second, she has decided to engage with real, ordinary people in the manner of the 'New Journalists' of the 1960s and 1970s, many of whom, as Nick Nuttall points out, 'participated' in the 'object of study' by interviewing people at great length – besides other research methods – for the purpose of achieving a fuller understanding of 'the thing or event'.[101] Further to this point, Rosalind Coward argues that the 'extended participant observations' of Norman Mailer, Joan Didion, Tom Wolfe and other New Journalists 'focus[ed] on "real" people rather than the "lofty" subjects of traditional journalism'.[102] In her exegesis of Mailer's *Armies of the Night* (1968), Coward avers that Mailer's 'participation in [anti-Vietnam War] protests' and his political 'partisanship enhanced his insight into the hatred of authority motivating the young people on the marches',[103] thereby comprehending dichotomies – 'ignorance and fear; brutality and evil, decency and foolhardy heroism',[104] as Peter Lennon puts it – far removed from the strictures of cultural demonology. As one who gave his life for the cause of Philippine independence, José Rizal shares something of Revilla's ethical and political commitment to fairly representing Filipinos for the objective of improving their lives. Don Crisostomo

Ibarra, the *méstizo* hero of Rizal's protest novel *Noli Me Tángere* (*The Social Cancer*) (first published 1887), dissects the reductionism of Manilaism's 'lazy native' model to the consternation of the Spanish clergymen he is dining with: 'Does this indolence actually, naturally, exist among the natives or is there some truth in what a foreign traveler says: that with this indolence we excuse our own, as well as our backwardness and our colonial system.'[105] With a consciousness of the mechanics of stereotyping that is way ahead of its time, Rizal claims that the Spanish colonial regime is projecting anxieties about its own negligence and inertia onto the subaltern population that it exploits and victimizes.

Other anti-Manilaist texts have answered Lisle's call for writers to 'present counter-examples' to contest the 'patronising and racist stereotypes' ubiquitous in Western travel writing.[106] As discussed earlier, a 200-year-old wraith that has yet to be exorcized from Manilaism is the narcissistic, populist *cacique* politician. Caroline S. Hau contends that sundry Filipino politicians and other establishment personages have played up to this image by writing self-aggrandizing autobiographies that express a 'desire to put oneself forward not as an abstract person but as a national subject who shares in the national history of "the people"'.[107] The motives of these ex-presidents, judges, lawyers and businessmen are less than honourable, given that their resort to categories such as 'the people' and 'the national community'[108] allows the 'plutocratic or authoritarian governments' they have supported to 'claim to exercise power in the interest of the majority' even when the opposite is true.[109] However, Hau also points to a counter-tradition of Philippine life writing that, while also drawing on the paradigms of 'history', the 'national subject' and 'the people', nonetheless 'offers an alternative way of imagining the nation in direct opposition to the prevailing official nationalist hegemony' by deconstructing the 'oppositions between public and private, between person and community, self and others' to '[recuperate] and [empower] politically marginalized voices'.[110] Hau therefore lauds the revolutionary activist Cesar Hernandez Lacara's 1988 Filipino-language autobiography *Sa tungki ng kaaway: Talambuhay ni Tatang* (*On the Tip of the Enemy's Nose: Autobiography of Tatang*) for its re-definition of individual agency as a means of achieving genuine political progress and social justice on behalf of a different conception of 'the people' as the benighted majority that has scarcely benefited more from nationalist hegemony than their forebears did from direct colonial rule. Although it is a novel rather than a work of life or travel writing, John Sayles's *A Moment in the Sun* arguably responds to Lisle's challenge above in the form of the character of Diosdado Concepcíon, the young *ilustrado* revolutionary who retains his principled dedication to the cause of Philippine freedom to almost the end of the war with the United States. 'If dying could drive the yanquis back across the sea,' he says to himself before he grudgingly surrenders to the invaders, 'he would find a way to die'.[111]

Hau's comments on agency could be transposed to the female characters in *State of War*, a novel by the feminist Ninotchka Rosca which was published the same year as Lacaba's account of anti-Marcos unrest. Breaking with the Manilaist preoccupation with supine Filipinas as embodying the Philippines' political status as an inferior connubial partner to the United States, *State of War*'s strong women are, so Patke and Holden dub them, 'enablers of history'[112] who variously wield sexual power over members of the Marcos-like governing elite of the country and plot terrorist actions against the same oligarchy. If it is true that, as Patke and Holden assert, these women are invested with Rosca's 'belief in the possibility of radical, even revolutionary, social change' that has 'not yet been subsumed by textual irony'[113] then there is plenty of textual irony in Cassandra Chase, the American photographer who features in the film script embedded in the main narrative of Gina Apostol's novel *Insurrecto* (2018). Chase is the metatextual reversal not of any particular stereotype peddled by Manilaism but of a specific Manilaist authorial persona, that of someone like Mary H. Fee, the high-handed Thomasite schoolteacher who came to Manila in 1910 to inculcate the new subjects with sturdy American values (see Chapter 3). Like Fee, Chase must assert herself in a male-dominated, militarized environment, but unlike Fee, she has only 'dislike' of 'this war' of colonial violence[114] and she is not afraid to express it by recommending to an army captain that he read Mark Twain's famed anti-imperialist treatise 'To the Person Sitting in the Darkness' (1901).

Another Filipino writer – this time a male one, Alfred A. Yuson – defies Manilaist gender assumptions from a different angle, at once interrogating normative ideas about male-female roles and the formal conventions of the macho colonial adventure idiom sketched out in Chapter 2. We saw earlier how Manilaism has often been subject to the prevailing trend of 'masculinist' memoir and travel writing under the sway of a 'predominantly male [. . .] mythology' of 'wander[ing] and conquer[ing]'[115] and 'heroic risk-taking'[116] to the exclusion of 'feminist'[117] perspectives on 'the politics of everyday life'[118] and the 'private sphere'.[119] By contrast, Yuson's short autobiographical piece 'Confessions of a Q.C. House-Husband' (1988; 2005) engages with, as Rosalind Coward avers, topics such as 'health, family, emotional life and sexual relationships' that have become more prominent in media discourses since the 'feminisation of journalism' that accompanied women's liberation in the middle of the twentieth century.[120] Yuson's tale of his experiences as a stay-at-home husband is framed as an adventure of sorts, with challenges to overcome, problems to solve and knowledge to be gained. But these activities are at odds with those of our Manilaist gentlemen soldiers, explorers, reporters and entrepreneurs. Instead of shooting up the Spanish navy in Manila Bay, sheltering from Japanese fighter bombers on Dewey Boulevard or grimacing at the rubbish dump-cum-shanty town of Smokey Mountain, Yuson redraws the textual map of Manila in rather more domestic terms, tending to the garden of the family home in UP Teachers' Village and going grocery shopping at the wet markets, fruit stalls and supermarkets of Quezon City. Whereas, according to Martin Green, colonial adventure literature was notable for its heroes using reason, the scientific method and other tools of the 'modern system' to overcome enemies in the hostile boondocks,[121] Yuson, a left-wing, Filipino 'new man', instead relies on his bargaining skills and Epicurean disposition to buy 'piping-hot, crispy-fried langka-laden stuff' and 'plump Baguio tomatoes' for the family cooking pot.[122] He undermines other Manilaist tropes too. Just as hard graft and a yearning for excellence characterize the young servicemen of Edward Stratemeyer's 'Old Glory' franchise, so Yuson asserts that shopping is 'what I do best' and takes his mission so (mock-)seriously that he refuses to divulge exact information about where certain cheap products can be found.[123] Not unlike the pulp fiction seam of Manilaism, Yuson's quest is fast-paced and action-oriented, albeit the action involves haggling and celebrity-spotting. The short, sharp transitions are between 'neighborhood grocer[ies]'[124] rather than battles, protests or nervy encounters with natives. In a riposte to the Manilaist's unshaking trust in the rectitude and importance of his/her mission, Yuson is candid about the failures of his sojourns: 'I walk back home in a deep slough of despond.'[125]

There is another key point to be made about Yuson's connections to the gender patterns of Manilaism. As we saw earlier, early Manilaist texts give the impression that writing about foreign lands is, above all, a testosterone-fuelled pursuit crucial to promoting the imperialist, masculinist values of strength, violence, honour, work and competition. While latter-day Manilaists – especially the foreign correspondents I have critiqued – may not share that particular predilection, they often fetishize writing as a manly, post-Hemingway enterprise in which the writer or reporter intervenes in bodily dangerous situations of war, crime or political disorder. The fetish is never openly admitted to but rather betokened by a hard-boiled narrative voice that uses litote and gallows humour to prove that the protagonist is relatively unfazed by the hazards confronting him (as with James Fenton's reportage on Duterte's drug war in Chapter 6), for to be a 'proper' man – and writer worth his salt – one must not show doubt or weakness in the face of Marcos's goons, Duterte's vigilantes or whichever other menace – also exclusively male – happens to be looming. This fetish appears in settings which are far removed from the domestic sphere of the home, the family and anywhere else one might traditionally expect to find women. Antithetically to all that, Yuson's narrative plays out exclusively in the domestic sphere and he is refreshingly self-deprecating about his status as a writer which, rather than granting him access to some glamorous, alpha-male lifestyle, has instead resulted in his becoming the eponymous house husband of his article's title. Without a shred of regret he writes, 'I only make a few thousand a week from my poetry' as compared to his wife who 'brings home the eight-to-five bacon',[126] thereby repositioning the writer in a weaker, less economically productive, 'feminine' role, at least according to the assumptions underpinning the classic nuclear family. Indeed, at the finale of Yuson's piece, writing poetry is listed alongside his other domestic duties: checking on his children, tending to the fishpond and making sure the 'red bilbergia [. . .] [are] abloom'.[127]

As discussed in Chapter 3, another Western discursive practice that dehumanizes subaltern subjects is what Ashcroft, Griffiths and Tiffin call the 'power which comes from the control of the language'.[128] In that same chapter, I argued that Archibald Clavering Gunter and his generation of Manilaists audaciously tried to assert linguistic control over the Philippines through re-naming phenomena and ventriloquizing Filipino characters in American English. While to their credit – and despite their other shortcomings – the later Manilaists James Fenton and P.J. O'Rourke capture something of the speech patterns of the Filipinos they interact with, other of their contemporaries lack such nuance. Regardless of their class background or educational level, all the indigenes in Buruma's book could be mistaken for fairly eloquent, middle-class, English-speaking Westerners. 'Well, during the Japanese times,' a retired mayor tells him, 'it was the Americans who saved us [. . .] . But then they helped Japan and left us on our own'.[129] More problematically, Duncan Alexander McKenzie semi-silences his subjects by seldom quoting their direct speech and instead preferring to paraphrase their statements. In contrast to this imposition of American or British English onto a different culture, other Western writers have sought to depict foreigners more fairly and faithfully by rendering their speech in authentic vernacular. As travel writing scholar Kári Gíslason advises, 'use the specific terms that the culture uses. This will give your writing credibility'.[130] In that spirit, literary critic Claudia Capancioni remarks of the British Victorian travel writer Janet Ross, 'Her Italian [which] . . . is always accurate even when it transcribes the phonetic pronunciation of local dialects . . . shows deep respect.'[131] In kindred style, John Sayles artfully approximates the various dialects of English spoken by white American, African American and Filipino characters involved in the Spanish–American and Philippine–American Wars. Modes of verbal communication specific to ethnicity and nationality appear both in the direct speech of the characters and in the third-person limited narrative voice recounting their thoughts and actions. One early paragraph relaying the contemplations of the student radical Diosdado Macapagal about his place within the Gordian social hierarchy of late Hispanic Manila is peppered with Spanish and Tagalog words ('dueñas', 'bombones', 'balintawak', 'indios').[132] From a *Kirkus* review that recognizes *A Moment in the Sun*'s debt to the 'radical-revisionist school' of historical research rooted in the lived experience of ordinary people,[133] we can infer that Sayles's aim here is to courteously grant a measure of autonomy to his characters.

While some Filipino writers have rejected English outright as 'symbolizing American linguistic and cultural imperialism'[134] and elected to work exclusively in local argots, others, like Jessica Zafra, have drawn attention to the dynamic hybridity of Tagalog which often subverts English words by abbreviating and conjoining them in order to signify Filipino social and cultural phenomena. With a jocose light touch, Zafra in her personal essay 'Dedma 101' (1994; 2005) surveys the myriad meanings of the Tagalog word 'dedma' meaning 'the attenuated form of the English words dead malice'.[135] Zafra's piece is, in part, structured like a multiple choice quiz presenting the (implied Filipina) reader with social scenarios in which 'dedma' could be relevant:

> 2. A friend who is habitually late arrives two hours after the appointed time. She begins babbling excuses for her tardiness, excuses you have heard countless times before. What will you do? a) Forgive her; after all, it's in her nature. b) Give her yet another lecture on good manners and right conduct. c) Dedma time![136]

Just as the language of the metropole can be turned against itself in this fashion, so can the doxa that animate metropolitan myths about the non-metropolitan world. Barbara Korte has coined the term 'inverted patterns of travel' to narratives in which a traveller-writer, who hails from a colonial or postcolonial society, journeys around 'the imperial centre' and comes to certain realizations about it that dispute the Western supremacist self-image.[137] For Korte, the Indian novelist R.K. Narayan's recollections of dwelling in and touring the United States, *My Dateless Diary* (1988), 'turns the notion of Western progressive civilisation upside down' by commenting irreverently on how far American society seems to be lagging behind India with regard to its attitude to time, its consumerist values and the quality of its fashion, cuisine and transport.[138] Korte alludes also to Caryl Phillips's ironizing ethnography, *The European Tribe* (1987), which implies that Europe's 'primitive' racism, nationalism and militarism undercuts its pretensions to the moral high ground when it disapproves of African cannibalism and Islamic misogyny. One notably sophisticated text that could also belong to this same inverted patterns of travel genus is Juan C. Laya's novel *His Native Soil* (1972), an early exploration of the Filipino migrant experience that deftly repudiates several abiding Manilaist illusions. Martin Romero is a young provincial Filipino who relocates to the United States with the idealistic expectation that he will find it a free, fair and just 'land of plenty'.[139] When he starts doing low-paid, low-status 'seasonal work'[140] in Washington, DC, he discovers a yawning disconnect between the romance and the reality; he falls prey to exploitation, social immobility and class and racial prejudice. He returns to the Philippines humiliated by his maltreatment as a non-white migrant and by his inability to find a good, white-collar job despite his American university education. According to Jennifer M. McMahon, Martin's tribulations uncover the fraudulence of American colonialism's promises to its Filipino subjects about democracy, 'racial tolerance', 'the transformative power of capitalism'[141] and 'the value of the work ethic'.[142] In a sense, the inverted pattern of travel technique is vulnerable to the *tu quoque* fallacy outlined in Chapter 6. The same modern liberal Manilaists who condemn President Duterte for lambasting the West's human rights record whenever one of its institutions lambastes his, might well charge a writer like Laya with dwelling on the socio-political defects of America while overlooking those of his home country. But, as I hinted at before, a party who invokes *tu quoque* in this way might prove that their opponent is insincere or opportunistic, but not that the charges they have retorted are false. Furthermore, asserting that it is hypocritical for your opponent to call you hypocritical does not automatically result in the exculpation of your own hypocrisy.

I want to end this chapter by briefly ruminating on Carlos Bulosan's classic roman-á-clef, *America Is in the Heart* (1943; 2014), which I think brings together some of the overriding themes of anti-Manilaism. Partly set in Manila but mostly taking place in the United States, the text is a fictionalization of the author's arduous experiences as a migrant labourer during the Great Depression of the 1930s. One particular scene, about halfway through the story, adroitly illustrates the need for consistent moral principles in pursuance of de-stereotyping Filipinos. The scene can also be read as a riposte to Manilaist reluctance to admit the damaging impacts of Western wealth and power on Filipinos, while blaming minority populations for this dialectical condition (as discussed previously, such appetite for blaming the victim has been virulent in constructions of the Chinese diaspora). Bulosan is working in the bakery section of a Seattle café when a curmudgeonly white businessman asks him in disbelief if he is 'reading books', thereby endorsing the stereotype that non-whites are uncivilized and illiterate. Bulosan replies that he would prefer to read than visit brothels and gambling dens in the evening, to which the businessman says, summoning another stereotype about Filipino immigrants as depraved, 'Well you bring it upon yourself [. . .] I mean prostitution and gambling.'[143] Bulosan then reminds his interrogator that he is victim-blaming Filipinos for indulging in vices that the white elite orchestrates and profits from: 'the gambling and prostitution are operated by three of the town's most respectable citizens.'[144] Appalled by this impertinent disclosure of his double standards, the American smashes Bulosan over the head with a bottle, prompting Bulosan to ward off his assailant with the wave of a knife. While this encounter clearly does not achieve what the social psychologists Son Hing, Li and Zanna call 'prejudice reduction'[145] in the American antagonist, the textual dramatization of his hypocrisy might have been calculated to reduce the reader's prejudices given that, as the literary critics Denise Cruz and Erin Suzuki argue, *America Is in the Heart* is an exposé of 'racism and violence' and should be understood in the context of the avowedly left-wing Bulosan's 'development of his activist consciousness'.[146]

The challenges that Bulosan and other writers in this chapter have mounted to Manilaist (and more generally Orientalist) myths and fantasies have, I think, a constructive social and political purpose much-needed in our present age of global catastrophe in which the centuries-old monstrosities of war, racism, ethnocentrism, jingoism, imperialism, authoritarianism and rapacious capitalism constitute new existential threats to humanity. I want to unpack this notion as a means of concluding this study, which will be the purpose of the next and final chapter.

Conclusion

Liberal Orientalism versus humanism, socialism and internationalism

This book has explored how, over several centuries, the Manilaist imagination has demeaned cultural forms and habits, slandered a plethora of individuals, cultures and subcultures; castigated the social and economic policies of both the Spanish colonial regime and post-independence administrations; and undermined or trivialized the aspirations of native anti-colonial and social justice movements. I have suggested causal relationships between certain social, political and economic formations and Manilaist strategies of signification, and explained how these strategies have been resisted by counter-hegemonic historiography, cultural criticism and creative writing.

Although certain of the older Manilaist observations I have considered may appear at face value passé and irrelevant to twenty-first-century concerns – for instance, contempt for the long obsolete Spanish Empire is now a redundant issue for most people – I nonetheless hope that, by tracing the evolution of these sentiments and identifying the linguistic and narrative tools actuating them, I have helped foster a better understanding of the contemporary Orientalist imagination, that is both an epiphenomenon of and a contributing factor to the ongoing tensions between the Euro-American West and the nations of the East. While the motives behind current Orientalisms may differ from those of their age of Empire forebears – states such as Russia and China are today more likely to be perceived as geopolitical competitors rather than potential colonial possessions – the deep mechanics of representation have altered little. The sanctimony, duplicity and 'reactionary forgetting'[1] that typify Manilaist reproofs of Spanish and Filipino administrations in Manila haunt the 'new Russophobia'[2] promulgated by the Western state-corporate media. Mainstream British and American journalists continually excise NATO's provocations from their doom-laden reporting on Russia's mistreatment of Crimea or Ukraine, or heckle 'the Evil Empire'[3] with charges of 'gangster'[4] capitalism while seldom acknowledging the United States' collusion in fashioning the modern Russian state after the disintegration of the USSR in 1989. Just as Manilaists condensed a heterogeneous metropolis of individual human beings into a handful of sweeping clichés, the survey research of Edina Lilla Mészáros reveals that EU citizens currently hold 'common misperceptions and stereotypes' about Russians as steadfastly 'cold', 'blunt', 'corrupt', alcoholic and 'still commie'.[5] As Western societies tussle with debt, stagnation, housing shortages, flatlining public services, unemployment and under-employment, the utterances of their mainstream media recall Manilaist Sinophobia: Chinese enterprise must be simultaneously envied, feared and grudgingly admired.[6] As we have already seen multiple times throughout this study, such slurs against Chinese, Russians and other non-Western peoples can only be tenable if the accusers remain spectacularly oblivious to the foibles and failings of their own societies.

If Tadiar is correct that 'the Philippine state's deployment and manipulation of [the] codes of international fantasy' has had the material impact of 'fundamentally [enabling] the systemic exploitation and oppression of the great majority of Filipino lives',[7] then it is fair to contend that Manilaism's deployment of representational codes has had a similar enabling effect on Western structures of oppression, and that critically analysing these codes is not just a pure academic affair of fattening the body of research into cultural mimesis. It is also vital to the political task of disputing the elite rhetoric that endorses the deadly direction our world geopolitics – which incorporate Philippine-Western relations – are drifting in. This task can make gains at the relatively small, interpersonal scale, as the social psychologists Son Hing, Li and Zanna discovered in their 2002 clinical study into 'prejudicial behaviour among aversive racists'. When their subjects were told about the 'subconscious' fallacies underlying their racist views towards Asians, those who had initially exhibited 'low [...] explicit and implicit prejudice' showed a 'reduction in prejudicial behaviour'.[8] While the outcome of this and other experiments give us cause to be optimistic that rational explanation can change individual minds about cultural clichés and stereotypes, it would be naïve to pin all our hopes on this patently limited strategy, as it is unlikely to convert enough of those prominent individuals who are the producers and curators of Orientalist discourses – and, of course, who reap rewards from its continued hegemony – to make much difference. And even if these people could be converted, the toxic ideas we are contending with are so socio-culturally deep seated and so closely aligned with the actual apparatuses of Western domination that the system would quickly find other stooges to replace them. The point is, then, to find ways of resisting the discourse on a much broader systemic level, and this has never been a more urgent imperative as we approach the end of the first quarter of the twenty-first century.

The climate emergency, the most pressing existential threat to all human life on Earth, cannot be disentangled from the injustices and inequalities of contemporary imperialist capitalism, even if the mainstream discourses concerning it are generally 'unsociological and depoliticised',[9] as John Narayan and Leon Sealey-Huggins aver. The poorest citizens of the Global South suffer disproportionately from an ecological mess that is largely the making of the elites of the Global North.[10] Profound social problems that have long blighted the South – poverty, war, disease, large-scale migration, inter alia – are being exacerbated by ecological disaster and a dystopian near future of famine, 'mass displacements' and 'resource wars within and between nations' will likely come to pass.[11] A further challenge to global peace and security is the trade war between the United States and China, which many commentators fear could escalate into a shooting war, given mounting tensions in the South China Sea.[12] For some years now, the West has already been in proxy conflict with Russia in Syria and Eastern Europe.[13] This 'new US-Russian Cold War', writes the historian Stephen F. Cohen, 'is more dangerous than was its 40-year predecessor that the world survived. The chances are even greater that this one could result, inadvertently or intentionally, in actual war between the two nuclear superpowers.'[14] When considering the economic motors of these new rivalries with Russia and China, it is hard not to think again of those early-twentieth-century critics of imperialism, J.A. Hobson, Nikolai Bukharin and V.I. Lenin. In their time, the global economy was monopolized by the advanced capitalist nations (Britain, the United States and Germany) that had prospered from exporting their surplus capital to the colonial periphery. By 1914, when the great powers had exhausted the profit opportunities within their own territorial borders, they were obliged by the logic of finance capitalism to compete for each other's resources, markets and trade routes.[15] The First World War was the devastating consequence. With some foresight, Bukharin observed that, from now on, international military conflict would be 'the method of competition between state capitalist trusts'.[16] A century later, history is repeating itself, but this time the price could be higher than even the 37 million who died in the Great War. Since the 2008 banking catastrophe, 'emerging and developing countries' led by China and Russia have seen their share of global GDP in terms of purchasing power rise from 44 per cent to 60 per cent.[17] China is now the world's largest manufacturer and fastest-growing consumer market, with the most total banking assets of all nations. That the general global rate of profit is now a paltry 17 per cent (compared to 43% in the 1870s) means there are very few financial opportunities for China, Russia, the United States and the EU to compete for.[18] By 2033, China is predicted to overtake the United States as the largest economy on Earth by the GDP index.[19] Such economic threats from Russia and China, as they are perceived by the United States and EU, are feeding the above-mentioned phobic discourses towards these nations and the provocative behaviour of the United States in Asia and NATO in Eastern Europe. Therefore, to interrogate this discourse is also to interrogate – and hopefully resist – a crazed economic zero-sum game that, given all its belligerents possess nuclear weapons, could lead to the war to end all wars. (Descriptions of the First World War as such turned out to be premature, sadly.) At the time of writing, the Coronavirus pandemic is wreaking unprecedented havoc across the globe and the World Trade Organization is warning that an economic catastrophe as grave as the Great Depression of the 1930s could follow in its wake.[20] This will only exacerbate the risk of hazardous East–West rivalries.

As we saw in Chapter 2, the United States continues to airbrush its imperial aggressions from the story it likes to tell itself about not being – nor ever having been – an empire. At first glance, a disquisition on Victorian boy's own stories may not be the most fruitful resource for understanding present East–West hostilities. But it is not entirely fruitless either. In demystifying the genealogy of American Orientalist idées fixes about Asia as an adversarial Other, we can learn about the self-justificatory logic behind the current exercise of American military, diplomatic, economic and cultural might. As the Filipino historiographer Oscar V. Campomanes avers, close inspection of period literature that articulates 'the history of [the US oppression of the Philippines beginning in] 1898'[21] can answer 'the question of what to teach'[22] today and therefore boost public awareness of this and other under-reported acts of American state terror. Furthermore, such research can sharpen our definitions of US imperialism's 'nature', 'temporality or duration' and 'its peculiar forms or formulations of territoriality'; all of which contribute to holding 'U.S. global power [. . .] critically accountable'.[23] And accountability is paramount, given the sheer extent of – and risks posed by – that power today, whether we quantify it in terms of the United States' current involvement in over 100 wars worldwide or its battle-ready troop presence in 172 nation states.[24] It is intriguing to wonder whether William McKinley and his gung-ho novelist counterparts could ever have anticipated their beloved America rising to such extraordinary hegemony.

In a similar vein, 100-year-old novels by white American gentlemen about Manila can potentially shine a light on the gendered aspect of modern-day Western imperialism. In addition to dramatizing Mazie Gordon's symbolic embrace of American values through romance and marriage, *Jack Curzon* frequently cites the social advantages enjoyed by American women of the 1890s, including limited suffrage, the right to stand for mayoral election[25] and the freedom to indulge 'the cigarette habit';[26] this despite the novel's twin masculinist narratives concerning the conquest of both the Philippines and a mixed race Filipina. Arguably, these articulations prefigure the contemporary discourses of Western NGOs, charities, women's magazines and reality television shows that, according to Mimi Thi Nguyen, 'represent women in the global South as needing modernization'[27] within a paradigm that 'constructs Western women as ethical and free' in opposition to their counterparts in 'patriarchal states or "backward" cultures'.[28] The current generation of 'liberal interventionists' espouses such canards to vindicate the West's disastrous wars-of-choice against Islamic and other purportedly 'primitive'[29] and 'patriarchal'[30] societies.[31] These same Western liberal opinion-formers subscribe to an updated version of benevolent assimilation that substitutes the language of paternalism, cultural improvement and interdependency with the vocabulary of secularism, international law, 'liberal democratic governance' and economic 'growth'.[32] In both the old and new conceptions of benevolent assimilation, a much more discursive *legerdemain* is needed to conceal or distract from the slaughter, torture, vandalism and displacement that are the unavoidable results of Western martial adventurism.

Finally – and perhaps most importantly – I hope that exposing the profound flaws in contemporary Manilaism's efforts 'to know, to name, to fix the other'[33] can contribute to a much-needed discursive riposte against a dangerously misguided Western (neo)liberal world view beset by a crisis that Pankaj Mishra explains eloquently here:

> It (liberalism) made human beings subordinate to the market, replacing social bonds with market relations and sanctifying greed. It propagated an ethos of individual autonomy and personal responsibility, while the exigencies of the market made it impossible for people to save and plan for the future. It burdened people with chronic debt and turned them into gamblers in the stock market. Liberal capitalism was supposed to foster a universal middle class and encourage bourgeois values of sobriety and prudence and democratic virtues of accountability. It achieved the opposite: the creation of a precariat with no clear long-term prospects, dangerously vulnerable to demagogues promising them the moon. Uncontrolled liberalism, in other words, prepares the grounds for its own demise.[34]

Crucially to the Philippine context, Mishra asserts that liberalism has always been the official ideology of 'the propertied white men'[35] at the forefront of

Western imperialism. The noble-sounding liberal ideals of universal freedom, equality and protection under the law were never compatible with the West's 'institutionalized hierarchies of race and class and bogus distinctions between civilized and uncivilized peoples'.[36] Such 'fatal contradictions', as Mishra calls them, are evident in the short-sighted and hypocritical representations of Jonathan Miller, Tom Smith and Michael Peel, as we saw in Chapter 6. By signalling what I believe are the two most egregious iterations of this hypocrisy – that the West bears little or no culpability for the ravages of *Dutertismo* and that the West's latest imperial wars are moral bagatelles next to Duterte's butchery – we can start to leave behind what Martin Green dubs 'the nationalist slogan'[37] school of moral arithmetic that always arrives at the same reckoning: one human life in one part of the world is worth more than another human life in another part of the world.[38] We would also be ready to transcend the brand of Western liberal exceptionalism that, through a highly selective reading of world affairs, almost always excuses Western oppression at home and abroad with its own spin on 'whataboutism'. We might have our problems in the United States and Western Europe, so the argument goes, but at least we enjoy certain rights, liberties and privileges that Filipinos, Chinese, Russians and so on do not. But it is easier for an elite Western politician or pundit to claim this than it is for, say, one of the 1 million African Americans currently condemned to 'forced labour' in the US prison-industrial complex.[39] Making such a claim also omits the fact that maintaining a prosperous liberal democracy that provides a certain level of care for its citizens is to the detriment of millions of other citizens of countries that are conveniently out of sight, out of mind. For Westerners to be able to earn relatively high wages, live in reasonably pleasant environments and afford cheap consumer goods is a sine qua non of a global economic and political system that is rigged in favour of the rich nations and costs the lives of 24,000 people in the poor nations every single day, who fall foul of preventable malnutrition, disease, overwork and pollution.[40] That neither Manilaism nor its related liberal discourses are especially worried about all this rather invalidates any gasconades they make for their commitment to universal humanism. In truth, their moral outlook is tribal and exclusionary, with some human lives worth more than others by dint of their value to a particular agenda of power. Ironically – for the Manilaist/Orientalist mindset, at least – this is where the elites of all nations whether East or West, 'neo-liberal' or 'neo-fascist'[41] have a good deal in common. For Duterte, the lives of innocent teenagers mowed down in Manila alleyways are worth literally nothing compared to the lives of those Filipinos who support him, and less still than the lives of the political powerbrokers who helped him win the 2016 election. Equally, while every American president in history has viewed the lives of poor (and generally non-white) people both within and without the Republic as expendable in the name of delivering security, prosperity and happiness to the majority of ordinary white American voters, poor, non-white lives matter even less than the lives of upper-class white Americans, a category to which all the presidents – with the exception of Barack Obama even if his policies were as imperialistic as, if not more so than, his predecessor's – mentioned in this book belong. While this absurdly lopsided, chauvinistic vision of humanism – that allows national/regional political, military and economic interests to dictate destructive policies towards other nations, regions, cultures or societies – obtains, various forms of violence and oppression will continue apace and could culminate in the kind of apocalyptic showdown with a foreign adversary that I touched on earlier.

Thus, a concerted effort by like-minded scholars to critique this style of thinking and its discursive manifestations could expand the parameters of the current debate, to move the language of global moral constancy and accountability out of what Daniel Hallin calls the 'sphere of deviance' and into 'the sphere of consensus'.[42] We should not be under any illusions as to how strenuous this project will be. The Western ideological state apparatuses that try to legitimize imperialism – the legacy media, the tech giants, think tanks, policy groups, large elements of academia – are insulating themselves from valid criticism with methods both old and new. Old in the sense that they often cohere with the tried and trusted techniques of excision, distortion and distraction examined earlier in this book, yet new in so far as they exploit popular uncertainties about modern digital communications platforms. Out of insecurity about their dwindling prominence in this revolutionary new ecosystem, state-corporate outlets from the *New York Times* to the BBC are reinventing themselves – rather unconvincingly – as bastions of neutrality, balance and accuracy in opposition to what they perceive as the ill-informed zealots on social and independent news media.[43] The casuistry and hypocrisy of this position will be evident to anyone with an awareness of the histories of these institutions. These histories feature 'star' reporters regurgitating lies told by politicians to gain public assent for military actions ranging from Gulf War I to Gulf War II, Vietnam to Libya. Other establishmentarian journalists, such as Jayson Blair and Janet Cooke, have indulged in blatant plagiarism and fabrication in order to uphold the 'news values' of their respective employers. More recently, British broadcasters and newspapers disgraced themselves by pursuing a smear campaign against former Labour Party leader Jeremy Corbyn, which at times strayed into libel territory.[44]

While Facebook and the other web behemoths do not face the same challenges to their relevance and financial viability as the legacy media, they are all too willing to recite the elite's *Weltenschauung*. In 2017–18, Facebook and Google altered their algorithms to censor leftist, anti-war and anti-imperialist journalism and scholarship under the cloak of a crusade against the poorly defined scourges of 'fake news' and 'post-truth' (I have yet to hear a convincing argument for when precisely we all lived in a 'truth' age). Casualties have included articles contesting dominant analyses of Venezuelan politics and materials posted on the Occupy London, and anti-fascist No Unite the Right and World Socialist websites.[45] As per the BBC and the *New York Times*, we might wonder with what moral authority Facebook prosecuted this purge given its own refusal, time and again, to submit to state regulation that might impede it from profiting fantastically from the posting of hate speech, extreme pornography, violent imagery and the like.[46]

If, against these odds, radical writers and thinkers could force a new sphere of consensus, self-respecting mainstream commentators might be compelled to *consistently* oppose all orchestrated mass-violence, whether committed, enabled or supported by the elites of Western or non-Western nations. Winning such a battle of ideas would not by itself be enough to make viable a genuine conception of humanism that does not arbitrarily and unjustly discriminate between human lives. Concrete political action is also needed to radically transform the material conditions of the globe so that there can no longer be any economic or political incentives for anyone – whatever material means they have, whatever colour they are, whatever part of the world they come from – who decides to fight, conquer, exploit, belittle or defame anyone else.

Notes

Introduction

1. Edward Said, *Orientalism* (London: Peregrine Books, 1985), p. 55.
2. Ibid., pp. 49–50.
3. Ibid., p. 53.
4. Ibid., p. 58.
5. Ibid., p. 11.
6. The few who have engaged with Manila include Andrew Pagan, 'From the Darkness to the Family: Evolving Orientalist Representations of the Katipunan in Euro-American Travel Literature, 1899–1917', *The Forum: Journal of History*, 4 (2012); Reynaldo C. Ileto, *Knowledge and Pacification: On the US Conquest and the Writing of Philippine History* (Manila: Ateneo de Manila University Press, 2017); Walton J. Netzorg, 'The Philippines in Mass-Market Novels', in *Asia in Western Fiction*, ed. by Robin W. Winks and James R. Rush (Manchester: Manchester University Press, 1990); Meg Wesling, *Empire's Proxy: American Literature and US Imperialism in the Philippines* (New York: New York University Press, 2011) and David Brody, *Visualizing American Empire: Orientalism & Imperialism in the Philippines* (London: University of Chicago Press, 2010), who has coined the term 'American Orientalism' to describe paintings, photographs and other semiotic repertoires that upheld a US imperialist attitude to the Philippines around the turn of the twentieth century.
7. Robert J.C. Young, *Postcolonialism: An Historical Introduction* (London: Wiley-Blackwell, 2001), p. 383.
8. Mathieu E. Courville, *Edward Said's Rhetoric of the Secular* (London: Bloomsbury, 2010), p. 79.
9. Benita Parry, *Postcolonial Studies: A Materialist Critique* (London: Routledge, 2004), p. 4.
10. Walter D. Mignolo, *The Idea of Latin America* (Oxford: Blackwell, 2009), p. 33.
11. Parry, p. 3.
12. Ibid., p. 4.
13. Andrew Bennett and Nicholas Royle, *An Introduction to Literature, Criticism and Theory* (Oxford: Pearson Education Limited, 2004), pp. 112–13.
14. Jennifer M. McMahon, *Dead Stars: American and Philippine Literary Perspectives on the American Colonization of the Philippines* (Quezon City: University of the Philippines Press, 2011), p. 5.

15 Harriet Efanador, 'Africa and Sustainable Development in the Age of Globalization: New Wine in Old Skin', *Journal of Sustainable Development in Africa*, 15.2 (2013): 12 (pp. 12–26).
16 Martin Green, *Dreams of Adventure, Deeds of Empire* (London and Oxford: Routledge and Kegan Paul Ltd, 1980), p. 10.
17 Ibid., p. 10.
18 Jonathan Crush, 'Gazing on Apartheid: Post-colonial Travel Narratives of the Golden City', in *Writing the City: Eden, Babylon and the New Jerusalem*, ed. Peter Preston and Paul Simpson (Oxford: Routledge, 1994), pp. 257–71 (pp. 258–61).
19 George A. Miller, *Interesting Manila* (Manila: Philippine Education Company, 1929), p. 9.
20 James Hamilton-Paterson, *Playing with Water* (Bungay: Sceptre, 1988), p. 136.
21 William Dampier, *A New Voyage Round the World* (London: James Knapton, 1697), p. 325.
22 José S. Arcilla, *An Introduction to Philippine History* (Manila: Ateneo de Manila University Press, 1998), p. 124.
23 Pankaj Mishra, *From the Ruins of Empire: The Revolt Against the West and the Remaking of Asia* (London: Penguin, 2013), p. 7.
24 Jan Romein, *The Asian Century: A History of Modern Nationalism in Asia* (Berkeley and Los Angeles: University of California Press, 1962), p. 228.
25 Niall Ferguson, *The War of the World: Twentieth-Century Conflict and the Descent of the West* (New York and London: Penguin, 2007), p. 14.
26 Amitav Acharya, 'The Myth of ASEAN Centrality?', *Contemporary Southeast Asia: A Journal of International and Strategic Affairs*, 39.2 (2017): 273 (pp. 273–79).
27 Mesrob Vartavarian, 'Imperial Ambiguities: The United States and Philippine Muslims', *South East Asia Research*, 26.2 (2018): 133 (pp. 132–46).
28 Jedidiah Morse and Richard C. Morse, *A New Universal Gazetteer*, 4th edn (New Haven: S. Converse, 1823), p. 223.
29 National Census and Statistics Office, '1980 Census of Population' (Manila: Republic of the Philippines National Economic and Development Authority, 1982) <https://psa.gov.ph/sites/default/files/1980%20Census%20of%20Population%20-%20Special%20Report%201.pdf> [accessed 13 March 2019] (p. xii).
30 I am referring here to the following sources: the anthology *Colonial Accounts* (2011); the archives of the University of Santo Tomas (UST), the Philippines' oldest university; and in John Newsome Crossley's study *The Dasmariñases, Early Governors of the Spanish Philippines* (2016).
31 The oldest text held in UST's Miguel de Benavides Library, *Relaciones de Pedro Teixera del Origen, Descendencia y Succession de los Reyes de Persia y de Harmuz* (1610), only makes brief mention of the Philippines. A 1691 text by Raymundo Berart analyses the accomplishments of the then archbishop of Manila, Phelipe

Pardo. Eighteenth-century Spanish holdings offer relatively uncritical descriptions of government initiatives such as the establishment of a hospice for beggars and prostitutes in Manila.

32 Miguel López de Legazpi, quoted in Renato Constantino, *A History of the Philippines: From Spanish Colonization to the Second World War* (New York: Monthly Review Press, 2010), p. 30.
33 Robin Blackburn, *The Making of New World Slavery* (London: Verso, 1997), p. 4.
34 Constantino, p. 30.
35 Francia, Luis H., *A History of the Philippines: From Indios to Bravos* (New York: Overlook Press, 2014), p. 67.
36 Pablo Feced Temprano, quoted in Paul A. Kramer, *The Blood of Government: Race, Empire, the United States, & the Philippines* (Chapel Hill: University of North Carolina Press, 2006), p. 47.
37 John Newsome Crossley, *The Dasmariñases, Early Governors of the Spanish Philippine* (Oxford: Routledge, 2016), p. ix.
38 Kramer, p. 51.
39 Dylan Rodriguez, *Suspended Apocalypse: White Supremacy, Genocide, and the Filipino Condition* (Minneapolis: University of Minnesota Press, 2010), p. 99.
40 Dampier, p. 307.
41 Jane H. Jack, "'A New Voyage Round the World': Defoe's "Roman á These"', *Huntington Library Quarterly*, 24.4 (1961): 324 (pp. 323–36).
42 Daniel Defoe, *A New Voyage Round the World by a Course Never Sailed Before* (London: A. Bettesworth, 1725), p. 264.
43 Constantino, pp. 113–16.
44 Robert MacMicking, *Recollections of Manilla and the Philippines during 1848, 1849 and 1850* (London: Richard Bentley, 1851), p. 181.
45 Ivan Goncharov, *The Voyage of the Frigate Pallada* (London: Folio Society, 1965), p. 177.
46 Ibid., p. 232.
47 Ibid., p. 233.
48 Ibid.
49 Barbara Korte, *English Travel Writing from Pilgrimages to Post-colonial Explorations* (London: Palgrave Macmillan, 2000), p. 92.
50 Goncharov, p. 234.
51 Ibid., p. 234.
52 Ibid., p. 223.
53 Sergei Mashinsky, *The Works of I.A. Goncharov in Six Volumes* (Moscow: Pravda, 1972), pp. 3–54.
54 Green, pp. 164–5.
55 Ibid., p. 166.

56 Fedor Jagor, *Travels in the Philippines* (London: Chapman and Hall, 1875), p. 36.
57 Ibid., p. 39.
58 Ibid., p. 37.
59 Volker Schult, 'Revolutionaries and Admirals: The German East Asia Squadron in Manila Bay', *Philippine Studies*, 50 (2002): 496–511 (p. 501).
60 Said, *Orientalism*, pp. 3–4.
61 Netzorg, pp. 175–95 (p. 175).
62 Debbie Lisle, *The Global Politics of Contemporary Travel Writing* (Cambridge: Cambridge University Press, 2006), p. 1.
63 Patrick Holland and Graham Huggan, *Tourists with Typewriters: Critical Reflections on Contemporary Travel Writing* (Ann Arbor: University of Michigan Press, 2000), p. 69.
64 Ibid., p. 77.
65 Said, *Orientalism*, p. 192.
66 Anonymous, 'Books and Authors', *Deseret News* (Salt Lake City, Utah), 30 July 1927. Newspapers.com <https://www.newspapers.com/image/594551916/?terms=%22walter%2Brobb%22%2B%22khaki%2Bcabinet%2Band%2Bold%2Bmanila%22> [accessed 19 May 2020] (para 1 of 3).

  Col. Joseph I. Greene, 'Pacific Thunder', *New York Times*, 21 March 1943. Times Machine. <https://timesmachine.nytimes.com/timesmachine/1943/03/21/83908334.html?pageNumber=37> [accessed 10 April 2020] (paras 11–12 of 12).
67 Walter Robb, *The Khaki Cabinet and Old Manila* (Manila: Sugar News Press, 1926), p. 118.
68 Edward Stratemeyer, *The Campaign of the Jungle or Under Lawton through Luzon* (Boston: Lee and Shepard, 1900), p. iv.
69 Anonymous, 'W.D. Boyce Was Pioneer Yellow Journalist', *The Bridgeport Times and Evening Farmer* (Bridgeport, Connecticut), 17 June 1912. Newspapers.com <https://www.newspapers.com/image/336885604/?terms=%22william%2Bd.%2Bboyce%22%2B%22labor%2Bunion%22> [accessed 19 May 2020] (paras 1–2 of 2).
70 David S. Roh, Betsy Huang and Greta A. Nui, 'Technologizing Orientalism', in *Techno-Orientalism: Imagining Asia in Speculative Fiction, History, and Media*, ed. David S. Roh, Betsy Huang and Greta A. Nui (New Brunswick: Rutgers University Press, 2015), pp. 1–20 (p. 3.)
71 Green, p. 38.
72 Ibid., p. 55.
73 Ileto, *Knowledge and Pacification*, p. 4.
74 Edward Said, *Culture and Imperialism* (London: Vintage, 1994), p. 307.
75 Bill Ashcroft, Gareth Griffiths and Helen Tiffin, *Key Concepts in Post-Colonial Studies* (London: Routledge, 1998), p. 115.
76 Brody, p. 103.

77 William McKinley, quoted in James H. Blount, *The American Occupation of the Philippines 1898–1912* (New York: G. P. Putnam's Sons, 1913), p. 149.
78 Daniel Burnham to William Taft, 24 June 1905, Burnham Papers, Chicago Art Institute Library.
79 Hamilton-Paterson, *Playing with Water*, p. 132.
80 Neferti Xina M. Tadiar, *Fantasy-Production: Sexual Economies and Other Philippine Consequences for the New World Order* (Hong Kong: Hong Kong University Press, 2004), p. 47.
81 Alain Grosrichard, *The Sultan's Court: European Fantasies of the East* (London and New York: Verso, 1998), p. 4.
82 Edward Said, 'A Window on the World', *Guardian*, 2 August. <https://www.theguardian.com/books/2003/aug/02/alqaida.highereducation> [accessed 12 February 2019] (paras 4–5 of 25).
83 Lisle, p. 77.
84 Said, *Orientalism*, p. 67.

Chapter 1

1 Tzvetan Todorov, *The Fantastic: A Structural Approach to a Literary Genre* (Ithaca, New York: Cornell University Press, 1975), p. 25.
2 Joan M. Ferrante, *The Political Vision of Dante* (Princeton, NJ: Princeton University Press, 1984), pp. 41–2.
3 Grosrichard, p. 67.
4 Green, p. 8.
5 Ibid., p. 40.
6 Ibid., p. 9.
7 Ibid.
8 Francia, *A History of the Philippines*, pp. 83–94.
9 Ibid., p. 94.
10 Nicholas Loney, *A Britisher in the Philippines or the Letters of Nicholas Loney* (Manila: National Library, 1964), p. 85.
11 Charles Wilkes, *Travel Accounts of the Islands (1832–58)* (Manila: Filipiniana Book Guild, 1974), p. 36.
12 Ibid., p. 36.
13 Charles Wilkes, *Round the World Embracing the Principal Events of the Narrative of the United States Exploring Expedition* (Philadelphia: Geo. W. Gorton, 1849), p. v.
14 Grosrichard, p. 68.
15 Ibid., p. 69.
16 Ibid.

17 Loney, p. 5.
18 Young, 2001, p. 36.
19 This may be explained by geopolitical tensions between Germany, on the one hand, and Britain and the United States, on the other hand, that would culminate in the inter-imperialist confrontation of the First World War. Archibald Clavering Gunter, *Jack Curzon (Being a Portion of the Records of the Managing Clerk of Martin, Thompson & Co., English Merchants Doing Business in Hong Kong, Manila, Cebu and the Straits Settlements)* (New York: Hurst, 1898), a Manilaist text that is considered in the next section, is almost as stacked with Teutophobic images as it is with Sinophobic or Hispanophobic ones.
20 Loney, p. 60.
21 Ibid.
22 Ibid., p. 62.
23 Mignolo, p. 57.
24 Ibid., p. 64.
25 Green, p. 30.
26 MacMicking, p. 51.
27 Grosrichard, p. 45.
28 Ibid., p. 43.
29 Ibid., pp. 106–7.
30 MacMicking, p. 69.
31 Ibid., p. 103.
32 Kevin McNamara, 'Introduction', in Kevin McNamara (ed.), *The Companion to the City in Literature* (Cambridge: Cambridge University Press, 2013), pp. 1–13 (p. 3).
33 Loney, p. 6.
34 Grosrichard, p. 79.
35 Miller, *Interesting Manila*, p. 48.
36 Ibid., p. 26.
37 Ibid., p. 48.
38 Ibid., p. 27.
39 Ibid., p. 51.
40 Ibid., p. 79.
41 Robb, p. 3.
42 Ibid., p. 126.
43 Clark Lee, *They Call It Pacific: An Eyewitness Story of Our War against Japan from Bataan to the Solomons* (New York: Viking Press, 1943), p. 24.
44 Ibid., p. 4.
45 Ibid., p. 47.
46 These include the fire of bombs and shells in Tolstoy's Borodino of cannonball and grenade explosions, Kurt Vonnegut's Dresden incinerated by napalm and

phosphorus, and Sarah Waters's Blitz-era London of air raid sirens and blazing buildings.
47 Lee, *They Call It Pacific*, p. 47.
48 Felix Konrad, *'Turkish Menace' to Exoticism and Orientalism: Islam as Antithesis of Europe (1453–1914)* (Mainz: Inst. f. Europ. Geschichte, 2011), p. 40.
49 Col. Joseph I. Greene, 'Pacific Thunder', *New York Times*, 21 March 1943. Times Machine. < https://timesmachine.nytimes.com/timesmachine/1943/03/21/83908334.html?pageNumber=37> [accessed 10 April 2020] (paras 11-12 of 12).
50 John Bechtel, *Perla of the Walled City* (Grand Rapids: W.M.B. Eerdmans, 1946), p. 1.
51 Ibid., p. 2.
52 'Rev. John Bechtel To Speak at Pavilion', *The Morning Call* (Paterson, New Jersey), 14 August 1944. Newspapers.com <https://www.newspapers.com/image/552802457/?terms=%22john%2Bbechtel%22%2Bpig's%2Bbirthday> [accessed 27 April 2020].
53 DeLoris Stevenson, *Land of the Morning* (St Louis: The Bethany Press, 1956), p. 144.
54 Ibid., p. 10.
55 Ibid., p. 14.
56 Krystyn R. Moon, '"There's no Yellow in the Red, White, and Blue": The Creation of Anti-Japanese Music during World War II', *Pacific Historical Review*, 72.3 (2003): 337 (pp. 333–52).
57 Ibid., pp. 337–8.
58 Arcilla, p. 124.
59 Said, *Orientalism*, p. 210.
60 Ibid., p. 26.
61 Ibid., p. 52.
62 Stevenson, p. 16.
63 Damon L. Woods, *The Philippines: A Global Studies Handbook* (Oxford: ABC Clio, 2006), p. 125.
64 Francia, *A History of the Philippines*, pp. 59–60.
65 'Manila Today Is No Longer Known as Tropical Paradise', *The Catholic Advance* (Wichita, Kansas), 10 May 1957. Newspapers.com <https://www.newspapers.com> [accessed 28 January 2019] (para 32 of 41).
66 Ibid., para 36 of 41.
67 Ibid., para 39 of 41.
68 Ibid., para 30 of 41.
69 These texts include Benjamin Appel, *Fortress in the Rice* (New York: Bobs-Merrill, 1951); John Benjamin Howell, *42 Months of Hell: My Life as a Prisoner of the Japanese, WWII* (Muskogee: Hoffmann Printing Company, 1969); Wanda Liles

Kellett, *Wings as Eagles* (New York: Vantage Press, 1954); Norman Mailer, *The Naked and the Dead* (New York: Rinehart & Company, 1948); Blanche Palmer, *Pilgrim of the Night* (Nashville: Southern Publishing Association, 1966).

70 These texts include Bernard Bancroft, *Bread upon the Waters* (Des Plaines: Regular Baptist Press, 1959); Albert Roland, *The Philippines* (New York: MacMillan, 1967), and David Joel Steinberg, *The Philippines: A Singular and Plural Place* (Boulder: Westview Press, 1969).

71 Samuel K. Tan, *A History of the Philippines* (Manila: University of the Philippines Press, 1987), pp. 82–3.

72 Frank Hindman Golay, *Face of Empire: United States-Philippine Relations, 1898–1946* (Manila: Ateneo de Manila University Press, 2010), pp. 454–77.

73 Romein, p. 228.

74 Mary Louise Pratt, *Imperial Eyes: Travel Writing and Transculturation* (London: Routledge, 1991), p. 217.

75 Ibid., p. 218.

76 Tom Angotti, *The New Century of the Metropolis: Urban Enclaves and Orientalism* (New York: Routledge, 2013), p. 11.

77 Ibid., p. 12.

78 Ibid., p. 17.

79 P.J. O'Rourke, *Holidays in Hell* (New York: Grove, 1989; repr. 2012), Amazon Kindle e-book (location 1708).

80 Ibid., location 1675.

81 Said, *Orientalism*, p. 8.

82 Christopher Hitchens, *For the Sake of Argument: Essays and Minority Reports* (London and New York: Atlantic Books, 2014), Amazon Kindle e-book (location 6610).

83 Ibid., location 6080.

84 Ibid., location 6065.

85 Ibid., location 6110.

86 Ian Buruma, *God's Dust: A Modern Asian Journey* (London: Vintage, 1991), p. 170.

87 Ibid., p. 107.

88 James Fenton, *All the Wrong Places: Adrift in the Politics of Southeast Asia* (New York: Atlantic Monthly Press, 1988; repr. London: Granta, 2005), p. 172.

89 Ibid., p. 164.

90 Ibid., p. 113.

91 Ibid.

92 Ibid., p. 124.

93 Ibid., p. 121.

94 Ibid., p. 163.

95 Ibid.

96 Buruma, p. 75.
97 O'Rourke, location 1625.
98 Maslyn Williams, *Faces of My Neighbour: Three Journeys into East Asia* (Sydney: William Collins Pty, 1979), p. 19.
99 Mark Kram, 'Lawdy, Lawdy, He's Great', *Sports Illustrated Online*, 13 October 1975 <https://www.si.com/boxing/2012/01/17/muhammad-ali-70th-kram> [accessed 28 September 2017] (para 9 of 23).
100 Ileto, *Knowledge and Pacification*, p. 289.
101 Ibid., pp. 267–87.
102 Ibid., p. 268.
103 Matthew 26:56, *New International Version* (Biblica, 2011) <www.biblegateway.com/versions/New-International-Version-NIV-Bible/#booklist> [accessed 27 June 2018].
104 David Hawkes, *The Faust Myth: Religion and the Rise of Representation* (London: Palgrave Macmillan, 2007).
105 Murray L. Weidenbaum and Samuel Hughes, The Bamboo Network: How Expatriate Chinese Entrepreneurs are Creating a New Economic Superpower in Asia (London and New York: Simon & Schuster, 1996), pp. 4–8.
106 Setsuho Ikehata and Lydia Yu-Jose, *Philippines-Japan Relations* (Quezon City: Ateneo De Manila University Press, 2003), pp. 580–1.
107 Kanako Kutsumi, 'Koreans in the Philippines: A Study of the Formation of Their Social Organization', in Virginia A. Miralao and Lorna P. Makil (eds), *Exploring Transnational Communities in the Philippines* (Manila: Philippine Social Science Council, 2007), pp. 58–73.
108 Alex Garland, *The Tesseract* (London: Viking, 1998; repr. London: Penguin, 2007), Amazon Kindle e-book (location 363).
109 Timothy Mo, *Renegade or Halo²* (London: Paddleless Press, 1999), pp. 57–8.
110 Fredric Jameson, *The Cultural Turn: Selected Writings on the Post-modern, 1983–1988* (London: Verso 1998), pp. 9–10.
111 Garland, location 679.
112 Ibid., location 1005.
113 Ibid., location 565.
114 Thomas A. Smith, 'The Pleasure of Hell in *City of God*', *Augustinian Studies*, 30 (1999): 195–204 (p. 197).
115 Garland, location 287.
116 Ibid., location 3152–3156.
117 James Hamilton-Paterson, *Ghosts of Manila* (London: Random House, 1994), p. 43.
118 Ibid., p. 8.
119 Ibid., p. 5.
120 Ibid., p. 8.

121 Dante Alighieri, *Inferno*, trans. Henry Wadsworth Longfellow (Mineola, New York: Dover Books, 2005), p. 49.
122 Hamilton-Paterson, *Ghosts of Manila*, p. 1.
123 Alighieri, p. 204.
124 Alberto Manguel, 'Gouging Out Hell's Entrails: Ghosts of Manila – James Hamilton-Paterson', *Independent Online*, 3 June 1994 <http://www.independent.co.uk/arts-entertainment/books/book-review-gouging-out-hells-entrails-ghosts-of-manila-james-hamilton-paterson-jonathan-cape-pounds-1420229.html> [accessed 25 September 2017] (para 3 of 8).
125 Hamilton-Paterson, *Ghosts of Manila*, p. 103.
126 Todorov, p. 25.
127 Hamilton-Paterson, *Ghosts of Manila*, p. 257.
128 Andrzej Wicher, 'Introduction', in Andrzej Wicher, Piotr Spyra and Joanna Matyjaszcyk (eds), *Basic Categories of Fantastic Literature Revisited* (Newcastle upon Tyne: Cambridge Scholars Publishing, 2014), pp. 1–7 (p. 3).
129 Todorov, p. 103.
130 Roh, Huang and Nui, p. 3.
131 Martin Jacques, *When China Rules The World: The End of the Western World and the Birth of a New Global Order* (London: Penguin, 2012), pp. 1–89.
132 Dan Brown, *Inferno* (New York: Transworld Digital, 2013), Amazon Kindle e-book (location 6151).
133 Ibid., location 6151.
134 Ibid., location 6147.
135 Ibid., location 6155.
136 Ibid., location 6152.
137 Ibid., location 6141.
138 Philip C. Tubeza, 'Aquino Back Home with $13-B Deals', *Philippine Daily Inquirer*, 3 September 2011. <https://globalnation.inquirer.net/11553/aquino-back-home-with-13-b-deals> [accessed 14 May 2019].
139 Tarra Quismundo, 'Japanese Lawmakers Give Aquino Standing Ovation', *Philippine Daily Inquirer*, 4 June 2015. <https://globalnation.inquirer.net/123973/japanese-lawmakers-give-aquino-standing-ovation> [accessed 14 May 2019].
140 Said, *Orientalism*, p. 6.
141 Ibid., p. 6.
142 Francis Tolentino, quoted in Kate Hodal, 'Manila Less Than Thrilled at Dan Brown's *Inferno*', *Guardian*, 24 May 2013. <https://www.theguardian.com/world/2013/may/24/manila-thrilled-dan-brown-inferno> [accessed 13 December 2018].
143 George H.W. Bush, quoted in Lawrence Freedman, 'The Gulf War and the New World Order', *Survival*, 33.3 (1991): 191–200 (pp. 195–6).
144 M.G.E. Kelly, *Biopolitical Imperialism* (London: Zero Books, 2015), p. 93.

145 Ibid., p. 123.
146 Ibid., p. 65.

Chapter 2

1 Reynaldo C. Ileto, 'The Philippine-American War: Friendship and Forgetting', in Angel Velasco Shaw and Luis H. Francia (eds), *Vestiges of War: The Philippine-American War and the Aftermath of an Imperial Dream 1899–1999* (New York: New York University Press, 2002), pp. 3–21 (p. 3).
2 Hugh Rockoff, *America's Economic Way of War: War and the US Economy from the Spanish-American War to the Persian Gulf War* (New York: Cambridge University Press, 2012), p. 83.
3 Ileto, *Friendship and Forgetting*, p. 3.
4 David J. Scheffer, 'Towards a Modern Doctrine of Humanitarian Intervention', *University of Toledo Law Review*, 23 (1992): pp. 253–74.
5 George Monbiot, 'Empire of Denial', *Guardian*, 1 June 2004. <https://www.theguardian.com/world/2004/jun/01/usa.comment> [accessed 3 April 2018]; Niall Ferguson, *Colossus: The Rise and Fall of the American Empire* (London: Penguin, 2009).
6 Roger Peace, 'Cultivating Critical Thinking: Five Methods for Teaching the History of U.S. Foreign Policy', *The History Teacher*, 43 (2010): pp. 265–73 (p. 266).
7 William McKinley, 'William McKinley, "Benevolent Assimilation" Letter, December 21st 1898', in *The Encyclopedia of the Spanish-American and Philippine-American Wars Vol. 1*, ed. Spencer C. Tucker (Santa Barbara, Denver and Oxford: ABC Clio), p. 924.
8 William McKinley, 'War Message', in *Papers Relating to Foreign Affairs*, ed. unnamed (Washington, DC: US Department of State, 1898), pp. 750–60 (p. 750).
9 Ibid., p. 758.
10 Ibid., p. 757.
11 Theodore Roosevelt, 'Special Message, January 4', in *The American Presidency Project*, ed. by Gerhard Peters and John T. Woolley. <http://www.presidency.ucsb.edu/ws/?pid=69417> (para 7).
12 Lyndon Johnson, 'Why We Are in Vietnam', in *Modern America: A Documentary History of the Nation since 1945*, ed. Gary Donaldson (New York: Routledge), pp. 117–20 (p. 118).
13 George W. Bush, *We Will Prevail: President George W. Bush on War, Terrorism and Freedom* (New York: Continuum, 2003), p. 233.
14 Barack Obama, 'Remarks by the President in Address to the Nation on Libya' (2011) <https://obamawhitehouse.archives.gov/the-press-office/2011/03/28/remarks-president-address-nation-libya> [accessed 25 February 2018] (para. 23 of 45).

15 Green, p. 145.
16 Constantino, p. 212.
17 Howard Zinn, *A People's History of the United States: 1492-Present* (New York: Harper Collins, 2001), Amazon Kindle e-book (location 5923); Ileto, *Knowledge and Pacification*, p. 110.
18 Rodriguez, pp. 98–9.
19 Ashcroft, Griffiths and Tiffin, *Key Concepts*, p. 47.
20 Ibid., p. 23.
21 Said, *Orientalism*, p. 167
22 H. Porter Abbott, *The Cambridge Introduction to Narrative* (Cambridge: Cambridge University Press, 2008), p. 69.
23 David Spurr, *Rhetoric of Empire: Colonial Discourse in Journalism, Travel Writing and Imperial Administration* (Durham: Duke University Press, 1993), p. 15.
24 Ibid., p. 16.
25 Ashcroft, Griffiths and Tiffin, *Key Concepts*, p. 228.
26 Loney, p. 4.
27 Ibid., p. 5.
28 Ashcroft, Griffiths and Tiffin, *Key Concepts*, p. 38.
29 MacMicking, p. 105.
30 Wilkes, *Travel Accounts*, p. 15.
31 Korte, p. 92.
32 Wilkes, p. 35.
33 Steven Pinker, *The Sense of Style: The Thinking Person's Guide to Writing in the 21st Century* (New York and London: Allen Lane, 2013), p. 26.
34 William Henry Thomes, *Life in the East Indies* (Boston and New York: Lee and Shepard, 1875), p. 11.
35 Ibid., p. 11.
36 Ibid.
37 Ibid., p. 12.
38 Special Dispatch to the Chronicle, 'Reminiscences of Early San Francisco: Close of the Life of a Popular Writer of Adventures on Land and Sea', *San Francisco Chronicle*, 7 March 1895. Newspapers.com <https://www.newspapers.com/image/27547168/?terms=%22william%2Bhenry%2Bthomes%22> [accessed 27 April 2020] (para 4 of 9).
39 Constantino, p. 139.
40 Said, *Orientalism*, p. 167.
41 Ibid., p. 167.
42 Ibid.
43 Ibid., p. 315.
44 MacMicking, p. 138.

45 Ibid.
46 Constantino, p. 190.
47 Francia, *A History of the Philippines*, pp. 105–12.
48 MacMicking, p. 140.
49 Ibid., p. 140.
50 Ibid., p. 139.
51 Sir John Bowring, *A Visit to the Philippine Islands* (London: Smith, Elder & Co., 1859), p. 99.
52 Wilkes, p. 35.
53 Gunter, p. 28.
54 Ibid., pp. 76–7.
55 Ibid., p. 67.
56 Green, p. 26.
57 Ibid., p. 21.
58 Ibid.
59 Norman Fairclough, *Language and Power* (Oxford: Routledge, 2013), p. 102.
60 Geoffrey K. Pullum, 'Fear and Loathing of the English Passive', *Language and Communication*, 37.2 (2014): pp. 1–6 (p. 1).
61 MacMicking, p. 180.
62 Stratemeyer, *The Campaign of the Jungle*, p. 51.
63 Ibid., p. 19.
64 Spurr, p. 38.
65 Ibid.
66 Fairclough, pp. 98–9.
67 Ibid., p. 97.
68 Ashcroft, Griffiths and Tiffin, *Key Concepts*, p. 34.
69 Fairclough, p. 105.
70 Stratemeyer, *The Campaign of the Jungle*, p. iv.
71 Fairclough, p. 64.
72 Edward Stratemeyer, *Under Dewey at Manila or The War Fortunes of a Castaway* (Boston: Lee and Shepard, 1898), p. iv.
73 Ibid., p. iii.
74 Ibid.
75 Ibid., p. 194.
76 Ibid., p. 281.
77 Tadiar, p. 32.
78 Ibid., p. 9.
79 Ibid., p. 4.
80 Stratemeyer, *The Campaign of the Jungle*, p. 51.
81 Sigmund Freud, *Totem and Taboo* (Oxford: Routledge, 2001), p. 27.

82 Robert J.C. Young, *Colonial Desire: Hybridity in Theory, Culture and Race* (London: Routledge, 1995).
83 Casey Blanton, *Travel Writing: The Self and the World* (New York: Routledge, 2002), p. 62.
84 Grosrichard, p. xiii.
85 Stratemeyer, *The Campaign of the Jungle*, pp. 51–2.
86 Green, p. 26.
87 Ibid., pp. 31–2.
88 Ibid., p. 27.
89 Ibid., p. 32.
90 Stratemeyer, *Under Dewey at Manila*, p. 7.
91 Edward Stratemeyer, *Under MacArthur at Luzon, or Last Battles in the Philippines* (Boston: Lee and Shepard Publishers, 1902), p. 311.
92 Ibid., p. 312.
93 Ibid.
94 Green, p. 130.
95 Ibid.
96 Ibid., pp. 130–1.
97 Ibid., p. 130.
98 Rockoff, p. 78.
99 Unnamed quoted in Zinn, location 3445.
100 Mark Twain, 'A Salutation to the Twentieth Century', *The New York Herald*, 30 December 1900, p. 12.
101 Roosevelt quoted in Rockoff, p. 70.

Chapter 3

1 McKinley quoted in Blount, p. 149.
2 Ibid., pp. 149–50.
3 Kramer, p. 161.
4 Twain, quoted in Zinn, location 5929.
5 Bart Moore-Gilbert, *Postcolonial Theory: Contexts, Practices, Politics* (Verso: London and New York, 2000), p. 50.
6 Kenan Malik, *The Meaning of Race: Race, History and Culture in Western Society* (New York: New York University Press, 1996), p. 81.
7 Wilkes, p. 17.
8 Said, *Culture and Imperialism*, p. 307.
9 Erika Lee, *The Making of Asian America: A History* (New York: Simon & Schuster, 2016), p. 19.

10 Ibid., pp. 21–3.
11 Ibid., p. 34.
12 Stratemeyer, *Under Dewey at Manila*, p. 233.
13 Ibid., p. 197.
14 O.F. Williams, quoted in 'To Govern the Philippines', *New York Times*, 30 May 1898. Times Machine. <https://timesmachine.nytimes.com/timesmachine/1898/05/30/102562537.html?action=click&contentCollection=Archives&module=LedeAsset&region=ArchiveBody&pgtype=article&pageNumber=2> [accessed 1 March 2019] (para 3 of 9).
15 Father Diaz, quoted in 'War Is Inevitable', *News and Observer* (Raleigh, North Carolina), 10 January 1899, 19th Century U.S. Newspapers. http://find.galegroup.com/ncnp/infomark.do?action=interpret&source=gale&prodId=NCNP&userGroupName=uniportsmouth&tabID=T003&docPage=article&searchType=BasicSearchForm&docId=GT3005815312&type=multipage&contentSet=LTO&version=1.0&finalAuth=true [accessed 2 March 2019] (para 12 of 19).
16 Charles King, *Ray's Daughter: A Story of Manila* (Philadelphia: J. P. Lippincott Company, 1901), p. 161
17 Anonymous, 'Noted Soldier Author Coming', *The Post-Crescent* (Appleton, Wisconsin), 17 March 1905, Newspapers.com https://www.newspapers.com/image/408148570/?terms=%22charles%2Bking%22%2B%22ray's%2Bdaughter%22 [accessed 29 April 2020].
18 Anonymous, 'Readable Books', *The Indianapolis News*, 17 December 1900, Newspapers.com <https://www.newspapers.com/image/40043165/?terms=%22charles%2Bking%22%2B%22ray's%2Bdaughter%22> [accessed 29 April 2020] (para 24 of 25).
19 Argonaut Editorial, '"War is Not Nice." "War is Hell."', *Los Angeles Times*, 29 May 1902, Newspapers.com. <https://www.newspapers.com/image/380006988/?terms=%22atrocity%22%2B%22filipino%22> [accessed 14 February 2019] (paras 36, 41 and 49 of 52).
20 Lee, *The Making of Asian America*, p. 175.
21 Ibid., p. 175.
22 'American Occupation of the Philippines', *Washington Register* (Washington, Kansas), 16 August 1900, Newspapers.com <https://www.newspapers.com/image/386177513/> [accessed 1 March 2019] (paras 56, 63 and 74 of 91).
23 Ashcroft, Griffiths and Tiffin, *Key Concepts*, p. 47.
24 Grosrichard, p. 38.
25 Ibid., p. 38.
26 Ibid., p. 41.
27 Ibid., p. 43.
28 Ibid., p. 48.

29 Benjamin Kidd, *Social Evolution* (New York: Grosset and Dunlap, 1894).
30 Benjamin Kidd, *The Control of the Tropics* (New York: McMillan, 1898), p. 20.
31 Ibid., pp. 50–1.
32 Dr Henry C. Rowland, 'Fighting Life in the Philippines', *McClure's Magazine*, July 1902, p. 149.
33 Ibid., p. 150.
34 Brody, pp. 69–75.
35 Grosrichard, p. 74.
36 Stratemeyer, *Under MacArthur at Luzon*, p. 203.
37 William D. Boyce, *United States Colonies and Dependencies Illustrated* (New York: Rand McNally), p. 230.
38 Ibid., p. 240.
39 T.G. Steward, 'Haven for Negroes', *The Cambridge City Tribune* (Cambridge City, Indiana), 26 June 1902, Newspapers.com <https://www.newspapers.com/image/15178351/?terms=filipino%2Bhappy> [accessed 22 February 2019] (para 11 of 19).
40 Ibid., para 7.
41 Senator George C. Perkins, quoted in 'Senator Perkins Tells of Work in Congress', *Oakland Tribune* (Oakland California), 12 May 1904, Newspapers.com <https://www.newspapers.com/image/71561537/?terms=filipino%2Bhappy> [accessed 22 February 2019] (para 27 of 31).
42 Brody, p. 111.
43 Ibid., p. 112.
44 Steward, para. 9.
45 Lee, *The Making of Asian America*, p. 178.
46 Ibid., p. 176.
47 Robb, p. 126.
48 Homer Clyde Stuntz, *The Philippines and the Far East* (New York: Jennings and Pye, 1904), pp. 124–5.
49 Ibid., p. 125.
50 Ibid., p. 216.
51 Ibid., p. 508.
52 Ibid., p. 98.
53 Ibid., pp. 99–104.
54 José S. Arcilla, 'Protestant Missionaries in the Philippines', *Philippine Studies*, 36 (1988): 105 (pp. 105–12).
55 Ileto, *Knowledge and Pacification*, p. 267.
56 Stratemeyer, *Under Dewey at Manila*, p. 248.
57 Frank G. Carpenter, *Through the Philippines and Hawaii* (New York: Doubleday, Doran and Company, 1929), p. 11.

58 Isagani Cruz, 'The First University', *The Philippine Star*, 17 December 2009. <https://www.philstar.com/campus/2009/12/17/532930/first-university> [accessed 20 December 2019].
59 Bureau of Insular Affairs-War Department, *Sixth Annual Report of the Philippine Commission, 1905 Part III* (Washington, DC: Washington Government Printing Office, 1906), p. 282.
60 Logoupal, 'Hotel de Oriente' (2005), <http://www.lougopal.com/manila/?p=535> [accessed 17 April 2019] (para 2 of 19).
61 'Manila Electric Company (Meralco) History' (2004) <http://www.funduniverse.com/company-histories/manila-electric-company-meralco-history/> [accessed 17 April 2019] (para 2 of 27).
62 Gunter, p. 17.
63 Ibid., p. 330.
64 Ibid., p. 331.
65 Ibid.
66 Vernadette Vicuña Gonzalez, *Securing Paradise: Tourism and Militarism in Hawai'I and the Philippines* (Durham, NC: Duke University Press, 2013), p. 12.
67 Ibid., p. 3.
68 Green, p. 30.
69 Boyce, p. 244.
70 Ibid., p. 224.
71 William Shakespeare, 'Hamlet', in *The Complete Works of William Shakespeare*, Vol. 3 (Ware: Wordsworth Editions, 1999), 3.2, p. 244.
72 Boyce, p. xi.
73 Ibid., p. xi.
74 Ashcroft, Griffiths and Tiffin, *Key Concepts*, p. 47.
75 McKinley, quoted in Boyce, p. 238.
76 Kramer, p. 165.
77 Boyce, p. 240.
78 Kramer, p. 168.
79 Yo Jackson, *Encyclopedia of Multicultural Psychology* (London and New Delhi: SAGE, 2006), p. 216.
80 Lee, *The Making of Asian America*, p. 174.
81 Marilyn Ibach, 'About This Collection', Library of Congress.com (2006) <https://www.loc.gov/collections/carpenter/about-this-collection/> [accessed 2 July 2020] (para 5 of 27).
82 Carpenter, p. 265.
83 Ibid., p. 265.
84 Ibid., p. 267.
85 Ibid., p. 269.

86 Roger Fowler, *Language in the News: Discourse and Ideology in the Press* (Oxford: Routledge, 1991), p. 11.
87 Ibid., p. 3.
88 Frantz Fanon, *The Wretched of the Earth* (London: Penguin Classics, 1990), p. 38.
89 King, p. 173.
90 Ibid., p. 174.
91 Ibid.
92 Carl H. Nightingale, *Segregation: A Global History of Divided Cities* (Chicago: University of Chicago Press, 2012), p. 301.
93 Gunter, p. 66.
94 Ibid., p. 66.
95 Spurr, p. 17.
96 Carpenter, p. 16.
97 Miller, *Interesting Manila*, p. 28.
98 Boyce, p. 229.
99 Stanley Karnow, *In Our Image: America's Empire in the Philippines* (New York: Foreign Policy Association, 1989), p. 25.
100 Jonathan Lee, *History of Asian Americans: Exploring Diverse Roots* (Westport, CT: Greenwood, 2015), p. 67.
101 Karnow, p. 25.
102 Bill Ashcroft, Gareth Griffiths and Helen Tiffin, *The Empire Writes Back: Theory and Practice in Post-Colonial Literatures* (Oxford: Routledge, 2002), p. 88.
103 Ibid., p. 38.
104 Ibid., p. 79.
105 Boyce, p. 220.
106 Mary H. Fee, *A Woman's Impression of the Philippines* (Chicago: A. C. McClurg & Co, 1912; repr. Manila: GCF Books, 1988), p. 36.
107 Lisle, p. 270.
108 Kári Gíslason, 'Travel Writing', in *The Cambridge Companion to Creative Writing*, ed. David Morley and Philip Neilsen (Cambridge: Cambridge University Press, 2012), pp. 87–101 (p. 91).
109 Massimo Canevacci, 'Digital Auratic Reproducibility: Ubiquitous Ethnographies and Communicational Metropolis', in *An Ethnography of Global Landscapes and Corridors*, ed. Loshini Naidoo (Rijeka: In Tech, 2012), pp. 249–60 (p. 252).
110 Gunter, p. 10.
111 Ibid., p. 126.
112 '*Jack Curzon*, or Mysterious Manila. By Archibald Clavering Gunter (London: George Routledge & Sons, Limited)', *Glasgow Herald*, 4 May 1899, Newspapers. com <https://www.newspapers.com/image/409221346> [accessed 27 April 2020] (para 1 of 1).

113 Ibid., para 1 of 1.
114 Hamilton-Paterson, *Ghosts of Manila*, p. 115.

Chapter 4

1 Pratt, p. 7.
2 Pārtha Caṭṭopādhyāẏa and Partha Chatterjee, *Nationalist Thought and the Colonial World: A Derivative Discourse* (London: Zed Books, 1986), p. 51.
3 Ileto, *Knowledge and Pacification*, p. 108.
4 William Gilbert Irwin, and Special Correspondence, 'Yankeefied Manila', *Atchison Daily Globe* (Atchison, Kansas), 1 December 1898, 19th Century U.S. Newspapers <http://find.galegroup.com/ncnp/infomark.do?&source=gale&prodId=NCNP&userGroupName=uniportsmouth&tabID=T003&docPage=article&searchType=BasicSearchForm&docId=GT3012437529&type=multipage&contentSet=LTO&version=1.0> [accessed 2 March 2019] (para 1 of 20).
5 Boyce, p. 229.
6 Ibid., p. 253.
7 Carpenter, p. 15.
8 Spurr, p. 15.
9 Irwin, and Special Correspondent, para 5 of 20.
10 Boyce, p. 251.
11 Fee, p. 36.
12 Homi K. Bhabha, *The Location of Culture* (Oxford: Routledge, 1994), p. 87.
13 Claire 'High Pockets' Phillips and Myron Goldsmith, *Manila Espionage* (Portland, OR: Binfords & Mort, 1947; repr. Los Angeles: Enhanced Media Publishing, 2017), p. 7.
14 Ibid., p. 8.
15 Ibid., p. 9.
16 Ibid., p. 12.
17 Ibid., p. 8.
18 Ibid., p. 10.
19 Ibid., p. 8.
20 Ibid.
21 Ibid.
22 Ian Jarvie, 'Dollars and Ideology: Will Hays' Economic Foreign Policy 1922–1945', *Film History*, 2.3 (1988): 207–21 (p. 210).
23 *The Catholic Advance*, para 1 of 41.
24 Stevenson, p. 14.
25 Ibid., p. 15.

26 Ibid., p. 144.
27 Williams, p. 17.
28 Ibid., p. 20.
29 Ibid., para 4 of 10.
30 *The Journal Herald* (Dayton, Ohio) (1966). 'In Manila Hotel: Beatle Suite Redecorated for LBJ', 24 October 1966, Newspapers.com <https://www.newspapers.com/image/395130443/?terms=manila> [accessed 9 April 2019] (para 2 of 10).
31 Tadiar, p. 12.
32 Ibid., p. 12.
33 Benedict Anderson, 'James Fenton's Slideshow', *New Left Review*, 158 (1986): pp. 1–11 (p. 3).
34 Ibid., p. 4.
35 Hamilton-Paterson, *Playing with Water*, p. 131.
36 Ibid., p. 126.
37 Williams, p. 17.
38 Hamilton-Paterson, *America's Boy*, p. 359.
39 Buruma, pp. 84–5.
40 Lisle, p. 77.
41 Ibid.
42 Buruma, p. 71.
43 Ibid., p. 170.
44 Hamilton-Paterson, *Playing with Water*, p. 129.
45 Ibid., p. 128.
46 Ibid.
47 Primitivo Mijares, *The Conjugal Dictatorship of Ferdinand and Imelda Marcos* (Manila: CreateSpace Independent Publishing Platform, 2016), p. 7.
48 Tadiar, pp. 1–2.
49 Ibid., p. 84.
50 Ibid.
51 Ibid., p. 83.
52 Timothy Mo, *Brownout on Breadfruit Boulevard* (London: Paddleless Press, 1997), p. 24.
53 Ibid., p. 21.
54 Ibid., p. 32.
55 Ibid., p. 35.
56 Ibid., p. 24.
57 Graham Huggan, *The Post-colonial Exotic: Marketing the Margins* (Oxford: Routledge, 2001), pp. 12–13.
58 Amrik Singh, 'Asia Pacific Tourism Industry: Current Trends and Future Outlooks', *Asia Pacific Journal of Tourism Research*, 4 (1997): 1–5 <https://www.hotel-online

.com/Trends/AsiaPacificJournal/AsiaPacificTourismOutlook_1997.html> [accessed 15 October 2017] (p. 2).
59 Trading Economics, *United States Exports* <https://tradingeconomics.com/united-states/exports> [accessed 25 September 2017].
60 John Connell, 'Beyond Manila: Walls, Malls, and Private Spaces', *Environment and Planning*, 31 (1999), 15–24 <doi: 10.1068/a310417> [accessed 25 September 2017] (p. 17).
61 Hamilton-Paterson, *Playing with Water*, p. 130.
62 Pico Iyer, *Video Night in Kathmandu* (New York: Alfred A. Knopf, 1988; repr. London: Black Swan, 1998), p. 179.
63 Ibid., p. 180.
64 Frances Hardy, 'Sex Victims of Marriage by Mail', *Daily Mail* (London, England), 25 July 1991, Daily Mail Historical Archive <http://find.galegroup.com/dmha/newspaperRetrieve.do?sgHitCountType=None&sort=DateAscend&tabID=T003&prodId=DMHA&resultListType=RESULT_LIST&searchId=R2&searchType=AdvancedSearchForm&currentPosition=9&qrySerId=Locale%28en%2C%2C%29%3AFQE%3D%28tx%2CNone%2C11%29sex+victims%3AAnd%3ALQE%3D%28da%2CNone%2C23%2901%2F01%2F1990+-+01%2F07%2F1992%24&retrieveFormat=MULTIPAGE_DOCUMENT&userGroupName=uniportsmouth&inPS=true&contentSet=LTO&&docId=&docLevel=FASCIMILE&workId=&relevancePageBatch=EE1861069764&contentSet=DMHA&callistoContentSet=DMHA&docPage=article&hilite=y> [accessed 1 March 2019] (para 1 of 24).
65 Sara Barrett, 'Video Brides Who Think Heaven Is Having a British Husband', *Daily Mail* (London, England), 14 March 1988, Daily Mail Historical Archive <http://find.galegroup.com/dmha/infomark.do?&source=gale&prodId=DMHA&userGroupName=uniportsmouth&tabID=T003&docPage=article&searchType=BasicSearchForm&docId=EE1861445926&type=multipage&contentSet=LTO&version=1.0> [accessed 5 March 2019] (para 27 of 39).
66 Rafe Bartholomew, *Pacific Rims: Beermen Ballin' in Flip-Flops and the Philippines' Unlikely Love Affair with Basketball* (New York: New American Library, 2010), p. 2.
67 Barrett, para 8.
68 Ibid., para 10.
69 Ibid., para 16.
70 Ibid., para 8.
71 Ibid., para 17.
72 Gustave Flaubert, quoted in Tadiar, p. 58.
73 Tadiar, p. 58.
74 Ibid., p. 47.
75 Ibid.
76 Barrett, para 1.
77 Said, *Orientalism*, p. 62.

Chapter 5

1. Luisa Yap, 'The Chinese in the Philippines', *China Perspectives*, 20 (1998): 53.
2. Ibid., p. 53.
3. Francia, *History of the Philippines*, p. 62.
4. Michael Clodfelter, *Warfare and Armed Conflicts: A Statistical Encyclopedia of Casualty and Other Figures, 1492–2015*, 4th edn (Jefferson, NC: McFarland), p. 61.
5. J. Neil Garcia, *Philippine Gay Culture* (Hong Kong: Hong Kong University Press, 2008), p. 387.
6. Edgar Wickberg, 'Anti-Sinicism and Chinese Identity Options in the Philippines', in *Essential Outsiders: Chinese and Jews in the Modern Transformation of Southeast Asia and Central Europe*, ed. by Daniel Chirot and Anthony Reid (Seattle: University of Washington Press, 1997), pp. 153–183 (p. 157).
7. Garcia, p. 387.
8. Richard T. Chu, *Chinese and Chinese Mestizos of Manila: Family, Identity, and Culture 1860s–1930s* (Leiden; Boston: Brill, 2010), p. 75.
9. Defoe, p. 268.
10. Caroline S. Hau, *Necessary Fictions: Philippine Literature and the Nation, 1946–1980* (Manila: Ateneo de Manila University Press, 2000), p. 152.
11. Chu, p. 55.
12. Van Den Berghe, quoted in Michael Banton, 'The Concept of Racism', in *Race and Racialism*, ed. Sami Zubaida (London: Tavistock Publications, 1970), pp. 86–101 (p. 87).
13. Stanford M. Lyman, 'The "Yellow Peril" Mystique: Origins and Vicissitudes of a Racist Discourse', *International Journal of Politics, Culture, and Society*, 13.4 (2000): 683–747 (p. 694).
14. Christopher Frayling, *The Yellow Peril: Dr Fu Manchu and the Rise of Chinaphobia* (London: Thames and Hudson Ltd, 2014).
15. Lee, *The Making of Asian America*, p. 29.
16. Ibid., p. 30.
17. Lyman, p. 689.
18. Wickberg, pp. 278–9.
19. Constantino, p. 118.
20. Wickberg, p. 279.
21. Elliott C. Arensmeyer, 'The Chinese Coolie Labor Trade and the Philippines: An Inquiry', *Philippine Studies*, 28.2 (1980): 187–98 (p. 190).
22. Peter Kwong and Dušanka Miščevic, *Chinese America: The Untold Story of America's Oldest New Community* (New York: The New Press, 2006), pp. 10–20.
23. Ibid., p. 35.
24. MacMicking, p. 23.

25 Wilkes, p. 462.
26 Ibid., p. 17.
27 London *Times*, quoted in Jenny Clegg, *Fu Manchu and the 'Yellow Peril': The Making of a Racist Myth* (Stoke-on-Trent, Trentham Books, 1994), p. 22.
28 Kwong and Miščevic, pp. 44–5.
29 David Nirenberg, *Anti-Judaism: The Western Tradition* (New York: W. W. Norton & Company, 2013), pp. 196–7.
30 Bryan Cheyette, *Constructions of 'the Jew' in English Literature and Society: Racial Representations, 1875–1945* (Cambridge: Cambridge University Press, 1995), p. 67.
31 Ibid., pp. 181–2.
32 Ibid., p. 151.
33 Chu, p. 56.
34 Ibid., p. 81.
35 Ibid., p. 83.
36 Sara Lipton, 'The Invention of the Jewish Nose', *The New York Review of Books*, 14 November 2014 <https://www.nybooks.com/daily/2014/11/14/invention-jewish-nose/> [accessed 2 February 2019] (para 8 of 13).
37 Sara Lipton, 'Creating the Stereotyped Root of Evil', *The Jewish Chronicle*, 11 December 2014 <https://www.thejc.com/culture/books/creating-the-stereotyped-root-of-evil-1.63514> [accessed 2 February 2019] (para 9 of 11).
38 Lipton, 'The Invention of the Jewish Nose', para 13.
39 Norton Kyshe, James William, *History of the Laws and Courts of Hong Kong* (London: T Fisher Unwin, 1898), p. 42.
40 Bowring, p. 144.
41 Ibid., p. 116.
42 Ibid., p. 163.
43 Thomes, p. 10.
44 Lee, *The Making of Asian America*, p. 32.
45 Ibid., p. 33.
46 Tan, pp. 141–2.
47 Gunter, p. 40.
48 Ibid., p. 40.
49 Ibid., p. 124.
50 Ibid.
51 'Jack Curzon', 1899.
52 H. Irving Hancock, *Uncle Sam's Boys in the Philippines, or Following the Flag against the Moros* (Philadelphia, PA: Henry Altemus Company, 1912), p. 18.
53 'H. Irving Hancock', *New York Times*, 13 March 1922, Times Machine <https://www.newspapers.com/image/26756120/?terms=%22h.%2Birving%2Bhancock%22%2Bobituary> [accessed 8 June 2020] (para 1 of 5).

54 Ibid., p. 19.
55 Ibid.
56 Ibid., p. 20.
57 Ibid., p. 70.
58 Ibid., p. 74.
59 Ibid., p. 218.
60 Chu, p. 86.
61 Ibid., p. 87.
62 Kwong and Miščevic, p. 128.
63 Boyce, p. 43.
64 Robb, p. 191.
65 Clegg, p. 2.
66 Kwong and Miščevic, pp. 117–22.
67 Robb, p. 238.
68 Muriel Bailey, 'Chinese and Their Ways in the Philippines', *The Atlanta Constitution*, 29 July 1900, Newspapers.com <https://www.newspapers.com/image/26845829/?terms=%22chinese%22%2B%22philippines%22%2B%22women%22> (para 14 of 24).
69 Ibid. (para 11 of 24).
70 Ibid. (para 13 of 24).
71 Ibid. (para. 2 of 24).
72 Frantz Fanon, *Black Skin, White Masks* (London: Pluto Press, 2008), p. 89.
73 Ibid., p. 84.
74 Ibid., p. 87.
75 Ibid., p. 84.
76 Robb, p. 118.
77 'Weekly Papers are Being Hit Very Hard', *The Labor World* (Duluth, Minnesota), 27 October 1906, Newspapers.com <https://www.newspapers.com/image/49590487/?terms=%22w.d.%2Bboyce%22%2B%22labor%2Bunion%22%2B%22newspaper%22> [accessed 8 June 2020] (para 4 of 7).
78 'Boyce Takes Stand', *The Times* (Streator, Illinois), 27 June 1902, Newspapers.com. <https://www.newspapers.com/image/542909162/?terms=%22w.d.%2Bboyce%22%2B%22labor%2Bunion%22> [accessed 8 June 2020] (para 1 of 5).
79 Boyce, p. 17.
80 Ibid., p. 112.
81 Hau, *Necessary Fictions*, p. 138.
82 Ibid., p. 136.
83 Raymond Nelson, *The Philippines* (London: Thames and Hudson, 1968), p. 116.
84 Tzvetan Todorov, *On Human Diversity: Nationalism, Racism and Exoticism in French Thought* (Cambridge, Massachusetts: Harvard University Press, 1993), p. 137.

85 Ibid., p. 138.
86 Mo, *Renegade or Halo²*, p. 134.
87 Mo, quoted in Boyd Tonkin, 'The Books Interview: Timothy Mo – Postcards from the Edge', *Independent Online*, 9 July 1999, <http://www.independent.co.uk/arts-entertainment/the-books-interview-timothy-mo-postcards-from-the-edge-1105400.html> [accessed 25 September 2017] (para 5 out of 22).
88 Mo, *Renegade or Halo²*, p. 20.
89 Mo, quoted in Tonkin, para 18.
90 Hau, *Necessary Fictions*, p. 157.
91 Mark Turner, 'The Kidnapping Crisis in the Philippines 1991–1993: Context and Management', *Journal of Contingencies and Crisis Management*, 3.1 (1995): 1–11 (p. 1).
92 Seth Mydans, 'Kidnapping of Ethnic Chinese Rises in Philippines', *New York Times*, 17 March 1996. <https://www.nytimes.com/1996/03/17/world/kidnapping-of-ethnic-chinese-rises-in-philippines.html> [accessed 8 June 2020] (para 6 of 31).
93 Turner, p. 2.
94 Ibid., p. 2.
95 Mydans (para 9 of 31).
96 Ibid., p. 167.
97 Kwong and Miščevic, p. 324.
98 Zengjun Peng, 'Representation of China: An Across Time Analysis of Coverage in the *New York Times* and *Los Angeles Times*', *Asian Journal of Communication*, 14.1 (2004): 53–67 (p. 60).
99 Zhuo Ban, Shaunak Sastry and Mohan Jyoti Dutta, '"Shoppers' Republic of China": Orientalism in Neoliberal U.S. News Discourse', Journal of International and Intercultural Communication, 6.4 (2013): 280–97 (p. 286).
100 Guy de Jonquières, *China's Challenges* (Brussels: ECIPE, 2012), p. 9.
101 Duncan Alexander McKenzie, *The Unlucky Country: The Republic of the Philippines in the 21st Century* (Balboa Press: Carlsbad, 2012), Amazon Kindle edition, location 438.
102 Ibid., location 3997.
103 Ibid., location 1319.
104 Ibid., location 3999–4001.
105 Ibid., location 4002–4003.
106 Ibid., location 3990.
107 Ibid., location 4016.
108 Tom Smith, 'President Duterte's anti-US Populism Is a Dangerously Isolationist Path', *Guardian*, 7 September 2016, <https://www.theguardian.com/commentisfree/2016/sep/07/duterte-anti-us-philippines-isolationist-foreign-policy-insult-barack-obama-china> [accessed 27 February 2019], para 7 of 10.

109 Seth Robson, 'Facility for US Forces Opens on Philippines' Main Island; Another Slated for Palawan', *Stars & Stripes*, 31 January 2019 <https://www.stripes.com/news/facility-for-us-forces-opens-on-philippines-main-island-another-slated-for-palawan-1.566695> [accessed 16 April 2019].

110 Daniel Workman, 'Philippines Top Trading Partners', <http://www.worldstopexports.com/philippines-top-import-partners/> [accessed 21 May 2020] (para 6 of 8).

111 Ankit Panda, 'In Sudden Step, Philippines Reverses Course of Ending US Visiting Forces Agreement – For Now', *The Diplomat*, 4 June 2020 <https://thediplomat.com/2020/06/in-sudden-step-philippines-reverses-course-on-ending-us-visiting-forces-agreement-for-now/> [accessed 3 July 2020] (para 1 of 13).

112 Demetri Sevastopolu and Michael Peel, 'Duterte Plays Cat-and-mouse Game with China', *Financial Times*, 8 May 2017 <https://www.ft.com/content/4375d4ee-340c-11e7-bce4-9023f8c0fd2e> [accessed 1 April 2019] (para 1 of 17).

113 Joint Communiqué, quoted in 'One and Only China', *The Manila Times*, 9 October 2017 <https://www.manilatimes.net/one-and-only-china/355384/> [accessed 18 April 2019] (para 3 of 11).

114 Malcolm Cook, 'Meet New Boss Duterte, Same as the Old Boss', *Nikkei Asian Review*, 15 January 2017 <https://asia.nikkei.com/Politics/Meet-new-boss-Duterte-same-as-the-old-boss> (para 12 of 16).

115 Jonathan Miller, *Duterte Harry: Fire and Fury in the Philippines* (Brunswick and London: Scribe, 2018), p. 294.

116 John Pilger, 'The Coming War on China', *New Internationalist*, 30 November 2016 <https://newint.org/features/2016/12/01/the-coming-war-on-china> [accessed 11 December 2018].

117 Tom Engelhardt, 'A New Map Shows the Alarming Spread of the US War on Terror', *The Nation*, 4 January 2018 <https://www.thenation.com/article/a-new-map-shows-the-alarming-spread-of-the-us-war-on-terror/> [accessed 11 December 2018].

118 Tadiar, p. 70.

119 Kelly, p. 96.

120 Jing Yu, 'Tibet, Xinjiang, and China's Strong State Complex', *The Diplomat*, 28 July 2016 <https://thediplomat.com/2016/07/tibet-xinjiang-and-chinas-strong-state-complex/> [accessed 7 April 2019].

121 Kelly, p. 96.

122 Bloomberg News, 'Chinese Money Triggers a Dizzying Rally in Manila Property', Bloomberg, 3 May 2018 <https://www.bloomberg.com/news/articles/2018-05-03/in-china-s-new-gambling-hot-spot-property-prices-are-on-a-tear> [accessed 5 April 2019] (paras 1–2 of 22).

123 Ibid., paras 21–2.

124 Hau, *Necessary Fictions*, p. 134.

125　Ibid., p. 166.
126　Ibid., p. 175.
127　Bloomberg News, 'Chinese Money', para 6.
128　Kate McGeown, 'Call Me: Tech Powers Philippines Call Centre Success', *BBC News*, 15 May 2012 <https://www.bbc.co.uk/news/business-18061909> [accessed 5 April 2019] (para 31 of 31).
129　Ibid., para 23.
130　Ibid., para 26.
131　Bloomberg News, 'Chinese Money', para 2.
132　See I. Sayson, 'World's Largest Ikea to Open in Manila as Company Bets on Asia', [online] Bloomberg.com (2019). Available at: https://www.bloomberg.com/news/articles/2018-11-20/world-s-largest-ikea-to-open-in-manila-as-company-bets-on-asia [Accessed 10 April 2019]; Hotel Resource, '390 Room Sheraton Manila Hotel Opens', [online] Hotelnewsresource.com (2019). Available at: https://www.hotelnewsresource.com/article103605.html [Accessed 10 April 2019]; E. Goldberg, 'Wing Zone to Open 12 New Units in Panama and the Philippines in 2019', [online] Franchising.com (2019). Available at: https://www.franchising.com/articles/wing_zone_to_open_12_new_units_in_panama_and_the_philippines_in_2019.html [Accessed 10 April 2019].
133　Miller, *Duterte Harry*, p. 296.
134　Walden Bello, 'Foreword', in *The Realm of the Punisher: Travels in Duterte's Philippines*, ed. Tom Sykes (Oxford: Signal Books, 2018), pp. xi–xv (p. ix).
135　Miller, *Duterte Harry*, p. 288.
136　John Chalmers, 'Duterte's War: Meth Gangs of China Stoke Philippines Drug Crisis', Reuters, 16 December 2016 <https://www.reuters.com/investigates/special-report/philippines-drugs-china/> [accessed 10 April 2019], (para 3 of 51).
137　Ibid., para 4.
138　Ibid., para 7.
139　Ibid., para 5.
140　Gunter, p. 54.
141　Miller, *Duterte Harry*, p. 96.
142　Rupert Hodder, 'The Economic Significance of the Chinese in the Philippines: An Analysis of Its Overstatement', *Philippine Studies*, 55.1 (2007): 88–115 (pp. 90–1).
143　Chalmers, para 7.
144　Ibid., para 6.
145　Jodesz Gavilan, 'LIST: Suspected Drug Lords Killed under Duterte Gov't', *Rappler.com*, 30 August 2016 <https://www.rappler.com/newsbreak/iq/144659-war-on-drugs-suspected-drug-lords-killed-duterte-administration-list> [accessed 19 January 2019] (para 4 of 10).
146　Pedro Bordalo, Katherine Coffman, Nicola Gennaioli and Andrei Shleifer, 'Stereotypes', *The Quarterly Journal of Economics*, doi:10.1093/qje/qjw029, pp. 1753–94 (p. 1754).

147 Ibid., p. 1754.
148 Kyodo, 'Official Death Toll in Philippine President Rodrigo Duterte's War on Drugs Exceeds 5,000', *South China Morning Post*, 18 December 2018 <https://www.scmp.com/news/asia/southeast-asia/article/2178601/official-death-toll-philippine-president-rodrigo-dutertes> [accessed 19 January 2019], (para 9 of 13).
149 Willem Koomen, 'Ingroup and Outgroup Stereotypes and Selective Processing', *European Journal of Social Psychology*, 27 (1997): 589–601 (p. 598).

Chapter 6

1 Oliver Holmes and agencies in Manila, 'Philippine Police Kill 32 in Bloodiest Night of Duterte's War on Drugs', *Guardian*, 16 August 2017 <https://www.theguardian.com/world/2017/aug/16/philippines-police-bloodiest-night-duterte-war-drugs> [accessed 6 February 2019].
2 Miller, *Duterte Harry*, p. 2.
3 Ileto, *Knowledge and Pacification*, p. 270.
4 James Fenton, 'Murderous Manila: On the Night Shift', *New York Review of Books*, 9 February 2017 <https://www.nybooks.com/articles/2017/02/09/murderous-manila-on-the-night-shift/> [accessed 6 February 2019] (para 1 of 38).
5 Pankaj Mishra, quoted in Francis Wade, '"The Liberal Order Is the Incubator for Authoritarianism": A Conversation with Pankaj Mishra', *Los Angeles Review of Books*, 15 November 2018 <https://lareviewofbooks.org/article/the-liberal-order-is-the-incubator-for-authoritarianism-a-conversation-with-pankaj-mishra/> [accessed 30 February 2019] (para 6 of 28).
6 Miller, *Duterte Harry*, p. 102.
7 Ibid., p. 55.
8 Ibid., p. 331.
9 Ibid., p. 93.
10 Fenton, *Murderous Manila*, para 4.
11 Miller, *Duterte Harry*, p. 82.
12 Ibid., p. 84.
13 Ibid., p. 82.
14 Ibid., p. 275.
15 Ibid., p. 117.
16 Ileto, *Knowledge and Pacification*, p. 283.
17 Tamara Pearson, 'Everything the Western Mainstream Media Outlets Get Wrong When Covering Poor Countries', *Counterpunch*, 11 January 2019 <https://www.counterpunch.org/2019/01/11/everything-the-western-mainstream-media-outlets-get-wrong-when-covering-poor-countries-2/> [accessed 17 April 2019] (para 6 of 26).

18 Reynaldo C. Ileto, 'Orientalism and the Study of Philippine Politics', delivered as 'The Third Burns Chair Lecture' (University of Hawai'i, 1 October 1997), p. 4.
19 Miller, *Duterte Harry*, p. 52.
20 Ibid., p. 23.
21 Ibid., p. 24.
22 Ibid., pp. 265–6.
23 Ibid., pp. 289–91.
24 Grosrichard, p. 72.
25 Ibid., p. 71.
26 Miller, *Duterte Harry*, p. 67.
27 Ibid., p. 57.
28 Ibid., p. 187.
29 Grosrichard, p. 70.
30 Ibid., pp. 76–7.
31 Miller, *Duterte Harry*, p. 77.
32 Grosrichard, p. 85.
33 Miller, *Duterte Harry*, p. 296.
34 Ibid., p. 112.
35 Ibid., p. 297.
36 Stuart Hall, 'The Spectacle of the "Other"', in Representation: Cultural Representations and Signifying Practices', in *Representation: Cultural Representations and Signifying Practices*, ed. Stuart Hall (London: Sage, 1997), pp. 227–46 (p. 229).
37 Grosrichard, p. 5.
38 Ibid., p. 11.
39 Miller, *Duterte Harry*, p. 15.
40 Ibid., p. 294.
41 Ibid., p. 113.
42 Grosrichard, p. 46.
43 Miller, *Duterte Harry*, p. 13.
44 Ibid., p. 14.
45 Ibid., p. 287.
46 Ibid., p. 288.
47 Ibid., p. 43.
48 Sebastian Horsley, *Dandy in the Underworld: An Unauthorised Autobiography* (London: Sceptre, 2008), p. 299.
49 Ibid., p. 298.
50 Michael Peel, 'Drugs and death in Davao: The making of Rodrigo Duterte', *Financial Times*, 2 February 2017 <https://www.ft.com/content/9d6225dc-e805-11e6-967b-c88452263daf≥ [accessed 12 February 2019] (para 5 of 17).

51 Miller, *Duterte Harry*, p. 15.
52 Ibid., p. 14.
53 Fenton, 'Murderous Manila', para 7.
54 Miller, *Duterte Harry*, p. 292.
55 Walden Bello, Marissa de Guzman, Mary Lou Malig and Herbert Docena, *The Anti-Development State: The Political Economy of Permanent Crisis in the Philippines* (London and New York: Zed Books, 2004), p. 113.
56 Walden Bello, 'How Neoliberalism Killed the Philippines' EDSA Republic', *Green Left Weekly*, 24 June 2016 <https://www.greenleft.org.au/content/walden-bello-how-neoliberalism-killed-philippines-edsa-republic> (para 17 of 39).
57 Bello, de Guzman, Malig and Docena, p. 113.
58 Bello, *The Realm of the Punisher*, p. xi.
59 Tadiar, p. 53.
60 Noam Chomsky, quoted in David Barsamian, 'Noam Chomsky Interview', *The Progressive*, 1 May 2004 <https://progressive.org/magazine/noam-chomsky-interview/> [accessed 19 April 2019] (para 20 of 53).
61 Michael Peel, 'Philippine Leader Rodrigo Duterte Mines Seam of Anti-US Sentiment', *Financial Times*, 5 October 2016 <https://www.ft.com/content/def867ce-8aca-11e6-8cb7-e7ada1d123b1> [accessed 27 March 2019].
62 Miller, *Duterte Harry*, p. 303.
63 Ibid., p. 133.
64 Ibid., p. 134.
65 E. San Juan, Jr., *U.S. Imperialism and Revolution in the Philippines* (New York and Basingstoke: Palgrave MacMillan, 2007), p. xxiv.
66 Miller, *Duterte Harry*, p. 308.
67 Tadiar, p. 72.
68 San Juan Jr., p. xiii.
69 Ibid., p. xxiv.
70 Miller, *Duterte Harry*, p. 305.
71 Ibid., p. 311.
72 Ibid., p. 309.
73 Rodriguez, p. 99.
74 Miller, *Duterte Harry*, p. 305.
75 Ibid., p. 303.
76 Ibid., p. 304.
77 Mirca Madianou, 'Migration and the Accentuated Ambivalence of Motherhood: The Role of ICTs in Filipino Transnational Families', *Global Networks*, 12.3 (2012): 277–95 (p. 281).
78 Ibid., pp. 285–6.
79 Miller, *Duterte Harry*, p. 312.

80 Ibid., p. 312.
81 Alexis Romero, 'Duterte: No Joint Expeditions with US During My Time', *Philippine Star*, 21 March 2018 <https://www.philstar.com/headlines/2018/03/21/1799010/duterte-no-joint-expeditions-us-during-my-time> [accessed 6 February 2019].
82 Jeremy Butterfield, *Fowler's Dictionary of Modern English Usage*, 4th edn (Oxford: Oxford University Press, 2015), p. 422.
83 Andrew Spear, 'Hypocrisy and Responsibility: On the Uses and Abuses of tu quoque for Life' (Michigan: Grand Valley State University, 2017) <https://www.gvsu.edu/seidman/ethics/module-news-view.htm?storyId=CD0BC3F2-D254-A741-C4495405CDC5B795&siteModuleId=9C6681B1-92E9-F4F1-7B4DF17EDBE5D2DC> [accessed 27 July 2017] (para 5 of 7).
84 Miller, *Duterte Harry*, p. 112.
85 United Nations, 'Delegations Accuse International Criminal Court of "Double Standards", "Selectivity", as General Assembly Adopts Resolution Welcoming Its Report', United Nations Meetings Coverage, 13 May 2016 <https://www.un.org/press/en/2016/ga11784.doc.htm> [accessed 9 January 2019].
86 Scott Turner, 'The Dilemma of Double Standards in U.S. Human Rights Policy', *Peace & Change: A Journal of Peace Research*, 28.4 (2003): 524–54.
87 Mary Kimani, 'International Criminal Court: Justice or Racial Double Standards?', *Global Policy Forum/Afrik.com*, 16 December 2009 <https://www.globalpolicy.org/component/content/article/164-icc/48775-international-criminal-court-justice-or-racial-double-standards-.html> [accessed 7 February 2019] (para 5 of 12).
88 Wolfgang Kaleck, 'Double Standards in International Criminal Justice: A Long Road Ahead Towards Universal Justice', *FICHL Policy Brief Series*, 37 (2015): 1–4 (p. 4).
89 Vicente Rafael, 'Duterte's Hobbesian World', Philippine Inquirer, 13 June 2016 <https://opinion.inquirer.net/95185/dutertes-hobbesian-world> [accessed 15 April 2019] (para 2 of 9).
90 Ibid., para 4.
91 Richard Seymour, 'Modi and Duterte', *Media Review*, teleSUR, 12 May 2017 <https://www.youtube.com/watch?v=sT65Nuh8OKc> [accessed 10 April 2019].
92 Modi and Duterte.
93 Modi and Duterte.
94 Miller, *Duterte Harry*, p. 290.
95 Euan McKirdy, 'Philippines Vows to "destroy" Islamist Extremism. Here's Why That Won't Be so Easy', *CNN*, 31 January 2019 <https://edition.cnn.com/2019/01/30/asia/duterte-islamist-extremism-problem-intl/index.html> [accessed 20 February 2019].
96 Miller, *Duterte Harry*, p. 160.

97 BBC News, 'Europe and Nationalism: A Country-by-country Guide', *BBC News*, 10 September 2018 <https://www.bbc.co.uk/news/world-europe-36130006> [accessed 29 January 2019] (para 26 of 50).

98 Pankaj Mishra, 'Bland Fanatics', *London Review of Books*, 37.23 (2015): 37–40 (p. 38).

99 Tom Smith, 'Those Standing Up to Duterte Are from a Long Line of Strong Filipinas', *Guardian*, 7 December 2016 <https://www.theguardian.com/commentisfree/2016/dec/07/rodrigo-duterte-strong-filipinas-philippines-cory-aquino-gloria-arroyo> [accessed 29 January 2019] (para 4 of 10).

100 HYPERLINK "https://www.bulatlat.com/author/alex/" Alexander Martin Remollino, 'Victims of Martial Law See in Arroyo a Tyrant Worse Than Marcos', *Bulatlat*, 21 September 2009 <https://www.bulatlat.com/2009/09/21/victims-of-martial-law-see-in-arroyo-a-tyrant-worse-than-marcos/> [accessed 29 January 2019] (para 11 of 25).

101 Murray Hiebert, 'How Do You Solve a Problem Like Duterte?', Nikkei Asian Review, 3 October 2016 <https://asia.nikkei.com/Politics/Murray-Hiebert-and-Conor-Cronin-How-do-you-solve-a-problem-like-Duterte> [accessed 30 January 2019] (para 3 of 12).

Chapter 7

1 Justin D. Edwards and Rune Graulund, *Mobility at Large: Globalization, Textuality and Innovative Travel Writing* (Liverpool: Liverpool University Press, 2012), p. 5.
2 Said, *Orientalism*, p. 24.
3 Ibid., p. 5.
4 Ibid., p. 4.
5 Ibid., p. 112.
6 Ibid., p. 200.
7 Lisle, p. 273.
8 Ibid., p. 270.
9 Ong, quoted in Sykes, pp. 133–4.
10 Said, *Orientalism* p. 24.
11 Ibid., p. 322.
12 Canevacci, p. 252 (pp. 249–60).
13 Lisle, p. 77.
14 Ibid., p. 72.
15 Edwards and Graulund, p. 10.
16 Williams, p. 23.
17 Ibid., p. 128.

18 Ibid., p. 129.
19 Luis H. Francia, *Eye of the Fish: A Personal Archipelago* (New York: Kaya Press, 2001), p. 3.
20 Celia Hunt and Fiona Sampson, *Writing: Self & Reflexivity* (Basingstoke: Palgrave MacMillan, 2006), p. 4.
21 Ibid., p. 113.
22 Ibid., p. 114.
23 Ibid., p. 17.
24 Ibid., p. 180.
25 Francia, *Eye of the Fish*, p. 23.
26 Tadiar, p. 5.
27 Ibid., p. 5.
28 Lisle, p. 270.
29 Rosalind Coward, *Speaking Personally: The Rise of Subjective and Confessional Journalism* (Basingstoke: Palgrave MacMillan, 2013), p. 22.
30 Miguel Syjuco, *Autoplagiarist: An Exegesis of the Novel Ilustrado* (Doctoral thesis, University of Adelaide, Australia, 2010). Retrieved from https://digital.library.adelaide.edu.au/dspace/bitstream/2440/77856/6/04whole.pdf [Accessed 3 July 2020], p. 5.
31 Ibid., p. 33.
32 Leonard R. Sussman, 'Dying (and Being Killed) on the Job: A Case Study of World Journalists, 1982–1989', *Journalism & Mass Communication Quarterly*, 68.1–12 (1991): 195–9 (p. 195); Raul Dancel, 'Philippines: Most Dangerous Place for Journalists in Asia', *Straits Times*, 2 November 2018 <https://www.straitstimes.com/asia/se-asia/most-dangerous-place-for-journalists-in-asia> [accessed 4 February 2019].
33 John Pilger, *Hidden Agendas* (London: Vintage, 1998), pp. 486–7.
34 Aries C. Rufo, *Altar of Secrets: Sex, Politics, and Money in the Philippine Catholic Church* (Manila: Journalism for Nation Building Foundation, 2013), p. 25.
35 Ibid., p. 24.
36 Ibid., p. 25.
37 Ibid., p. 26.
38 Michele Elam, 'Mixed Race and Cultural Memory: Carl Hancock Rux's *Talk*', in *Signatures of the Past: Cultural Memory in Contemporary Anglophone North American Drama*, ed. Marc Maufort and Caroline De Wagter (New York: Peter Lang, 2010), pp. 83–101 (p. 95).
39 F. Sionil José, *Dusk* (New York: Modern Library, 2013), Amazon Kindle e-book, location 2954.
40 Ibid., location 2971.
41 Ibid., locations 3271–3273.

42 John Sayles, *A Moment in the Sun* (San Francisco: McSweeney's, 2011), Amazon Kindle edition, location 8604.
43 Ibid., locations 8604–8605.
44 Ibid., location 8608.
45 Nick Joaquin ('Quijano de Manila'), *Language of the Street and Other Essays* (Manila: National Bookstore, 1980), p. 87.
46 See Daniel A. Bell and Avner de-Shalit, *The Spirit of Cities: Why the Identity of a City Matters in a Global Age* (Princeton: Princeton University Press, 2011), p. 1 for a definition of 'civicism' as 'the sentiment of urban pride', or a feeling of patriotism about a city rather than a nation.
47 Joaquin, p. 87.
48 Ashcroft, Griffiths and Tiffin, *Key Concepts*, p. 159.
49 William McKinley, quoted in Jessica Hagedorn, *Dogeaters* (London: Penguin, 1991), p. 71.
50 Hagedorn, pp. 71–2.
51 Tadiar, p. 3.
52 Gina Apostol, *Insurrecto* (New York: Soho Press, 2018), p. 7.
53 Simon Dentith, *Parody* (London: Routledge, 2000), p. 20.
54 Jose F. Lacaba, 'The January 30 Insurrection', in *Creative Nonfiction: A Reader*, ed. Cristina Pantoja Hidalgo (Quezon City: The University of the Philippines Press, 2005), pp. 11–18 (p. 15).
55 Ibid., p. 17.
56 Ibid., p. 18.
57 Ibid.
58 Ibid., p. 15.
59 Jeremy Black and Donald M. MacRaild, *Studying History* (London: Palgrave MacMillan, 2017), p. 105.
60 Rajeev S. Patke and Philip Holden, *The Routledge Concise History of Southeast Asian Writing in English* (London: Routledge, 2009), p. 66.
61 Lisle, p. 273.
62 Ibid., p. 272.
63 Amadis Ma. Guerrero, *Traveler's Choice: North to South* (Manila: Anvil, 1994), p. 77.
64 Bartholomew, p. 383.
65 Edwards and Graulund, p. 10.
66 Lisle, p. 270.
67 Ibid., p. 33.
68 Bartholomew, pp. 57–8.
69 Ibid., p. 59.
70 Ibid., p. 61.

71 Ibid., p. 3.
72 Ibid., p. 382.
73 Ibid., p. 384.
74 Huggan and Holland, p. 40.
75 Anita Feleo and David Sheniak, *Two for the Road* (Manila: Anvil, 1998), p. 64.
76 Ibid., p. 68.
77 Ibid., p. 64.
78 Ibid., pp. 63–124.
79 Francia, *Eye of the Fish*, p. 5.
80 Ibid., p. 22.
81 Williams, p. 129.
82 Ibid., p. 121.
83 Tom Bamforth, *Deep Field: Dispatches from the Front Line of Aid Relief* (New York: Abrams, 2014), p. 139.
84 Ibid., p. 143.
85 Samuel Lynn Hynes, *The Auden Generation: Literature and Politics in England in the 1930's* (London: The Bodley Head, 1976), p. 144.
86 Jose Y. Dalisay, *Soledad's Sister* (Manila: Anvil, 2008), p. 1.
87 Tadiar, p. 50.
88 Dalisay, p. 4.
89 Ibid., p. 189.
90 Kelly, p. 93.
91 Ibid., p. 123.
92 Ibid., p. 65.
93 Jack Shaheen, *Reel Bad Arabs: How Hollywood Vilifies a People* (New York: Olive Branch Press), p. 4.
94 Ibid., p. 11.
95 Ibid., p. 33.
96 Ibid., p. 35.
97 Linda A. Revilla, 'Young Filipinos Lack Strong Ties to Culture', Honolulu Star-Bulletin, 20 April 1996. Newspapers.com <https://www.newspapers.com> [accessed 28 January 2019] (para 1 of 21).
98 Ibid., para 2.
99 Ibid., para 6.
100 Ibid., para 21.
101 Nick Nuttall, 'Cold-blooded Journalism', in *The Journalistic Imagination: Literary Journalists from Defoe to Capote and Carter*, ed. Richard Keeble and Sharon Wheeler (Oxford: Routledge, 2007), pp. 129–52 (p. 135).
102 Coward, p. 57.
103 Ibid., p. 58.

104 Peter Lennon, quoted in Coward, p. 58.
105 José Rizal, *The Social Cancer (Noli Me Tangere)*, trans. Charles Derbyshire (Manila: Philippine Education Company, 1912; repr. Project Gutenberg: Salt Lake City, 2004), Amazon kindle edition (location 800).
106 Lisle, p. 270.
107 Caroline S. Hau, *On the Subject of the Nation: Filipino Writings from the Margins, 1981–2004* (Quezon City: Ateneo de Manila University Press, 2004), p. 116.
108 Ibid., p. 111.
109 Ibid., p. 111.
110 Ibid., p. 118.
111 Sayles, location 15372.
112 Patke and Holden, p. 87.
113 Ibid., p. 87.
114 Apostol, p. 140.
115 Holland and Huggan, p. 112.
116 Susan Bassnett, 'Travel Writing and Gender', in *The Cambridge Companion to Travel Writing*, ed. Peter Hulme and Tim Youngs (Cambridge: Cambridge University Press, 2002), pp. 225–32 (p. 225).
117 Holland and Huggan, p. 112.
118 Teresa de Lauretis, *Feminist Studies, Critical Studies* (Bloomington: Indiana University Press, 1986), p. 12.
119 Holland and Huggan, p. 112.
120 Coward, p. 82.
121 Green, p. 23.
122 Alfred A. Yuson, 'Confessions of a Q.C. House-Husband', in *Creative Nonfiction: A Reader*, ed. Cristina Pantoja Hidalgo (Quezon City: The University of the Philippines Press, 2005), pp. 39–44 (p. 41).
123 Ibid., p. 40.
124 Ibid., p. 42.
125 Ibid., p. 43.
126 Ibid., p. 40.
127 Ibid., p. 44.
128 Ashcroft, Griffiths and Tiffin, *Empire Writes Back*, p. 88.
129 Buruma, p. 6.
130 Kári Gíslason, 'Travel Writing', in *The Cambridge Companion to Creative Writing*, ed. David Morley and Philip Neilsen (Cambridge: Cambridge University Press, 2012), pp. 87–101 (p. 91).
131 Claudia Capancioni, 'Victorian Women Writers and the Truth of the "Other Side of Italy"', in *Women, Travel Writing, and Truth*, ed. Claire Bloom Saunders (Oxford: Routledge, 2014), pp. 109–24 (p. 114).

132 Sayles, location 424.
133 'Kirkus Review: A Moment in the Sun', *Kirkus*, 18 April 2011 <https://www.kirkusreviews.com/book-reviews/john-sayles/moment-sun/> [accessed 27 July 2017] (para 2 of 3).
134 Frances Doplon, 'Code-Switching in Philippine Tabloids: Subservience and Resistance in a Post-Colonial Society', *Philippine Journal of Linguistics*, 38 (2007): 1–22 (p. 4).
135 Jessica Zafra, 'Dedma 101', in *Creative Nonfiction: A Reader*, ed. Cristina Pantoja Hidalgo (Quezon City: The University of the Philippines Press, 2005), pp. 27–30 (p. 27).
136 Ibid., p. 29.
137 Korte, p. 159.
138 Ibid., p. 160.
139 Juan C. Laya, *His Native Soil* (Quezon City: Kayumanggi Publishers, 1972), p. 115.
140 Ibid., p. 115.
141 McMahon, p. 70.
142 Ibid., p. 85.
143 Carlos Bulosan, *America Is in the Heart: A Personal History* (Seattle: University of Washington Press, 2014), p. 163.
144 Ibid., p. 163.
145 Leanne S. Son Hing, Winnie Li and Mark P. Zanna, 'Inducing Hypocrisy to Reduce Prejudicial Responses among Aversive Racists', *Journal of Experimental Social Psychology*, 38 (2002): 71–8, (p. 71).
146 Denise Cruz and Erin Suzuki, 'America's Empire and the Asia-Pacific', *The Cambridge Companion to Asian American Literature*, ed. Crystal Parikh and Daniel Y. Kim (Cambridge: Cambridge University Press, 2015), p. 20.

Conclusion

1 Elam, p. 95.
2 Andrei P. Tsygankov, *Russophobia: Anti-Russian Lobby and American Foreign Policy* (New York: Palgrave MacMillan, 2009), p. 21.
3 Ibid., p. 32.
4 Ibid., p. 155.
5 Edina Lilla Mészáros, 'The EU-Russia "Uncommon Spaces" Stereotypes and Growing Russophobia: Does Cultural Diplomacy Stand a Chance in Shaping Future EU-Russia Relations?', in *Culture and Paradiplomatic Identity: Instruments in Sustaining EU Policies*, ed. Alina Stoica, Ioan Horga and Maria Manuela Tavares Ribeiro (Newcastle-upon-Tyne: Cambridge Scholars, 2016), pp. 52–67 (p. 53).

6 Roh, Huang and Nui, p. 12.
7 Tadiar, p. 18.
8 Son Hing, Li and Zanna, p. 71.
9 John Narayan and Leon Sealey-Higgins, 'Whatever Happened to the Idea of Imperialism?', *Third World Quarterly*, 38.11 (2017): 2387–95 (p. 2395).
10 Kelly, p. 124.
11 Henri-Count Evans and Rosemary Musvipwa, 'The Sustainable Development Goals, the Paris Agreement and the Addis Agenda: Neo-liberalism, Unequal Development and the Rise of a New Imperialism', in *Knowledge for Justice: Critical Perspectives from Southern African-Nordic Research Partnerships*, ed. Tor Halvorsen, Hilde Ibsen, Henri-Count Evans and Sharon Penderis (Cape Town: African Minds, 2017), pp. 37–56 (p. 37).
12 Michael T. Klare, 'The United States Is Pushing toward War with China', The Nation, 19 June 2018 <https://www.thenation.com/article/united-states-pushing-towards-war-china> [accessed 15 April 2019].
13 Richard Gowan, 'Despite the Rising Stakes, Russia and the West Opt for Indefinite Proxy Conflict', *World Politics Review*, 22 October 2018 <https://www.worldpoliticsreview.com/articles/26547/despite-the-rising-stakes-russia-and-the-west-opt-for-indefinite-proxy-conflict> [accessed 15 April 2019].
14 Stephen F. Cohen, 'War with Russia?', *The Nation*, 3 December 2018. <https://www.thenation.com/article/cold-war-russia/> [accessed 15 April 2019] (para 2 of 25).
15 Sally Campbell, 'Why Does Capitalism Lead to War?', *Socialist Review*, 1 September 2014 <http://socialistreview.org.uk/394/why-does-capitalism-lead-war> [accessed 15 April 2019].
16 Nikolai Bukharin, quoted in Campbell, para 11 of 31.
17 Christine Lagarde, 'The Role of Emerging Markets in a New Global Partnership for Growth by IMF Managing Director Christine Lagarde', *imf.org*, 4 February 2016 <https://www.imf.org/en/News/Articles/2015/09/28/04/53/sp020416#P26_3020> [accessed 15 April 2019] (para 12 of 95).
18 Michael Roberts, 'A World Rate of Profit', in *11th Society of Heterodox Economists Conference* (Sydney: Society of Heterodox Economists, 2012), pp. 1–14.
19 Fergal O'Brien, 'China to Overtake U.S. Economy by 2032 as Asian Might Builds', Bloomberg News, 26 December 2017 <www.bloomberg.com/news/articles/2017-12-26/china-to-overtake-u-s-economy-by-2032-as-asian-might-builds> [accessed 16 April 2019].
20 Larry Elliott, 'Coronavirus Putting World on Track for New Great Depression, Says WTO', *Guardian*, 8 April 2020 <https://www.theguardian.com/world/2020/apr/08/coronavirus-putting-world-on-track-for-new-great-depression-says-who> [accessed 10 April 2020].
21 Oscar V. Campomanes, '1898 and the Nature of the New Empire', *Radical History Review*, 73 (1999): 130–46 (p. 131).

22 Ibid., p. 132.
23 Ibid.
24 The Editorial Board, 'America's Forever Wars', *New York Times*, 22 October 2017 <https://www.nytimes.com/2017/10/22/opinion/americas-forever-wars.html> [accessed 16 April 2019] (para 1 of 13).
25 Gunter, p. 29.
26 Ibid., p. 85.
27 Mimi Thi Nguyen, 'The Biopower of Beauty: Humanitarian Imperialisms and Global Feminisms in an Age of Terror', *Signs: Journal of Women in Culture and Society*, 36.2 (2011): 359–83 (p. 374).
28 Ibid., p. 371.
29 Andrew Urban, 'The Peaceful Majority Are Irrelevant', *The Spectator*, 1 July 2017, <https://www.spectator.co.uk/2017/07/the-peaceful-majority-are-irrelevant/> [accessed 20 April 2019] (para 1 of 22).
30 Janice Turner, 'Is Sherin Khankan the Future of Islam?', *The Times*, 2 June 2018, <https://www.thetimes.co.uk/article/is-sherin-khankan-the-future-of-islam-wfrzfrwzd> [accessed 17 April 2019] (para 5 of 25).
31 Luke Savage, 'New Atheism, Old Empire', *Jacobin*, 2 December 2014, <www.jacobinmag.com/2014/12/new-atheism-old-empire/> [accessed 16 April 2019].
32 David Bosco, 'What Divides Neocons and Liberal Interventionists', *Foreign Policy*, 9 April 2012, <https://foreignpolicy.com/2012/04/09/what-divides-neocons-and-liberal-interventionists/> [accessed 16 April 2019].
33 Ashcroft, Griffiths and Tiffin, *Key Concepts*, p. 169.
34 Mishra, 'The Liberal Order', para 9.
35 Ibid., para 11.
36 Ibid., para 12.
37 Green, p. 28.
38 This formulation originates, according to Green, in 'Shakespeare's Henry V [who] said that one Englishman was worth three Frenchmen' and Columbus' claim that 'with a magnification suitable to the greater cultural gap, [. . .] a thousand Indians would not stand before three Spaniards.' (p. 28).
39 Erik Loomis, 'Serving Time Should Not Mean "Prison Slavery"', *New York Times*, 30 August 2018, <https://www.nytimes.com/2018/08/30/opinion/national-prison-strike-slavery-.html> [accessed 30 August 2018].
40 T.J. Coles and Matt Alford, *Union Jackboot: What Your Media and Professors Don't Tell You about British Foreign Policy* (London: CreateSpace, 2018), p. 132.
41 Cornel West, 'Goodbye, American Neoliberalism: A New Era Is Here', *Guardian*, 17 November 2016 <https://www.theguardian.com/commentisfree/2016/nov/17/american-neoliberalism-cornel-west-2016-election> [accessed 18 April 2019].
42 Daniel C. Hallin, *The Uncensored War: The Media and Vietnam* (New York and Oxford: Oxford University Press, 1986), pp. 116–18.

43 'Beyond Fake News 2020', BBC.co.uk <https://www.bbc.co.uk/academy/en/collections/fake-news#> [accessed 8 June 2020].

44 Alexander Sobiesky, 'Corbyn Spy Smears Highlight Ruling Class Panic', *Socialist Appeal*, 2 March 2018 <https://www.socialist.net/corbyn-spy-smears-highlight-ruling-class-panic.htm> [accessed 8 June 2020].

45 Alan McLeod, 'Facebook Also Censoring the Left Isn't Just a Worry—It's a Reality', Truthdig.com, 23 August 2018 <https://www.truthdig.com/articles/that-facebook-will-turn-to-censoring-the-left-isnt-a-worry-its-a-reality/> [accessed 8 June 2020]; Daisuke Wakabayashi, 'As Google Fights Fake News, Voices on the Margins Raise Alarm', *New York Times*, 26 September 2017 <https://www.nytimes.com/2017/09/26/technology/google-search-bias-claims.html> [accessed 8 June 2020].

46 Richard Seymour, *The Twittering Machine* (London: The Indigo Press, 2019).

Bibliography

Abbott, H. Porter. 2008. *The Cambridge Introduction to Narrative*, 2nd edn (Cambridge: Cambridge University Press).
Acharya, Amitav. 2017. 'The Myth of ASEAN Centrality?', *Contemporary Southeast Asia: A Journal of International and Strategic Affairs*, 39.2: 273–9.
'American Occupation of the Philippines'. 1900. *Washington Register* (Washington, Kansas), 16 August <https://www.newspapers.com/image/386177513/> [accessed 1 March 2019].
Anderson, Benedict. 1997. 'First Filipino', *London Review of Books*, 19: 22–3.
Anderson, Benedict. 1986. 'James Fenton's Slideshow', *New Left Review*, 158: 1–11.
Angotti, Tom. 2013. *The New Century of the Metropolis: Urban Enclaves and Orientalism* (New York: Routledge).
Apostol, Gina. 2018. *Insurrecto* (New York: Soho Press).
Appel, Benjamin. 1951. *Fortress in the Rice* (New York: Bobs-Merrill).
Alighieri, Dante. 1320. *Inferno*, trans. Henry Wadsworth Longfellow (Mineola, New York: Dover Books; repr. 2005).
Arcilla, José S. 1998. *An Introduction to Philippine History* (Quezon City: Ateneo de Manila University Press).
Arcilla, José S. 1988. 'Protestant Missionaries in the Philippines', *Philippine Studies*, 36: 105–12.
Arensmeyer, Elliott C. 1980. 'The Chinese Coolie Labor Trade and the Philippines: An Inquiry', *Philippine Studies*, 28.2: 187–98.
Argonaut Editorial. 1902. '"War is Not Nice." "War is Hell."', *Los Angeles Times*, 29 May <https://www.newspapers.com/image/380006988/?terms=%22atrocity%22%2B%22filipino%22> [accessed 14 February 2019].
Ashcroft, Bill, Gareth Griffiths and Helen Tiffin. 1998. *Key Concepts in Post-Colonial Studies* (Oxford: Routledge).
Bailey, Muriel. 1900. 'Chinese and Their Ways in the Philippines', *The Atlanta Constitution*, 29 July, Newspapers.com <https://www.newspapers.com/image/26845829/?terms=%22chinese%22%2B%22philippines%22%2B%22women%22> [accessed 8 June 2020].
Bamforth, Tom. 2014. *Deep Field: Dispatches from the Front Line of Aid Relief* (New York: Abrams).
Ban, Zhuo, Shaunak Sastry and Mohan Jyoti Dutta, '"Shoppers' Republic of China": Orientalism in Neoliberal U.S. News Discourse', *Journal of International and Intercultural Communication*, 6.4: 280–97.
Bancroft, Bernard. 1959. *Bread Upon the Waters* (Des Plaines: Regular Baptist Press).

Barrett, Sara. 1988. 'Video Brides Who Think Heaven Is Having a British Husband', *Daily Mail* (London, England), 14 March, Daily Mail Historical Archive <http://find.galegroup.com/dmha/infomark.do?&source=gale&prodId=DMHA&userGroupName=uniportsmouth&tabID=T003&docPage=article&searchType=BasicSearchForm&docId=EE1861445926&type=multipage&contentSet=LTO&version=1.0> [accessed 5 March 2019].

Bartholomew, Rafe. 2010. *Pacific Rims: Beermen Ballin' in Flip-Flops and the Philippines' Unlikely Love Affair with Basketball* (New York: New American Library).

Bassnett, Susan. 2002. 'Travel Writing and Gender', in Peter Hulme and Tim Youngs (eds), *The Cambridge Companion to Travel Writing* (Cambridge: Cambridge University Press), 225–32.

Baudrillard, Jean. 1988. *Selected Writings* (Redwood City: Stanford University Press).

BBC News. 2018. 'Europe and Nationalism: A Country-by-country Guide', *BBC News*, 10 September <https://www.bbc.co.uk/news/world-europe-36130006> [accessed 29 January 2019].

Bell, Daniel A. and Avner de-Shalit. 2011. *The Spirit of Cities: Why the Identity of a City Matters in a Global Age* (Princeton: Princeton University Press).

Bello, Walden. 2018. 'Foreword', in *The Realm of the Punisher: Travels in Duterte's Philippines* by Tom Sykes (Oxford: Signal Books, 2018), xi–xv.

Bello, Walden, Marissa de Guzman, Mary Lou Malig and Herbert Docena. 2004. *The Anti-Development State: The Political Economy of Permanent Crisis in the Philippines* (London and New York: Zed Books).

Bennett, Andrew and Nicholas Royle. 2004. *An Introduction to Literature, Criticism and Theory* (Oxford: Pearson Education Limited).

'Beyond Fake News 2020'. 2020. BBC.co.uk <https://www.bbc.co.uk/academy/en/collections/fake-news#> [accessed 8 June 2020].

Bhabha, Homi K. 1994. *The Location of Culture* (Oxford: Routledge).

Bhabha, Homi K. 1984. 'Of Mimicry and Man: The Ambivalence of Colonial Discourse', Discipleship: A Special Issue on Psychoanalysis, 28: 125–33.

Black, Jeremy and Donald M. MacRaild. 2017. *Studying History* (London: Palgrave MacMillan).

Blackburn, Robin. 1997. *The Making of New World Slavery* (London: Verso).

Blanton, Casey. 2002. *Travel Writing: The Self and the World* (New York: Routledge).

'Books and Authors'. 1927. *Deseret News* (Salt Lake City, Utah), 30 July, Newspapers.com <https://www.newspapers.com/image/594551916/?terms=%22walter%2Brobb%22%2B%22khaki%2Bcabinet%2Band%2Bold%2Bmanila%22> [accessed 19 May 2020].

Bloomberg News. 2018. 'Chinese Money Triggers a Dizzying Rally in Manila Property', Bloomberg, 3 May <https://www.bloomberg.com/news/articles/2018-05-03/in-chinas-new-gambling-hot-spot-property-prices-are-on-a-tear> [accessed 5 April 2019].

Bordalo, Pedro, Katherine Coffman, Nicola Gennaioli and Andrei Shleifer, 'Stereotypes', *The Quarterly Journal of Economics*, doi:10.1093/qje/qjw029, 1753–94.

Bosco, David. 2012. 'What Divides Neocons and Liberal Interventionists', *Foreign Policy*, 9 April <https://foreignpolicy.com/2012/04/09/what-divides-neocons-and-liberal-interventionists/> [accessed 16 April 2019].

Bowring, Sir John. 1859. *A Visit to the Philippine Islands* (London: Smith, Elder & Co.).

'Boyce Takes Stand'. 1902. *The Times* (Streator, Illinois), June 27, Newspapers.com. <https://www.newspapers.com/image/542909162/?terms=%22w.d.%2Bboyce%22%2B%22labor%2Bunion%22> [accessed 8 June 2020].

Boyce, William D. 1914. *United States Colonies and Dependencies Illustrated* (New York: Rand McNally and Co).

Brody, David. 2010. *Visualizing American Empire: Orientalism & Imperialism in the Philippines* (Chicago and London: University of Chicago Press).

Brown, Dan. 2013. *Inferno* (New York: Transworld Digital), Amazon Kindle e-book.

Bukharin, Nikolai, quoted in Sally Campbell. 2014. 'Why Does Capitalism Lead to War?', *Socialist Review*, 1 September <http://socialistreview.org.uk/394/why-does-capitalism-lead-war> [accessed 15 April 2019].

Bulosan, Carlos. 2014. *America Is in the Heart: A Personal History* (Seattle: University of Washington Press).

Bureau of Insular Affairs-War Department. 1906. *Sixth Annual Report of the Philippine Commission, 1905 Part III* (Washington, DC: Washington Government Printing Office).

Burnham, Daniel to William Taft. 1905. Burnham Papers, Chicago Art Institute Library.

Buruma, Ian. 1988. *God's Dust: A Modern Asian Journey* (London: Vintage; repr. 1991).

Bush, George H.W. 1991. Quoted in Freedman, Lawrence, 'The Gulf War and the New World Order', *Survival*, 33.3: 195–6.

Bush, George W. 2003. *We Will Prevail: President George W. Bush on War, Terrorism and Freedom* (New York: Continuum).

Butterfield, Jeremy. 2015. *Fowler's Dictionary of Modern English Usage*, 4th edn (Oxford: Oxford University Press).

Campbell, Sally. 2014. 'Why Does Capitalism Lead to War?', *Socialist Review*, 1 September <http://socialistreview.org.uk/394/why-does-capitalism-lead-war> [accessed 15 April 2019].

Campomanes, Oscar V. 1999. '1898 and the Nature of the New Empire', *Radical History Review*, 73: 130–46.

Canevacci, Massimo. 2012. 'Digital Auratic Reproducibility: Ubiquitous Ethnographies and Communicational Metropolis', in Loshini Naidoo (ed.), *An Ethnography of Global Landscapes and Corridors* (Rijeka: In Tech), 249–60.

Capancioni, Claudia. 2014. 'Victorian Women Writers and the Truth of the "Other Side of Italy"', in Claire Bloom Saunders (ed.), *Women, Travel Writing, and Truth* (Oxford: Routledge), 109–24.

Carpenter, Frank G. 1929. *Through the Philippines and Hawaii* (New York: Doubleday, Doran and Company).

Caṭṭopādhyāẏa, Pārtha and Partha Chatterjee. 1986. *Nationalist Thought and the Colonial World: A Derivative Discourse* (London: Zed Books).

Chalmers, John. 2016. 'Duterte's War: Meth Gangs of China Stoke Philippines Drug Crisis', Reuters. 16 December <https://www.reuters.com/investigates/special-report/philippines-drugs-china/> [accessed 10 April 2019].

Cheyette, Bryan. 1995. *Constructions of 'the Jew' in English Literature and Society: Racial Representations, 1875–1945* (Cambridge: Cambridge University Press).

Chomsky, Noam, quoted in David Barsamian. 2004. 'Noam Chomsky Interview', *The Progressive*, 1 May <https://progressive.org/magazine/noam-chomsky-interview/> [accessed 19 April 2019].

Chu, Richard T. 2010. *Chinese and Chinese Mestizos of Manila: Family, Identity, and Culture 1860s–1930s* (Leiden; Boston: Brill).

Clodfelter, Michael. 2017. *Warfare and Armed Conflicts: A Statistical Encyclopedia of Casualty and Other Figures, 1492–2015*, 4th edn (Jefferson, NC: McFarland).

Cohen, Stephen F. 2018. 'War with Russia?', *The Nation*, 3 December <https://www.thenation.com/article/cold-war-russia/> [accessed 15 April 2019].

Coles, T.J. and Matt Alford 2018. *Union Jackboot: What Your Media and Professors Don't Tell You about British Foreign Policy* (London: CreateSpace).

Connell, John. 1999. 'Beyond Manila: Walls, Malls, and Private Spaces', *Environment and Planning*, 31: 15–24, <doi: 10.1068/a310417>.

Constantino, Renato. 2010. *A History of the Philippines: From Spanish Colonization to the Second World War* (New York: Monthly Review Press).

Cook, Malcolm. 2017. 'Meet New Boss Duterte, Same as the Old Boss', *Nikkei Asian Review*, 15 January <https://asia.nikkei.com/Politics/Meet-new-boss-Duterte-same-as-the-old-boss>.

Courville, Mathieu E. 2010. *Edward Said's Rhetoric of the Secular* (London: Bloomsbury).

Coward, Rosalind. 2013. *Speaking Personally: The Rise of Subjective and Confessional Journalism* (Basingstoke: Palgrave MacMillan).

Crossley, John Newsome. 2016. *The Dasmariñases, Early Governors of the Spanish Philippines* (Oxford: Routledge).

Crush, Jonathan. 1994. 'Gazing on Apartheid: Post-colonial Travel Narratives of the Golden City', in Peter Preston and Paul Simpson (ed.), *Writing the City: Eden, Babylon and the New Jerusalem* (Oxford: Routledge), 257–71.

Cruz, Denise and Erin Suzuki, 'America's Empire and the Asia-Pacific', in Crystal Parikh and Daniel Y. Kim (eds), *The Cambridge Companion to Asian American Literature* (Cambridge: Cambridge University Press, 2015), 17–27.

Cruz, Isagani. 2009. 'The First University', *The Philippine Star*, 17 December. <https://www.philstar.com/campus/2009/12/17/532930/first-university> [accessed 12 December 2019].

Dalisay, Jose Y. 2008. *Soledad's Sister* (Manila: Anvil).

Dampier, William. 1697. *A New Voyage Round the World* (London: James Knapton).

Dancel, Raul. 2018. 'Philippines: Most Dangerous Place for Journalists in Asia', *Straits Times*, 2 November <https://www.straitstimes.com/asia/se-asia/most-dangerous-place-for-journalists-in-asia> [accessed 4 February 2019].

Defoe, Daniel. 1725. *A New Voyage Round the World by a Course Never Sailed Before*, (London: A. Bettesworth).

Den Berghe, Van, quoted in Michael Banton. 1970. 'The Concept of Racism', in Sami Zubaida (ed.), *Race and Racialism* (London: Tavistock Publications), 86–101.

Dentith, Simon. 2000. *Parody* (London: Routledge).

Diaz, Father. 1899. Quoted in 'War Is Inevitable', News and Observer (Raleigh, North Carolina), 10 January <http://find.galegroup.com/ncnp/infomark.do?action=interpret&source=gale&prodId=NCNP&userGroupName=uniportsmouth&tabID=T003&docPage=article&searchType=BasicSearchForm&docId=GT3005815312&type=multipage&contentSet=LTO&version=1.0&finalAuth=true> [accessed 2 March 2019].

Doplon, Frances. 2007. 'Code-Switching in Philippine Tabloids: Subservience and Resistance in a Post-Colonial Society', *Philippine Journal of Linguistics*, 38: 1–22.

The Editorial Board. 2017. 'America's Forever Wars', *New York Times*, 22 October <https://www.nytimes.com/2017/10/22/opinion/americas-forever-wars.html> [accessed 16 April 2019].

Edwards, Justin D. and Rune Graulund. 2012. *Mobility at Large: Globalization, Textuality and Innovative Travel Writing* (Liverpool: Liverpool University Press).

Efanador, Harriet, 'Africa and Sustainable Development in the Age of Globalization: New Wine in Old Skin', *Journal of Sustainable Development in Africa*, 15.2: 12–26.

Elam, Michele. 2010. 'Mixed Race and Cultural Memory: Carl Hancock Rux's *Talk*', in Marc Maufort and Caroline De Wagter (eds), *Signatures of the Past: Cultural Memory in Contemporary Anglophone North American Drama* (New York: Peter Lang), 83–101.

Elliott, Larry. 2020. 'Coronavirus Putting World on Track for New Great Depression, Says WTO', *Guardian*, 8 April 2020 <https://www.theguardian.com/world/2020/apr/08/coronavirus-putting-world-on-track-for-new-great-depression-says-who> [accessed 10 April 2020].

Engelhardt, Tom. 2018. 'A New Map Shows the Alarming Spread of the US War on Terror', *The Nation*, 4 January <https://www.thenation.com/article/a-new-map-shows-the-alarming-spread-of-the-us-war-on-terror/> [accessed 11 December 2018].

Evans, Henri-Count and Rosemary Musvipwa. 2017. 'The Sustainable Development Goals, the Paris Agreement and the Addis Agenda: Neo-liberalism, Unequal Development and the Rise of a New Imperialism', in Tor Halvorsen, Hilde Ibsen, Henri-Count Evans and Sharon Penderis (eds), *Knowledge for Justice: Critical Perspectives from Southern African-Nordic Research Partnerships* (Cape Town: African Minds), 37–56.

Fairclough, Norman. 2013. *Language and Power* (Oxford: Routledge).

Fanon, Frantz. 2008. *Black Skin, White Masks* (London: Pluto Press, 2008).

Fanon, Frantz. 1990. *The Wretched of the Earth* (London: Penguin Classics).

Fee, Mary H. 1912. *A Woman's Impression of the Philippines* (Chicago: A. C. McClurg & Co; repr. Manila: GCF Books, 1988).

Feleo, Anita and David Sheniak. 1998. *Two for the Road* (Manila: Anvil).
Fenton, James. 1989. *All the Wrong Places: Adrift in the Politics of Southeast Asia* (London: Granta; repr. 2005).
Fenton, James. 2017. 'Murderous Manila: On the Night Shift'. 2017. *New York Review of Books*, 9 February <https://www.nybooks.com/articles/2017/02/09/murderous-manila-on-the-night-shift/> [accessed 6 February 2019].
Ferguson, Niall. 2009. *Colossus: The Rise and Fall of the American Empire* (London: Penguin).
Ferguson, Niall. 2007. *The War of the World: Twentieth-Century Conflict and the Descent of the West* (New York and London: Penguin).
Ferrante, Joan M., *The Political Vision of Dante* (Princeton, NJ: Princeton University Press, 1984).
Flaubert, Gustave, quoted in Tadiar, Neferti Xina M. 2004. *Fantasy-Production: Sexual Economies and Other Philippine Consequences for the New World Order* (Hong Kong: Hong Kong University Press).
Fowler, Roger. 1991. *Language in the News: Discourse and Ideology* in the Press (Oxford: Routledge).
Francia, Luis H. 2001. *Eye of the Fish: A Personal Archipelago* (New York: Kaya Press).
Francia, Luis H. 2014. *A History of the Philippines: From Indios to Bravos* (New York: Overlook Press).
Frayling, Christopher. 2014. *The Yellow Peril: Dr Fu Manchu and the Rise of Chinaphobia* (London: Thames and Hudson Ltd).
Freud, Sigmund. 2001. *Totem and Taboo* (Oxford: Routledge).
Garcia, J. Neil. 2008. *Philippine Gay Culture* (Hong Kong: Hong Kong University Press).
Garland, Alex. 1998. *The Tesseract* (London: Penguin; repr. 2007), Amazon Kindle e-book.
Gavilan, Jodesz. 2016. 'LIST: Suspected drug lords killed under Duterte gov't', *Rappler.com*, 30 August <https://www.rappler.com/newsbreak/iq/144659-war-on-drugs-suspected-drug-lords-killed-duterte-administration-list> [accessed 19 January 2019].
Gíslason, Kári. 2012. 'Travel Writing', in David Morley and Philip Neilsen (ed.), *The Cambridge Companion to Creative Writing* (Cambridge: Cambridge University Press), 87–101.
Goncharov, Ivan. 1965. *The Voyage of the Frigate Pallada* (London: Folio Society).
Gonzalez, Vernadette Vicuña. 2013. *Securing Paradise: Tourism and Militarism in Hawai'I and the Philippines* (Durham, NC: Duke University Press).
Golay, Frank Hindman. 2010. *Face of Empire: United States-Philippine Relations, 1898–1946* (Quezon City: Ateneo de Manila University Press).
Goldberg, E. 2019. 'Wing Zone To Open 12 New Units in Panama and the Philippines in 2019', Franchising.com, 2 May <https://www.franchising.com/articles/wing_zone_to_open_12_new:units_in_panama_and_the_philippines_in_2019.html> [accessed 10 April 2019].

Gowan, Richard. 2018. 'Despite the Rising Stakes, Russia and the West Opt for Indefinite Proxy Conflict', *World Politics Review*, 22 October <https://www.worldpoliticsreview.com/articles/26547/despite-the-rising-stakes-russia-and-the-west-opt-for-indefinite-proxy-conflict> [accessed 15 April 2019].

Green, Martin. 1980. *Dreams of Adventure, Deeds of Empire* (London and Oxford: Routledge and Kegan Paul Ltd).

Greene, Col. Joseph I. 1943. 'Pacific Thunder', *New York Times*, 21 March. <https://timesmachine.nytimes.com/timesmachine/1943/03/21/83908334.html?pageNumber=37> [accessed 10 April 2020].

Grosrichard, Alain. 1998. *The Sultan's Court: European Fantasies of the East* (London and New York: Verso).

Guerrero, Amadis Ma. 1994. *Traveler's Choice: North to South* (Manila: Anvil).

Gunter, Archibald Clavering. 1898. *Jack Curzon (Being a Portion of the Records of the Managing Clerk of Markrtin, Thompson & Co., English Merchants Doing Business in Hong Kong, Manila, Cebu and the Straits Settlements)* (New York: Hurst).

Hall, Stuart. 1997. 'The Spectacle of the "Other"', in Stuart Hall (ed.), *Representation: Cultural Representations and Signifying Practices* (London: Sage, 1997), 227–46.

Hallin, Daniel C. *The Uncensored War: The Media and Vietnam* (New York and Oxford: Oxford University Press, 1986).

Hamilton-Paterson, James. 1998a. *America's Boy: The Marcoses and the Philippines* (London: Granta).

Hamilton-Paterson, James. 1994. *Ghosts of Manila* (London: Random House).

Hamilton-Paterson, James. 1998b. *Playing with Water: Alone on a Philippine Island* (London: Sceptre).

Hancock, H. Irving. 1912. *Uncle Sam's Boys in the Philippines, or Following the Flag against the Moros* (Philadelphia, PA: Henry Altemus Company).

Hardy, Frances. 1991. 'Sex Victims of Marriage by Mail', *Daily Mail* (London, England), 25 July, Daily Mail Historical Archive <http://find.galegroup.com/dmha/newspaperRetrieve.do?sgHitCountType=None&sort=DateAscend&tabID=T003&prodId=DMHA&resultListType=RESULT_LIST&searchId=R2&searchType=AdvancedSearchForm&currentPosition=9&qrySerId=Locale%28en%2C%2C%29%3AFQE%3D%28tx%2CNone%2C11%29sex+victims%3AAnd%3ALQE%3D%28da%2CNone%2C23%2901%2F01%2F1990+-+01%2F07%2F1992%24&retrieveFormat=MULTIPAGE_DOCUMENT&userGroupName=uniportsmouth&inPS=true&contentSet=LTO&&docId=&docLevel=FASCIMILE&workId=&relevancePageBatch=EE1861069764&contentSet=DMHA&callistoContentSet=DMHA&docPage=article&hilite=y> [accessed 1 March 2019].

Hau, Caroline S. 2000. *Necessary Fictions: Philippine Literature and the Nation, 1946–1980* (Manila: Ateneo de Manila University Press).

Hau, Caroline S. 2004. *On the Subject of the Nation: Filipino Writings from the Margins, 1981–2004* (Quezon City: Ateneo de Manila University Press).

Hawkes, David. 2007. *The Faust Myth: Religion and the Rise of Representation* (London: Palgrave Macmillan).

Hiebert, Murray. 2016. 'How Do You Solve a Problem Like Duterte?', *Nikkei Asian Review*, 3 October 2016 <https://asia.nikkei.com/Politics/Murray-Hiebert-and-Conor-Cronin-How-do-you-solve-a-problem-like-Duterte> [accessed 30 January 2019].

'H. Irving Hancock'. 1922. The New York Times, 13 March, Timesmachine.com <https://www.newspapers.com/image/26756120/?terms=%22h.%2Birving%2Bhancock%22%2Bobituary> [accessed 8 June 2020].

Hitchens, Christopher. 2014. *For the Sake of Argument: Essays and Minority Reports* (London and New York: Atlantic Books), Amazon Kindle e-book.

Hodder, Rupert. 2007. 'The Economic Significance of the Chinese in the Philippines: An Analysis of Its Overstatement', *Philippine Studies*, 55.1: 90–1.

Holmes, Oliver and agencies in Manila. 2017. 'Philippine Police Kill 32 in Bloodiest Night of Duterte's War on Drugs', *Guardian*, 16 August <https://www.theguardian.com/world/2017/aug/16/philippines-police-bloodiest-night-duterte-war-drugs> [accessed 6 February 2019].

Horsley, Sebastian. 2008. *Dandy in the Underworld: An Unauthorised Autobiography* (London: Sceptre).

Hotel Resource. 2019. '390 Room Sheraton Manila Hotel Opens', Hotelnewsresource.com, 14 October <https://www.hotelnewsresource.com/article103605.html> [accessed 10 April 2019].

Howell, John Benjamin. 1969. *42 Months of Hell: My Life as a Prisoner of the Japanese, WWII* (Muskogee, Wisconsin: Hoffmann Printing Company).

Huggan, Graham. 2001. *The Post-colonial Exotic: Marketing the Margins* (Oxford: Routledge).

Hunt, Celia and Fiona Sampson. 2006. *Writing: Self & Reflexivity* (Basingstoke: Palgrave MacMillan).

Hynes, Samuel Lynn. 1976. *The Auden Generation: Literature and Politics in England in the 1930's* (London: The Bodley Head).

Ibach, Marilyn. 2006. 'About This Collection', Library of Congress.com <https://www.loc.gov/collections/carpenter/about-this-collection/> [accessed 2 July 2020] (para. 5 of 27).

Ikehata, Setsuho and Lydia Yu-Jose. 2003. *Philippines-Japan Relations* (Quezon City: Ateneo De Manila University Press).

Ileto, Reynaldo C. 2017. *Knowledge and Pacification: On the U.S. Conquest and the Writing of Philippine History* (Manila: Ateneo de Manila University Press).

Ileto, Reynaldo C. 1997. 'Orientalism and the Study of Philippine Politics', delivered as 'The Third Burns Chair Lecture' (University of Hawai'i).

Ileto, Reynaldo C. 2002. 'The Philippine-American War: Friendship and Forgetting', in Angel Velasco Shaw and Luis H. Francia (eds), *Vestiges of War: The Philippine-American War and the Aftermath of an Imperial Dream 1899–1999* (New York: New York University Press), 3–21.

Irwin, William Gilbert and Special Correspondence. 1898. 'Yankeefied Manila', *Atchison Daily Globe* (Atchison, Kansas), 1 December, 19th Century U.S. Newspapers <http://find.galegroup.com/ncnp/infomark.do?&source=gale&prodId=NCNP&userGroupName=uniportsmouth&tabID=T003&docPage=article&searchType=BasicSearchForm&docId=GT3012437529&type=multipage&contentSet=LTO&version=1.0> [accessed 2 March 2019].

Iyer, Pico. 1988. *Video Night in Kathmandu* (London: Black Swan; repr. 1998).

'Jack Curzon, or Mysterious Manila. By Archibald Clavering Gunter (London: George Routledge & Sons, Limited)'. 1899. *The Glasgow Herald*, 4 May 1899, Newspapers.com <https://www.newspapers.com/image/409221346> [accessed 27 April 2020].

Jack, Jane H. 1961. '"A New Voyage Round the World": Defoe's "Roman á These"', *Huntington Library Quarterly*, 24.4: 323–36.

Jackson, Yo. 2006. *Encyclopedia of Multicultural Psychology* (London and New Delhi: SAGE).

Jacques, Martin. 2012. *When China Rules The World: The End of the Western World and the Birth of a New Global Order* (London: Penguin).

Jagor, Fedor. 1875. *Travels in the Philippines* (London: Chapman and Hall).

Jameson, Fredric. 1998. *The Cultural Turn: Selected Writings on the Postmodern, 1983–1988* (London: Verso).

Jarvie, Ian. 1988. 'Dollars and Ideology: Will Hays' Economic Foreign Policy 1922–1945', *Film History*, 2.3: 207–21.

Joaquin, Nick ('Quijano de Manila'). 1980. *Language of the Street and Other Essays* (Manila: National Bookstore).

Johnson, Lyndon. 1966. 'Why We Are in Vietnam', in Gary Donaldson (ed.), *Modern America: A Documentary History of the Nation since 1945* (New York: Routledge), 117–20.

Joint Communiqué, quoted in 'One and Only China'. 2017. *The Manila Times*, 9 October <https://www.manilatimes.net/one-and-only-china/355384/> [accessed 18 April 2019].

De Jonquières, Guy. 2012. *China's Challenges* (Brussels: ECIPE).

José, F. Sionil. 2013. *Dusk* (New York: Modern Library), Amazon Kindle e-book.

The Journal Herald (Dayton, Ohio). 1966. 'In Manila Hotel: Beatle Suite Redecorated for LBJ', 24 October, Newspapers.com <https://www.newspapers.com/image/395130443/?terms=manila> [accessed 9 April 2019].

Kaleck, Wolfgang. 2015. 'Double Standards in International Criminal Justice: A Long Road Ahead Towards Universal Justice', *FICHL Policy Brief Series*, 37: 1–4.

Karnow, Stanley. 1989. *In Our Image: America's Empire in the Philippines* (New York: Foreign Policy Association).

Kellett, Wanda Liles. 1954. *Wings as Eagles* (New York: Vantage Press).

Kidd, Benjamin. 1898. *The Control of the Tropics* (New York: McMillan).

Kidd, Benjamin. 1894. Social Evolution (New York: Grosset and Dunlap).

Kimani, Mary. 2009. 'International Criminal Court: Justice or Racial Double Standards?', *Global Policy Forum/Afrik.com*, 16 December <https://www.globalpolicy.org/component/content/article/164-icc/48775-international-criminal-court-justice-or-racial-double-standards-.html> [accessed 7 February 2019].

King, Charles. 1901. *Ray's Daughter: A Story of Manila* (Philadelphia: J. P. Lippincott).

Kirkus. 2017. 'Kirkus Review: A Moment in the Sun' <https://www.kirkusreviews.com/book-reviews/john-sayles/moment-sun/> [accessed 27 July 2017].

Klare, Michael T. 2018. 'The United States Is Pushing Toward War With China', *The Nation* <https://www.thenation.com/article/united-states-pushing-towards-war-china> [accessed 15 April 2019].

Konrad, Felix. 2011. *"Turkish Menace" to Exoticism and Orientalism: Islam as Antithesis of Europe (1453–1914)* (Mainz: Inst. f. Europ. Geschichte).

Koomen, Willem. 1997. 'Ingroup and Outgroup Stereotypes and Selective Processing', *European Journal of Social Psychology*, 27: 589–601.

Korte, Barbara. 2000. *English Travel Writing from Pilgrimages to Postcolonial Explorations* (London: Palgrave Macmillan).

Kram, Mark. 1975. 'Lawdy, Lawdy, He's Great,' Sports Illustrated Online, 17 January 2012 <https://www.si.com/boxing/2012/01/17/muhammad-ali-70th-kram> [accessed 28 September 2017].

Kramer, Paul A. 2006. *The Blood of Government: Race, Empire, the United States, & the Philippines* (Chapel Hill, CA: University of North Carolina Press).

Kutsumi, Kanako. 2007. 'Koreans in the Philippines: A Study of the Formation of Their Social Organization', in Miralao, Virginia A. and Lorna P. Makil (eds), *Exploring Transnational Communities in the Philippines* (Manila: Philippine Social Science Council), 58–73.

Kwong, Peter and Dušanka Miščevic. 2006. *Chinese America: The Untold Story of America's Oldest New Community* (New York: The New Press).

Kyodo. 2018. 'Official Death Toll in Philippine President Rodrigo Duterte's War on Drugs Exceeds 5,000', *South China Morning Post*, 18 December <https://www.scmp.com/news/asia/southeast-asia/article/2178601/official-death-toll-philippine-president-rodrigo-dutertes> [accessed 19 January 2019].

Lacaba, Jose F. 1970. 'The January 30 Insurrection, in Cristina Pantoja Hidalgo (ed.), *Creative Nonfiction: A Reader* (Quezon City: The University of the Philippines Press, 2005), 11–18.

Lagarde, Christine. 2016. 'The Role of Emerging Markets in a New Global Partnership for Growth by IMF Managing Director Christine Lagarde', *imf.org*, 4 February <https://www.imf.org/en/News/Articles/2015/09/28/04/53/sp020416#P26_3020> [accessed 15 April 2019].

De Lauretis, Teresa. 1986. *Feminist Studies, Critical Studies* (Bloomington, IN: Indiana University Press).

Laya, Juan C. 1972. *His Native Soil* (Quezon City: Kayumanggi Publishers).

Lee, Clark. 1943. *They Call It Pacific: An Eyewitness Story of Our War Against Japan from Bataan to the Solomons* (New York: Viking Press).

Lee, Erika. 2016. *The Making of Asian America: A History* (New York: Simon & Schuster, 2016).

Lee, Jonathan. 2015. *History of Asian Americans: Exploring Diverse Roots* (Westport, CT: Greenwood).

De Legazpi, Miguel López. 1570. Quoted in Renato Constantino, *A History of the Philippines: From Spanish Colonization to the Second World War* (New York: Monthly Review Press).

Lennon, Peter. 2013. Quoted in Coward, Rosalind, *Speaking Personally: The Rise of Subjective and Confessional Journalism* (Basingstoke: Palgrave MacMillan).

Lipton, Sara. 2014. 'Creating the Stereotyped Root of Evil', *The Jewish Chronicle*, 11 December <https://www.thejc.com/culture/books/creating-the-stereotyped-root-of-evil-1.63514> [accessed 2 February 2019].

Lipton, Sara. 'The Invention of the Jewish Nose', *The New York Review of Books*, 14 November <https://www.nybooks.com/daily/2014/11/14/invention-jewish-nose/> [accessed 2 February 2019].

Lisle, Debbie. 2006. *The Global Politics of Contemporary Travel Writing* (Cambridge: Cambridge University Press).

Logoupal. 2005. 'Hotel de Oriente' <http://www.lougopal.com/manila/?p=535> [accessed 17 April 2019].

London Times, quoted in Jenny Clegg. 1994. *Fu Manchu and the 'Yellow Peril': The Making of a Racist Myth* (Stoke-on-Trent: Trentham Books).

Loney, Nicholas. 1964. *A Britisher in the Philippines or the Letters of Nicholas Loney* (Manila: National Library).

Loomis, Erik. 2018. 'Serving Time Should Not Mean "Prison Slavery"', *New York Times*, 30 August <https://www.nytimes.com/2018/08/30/opinion/national-prison-strike-slavery-.html> [accessed 30 August 2018].

Lyman, Stanford M. 2000. 'The "Yellow Peril" Mystique: Origins and Vicissitudes of a Racist Discourse', *International Journal of Politics, Culture, and Society*, 13.4: 683–747.

MacMicking, Robert. 1851. *Recollections of Manilla and the Philippines during 1848, 1849 and 1850* (London: Richard Bentley).

Madianou, Mirca. 2012. 'Migration and the Accentuated Ambivalence of Motherhood: The Role of ICTs in Filipino Transnational Families', *Global Networks*, 12.3: 277–95.

Mailer, Norman. 1948. *The Naked and the Dead* (New York: Rinehart & Company).

Malik, Kenan. 1996. *The Meaning of Race: Race, History and Culture in Western Society* (London: Palgrave MacMillan).

Manguel, Alberto. 1994. 'Gouging Out Hell's Entrails: Ghosts of Manila – James Hamilton-Paterson', *Independent Online*, 3 June <http://www.independent.co.uk/arts-entertainment/books/book-review-gouging-out-hells-entrails-ghosts-of-manila-james-hamilton-paterson-jonathan-cape-pounds-1420229.html> [accessed 25 September 2017].

'Manila Electric Company (Meralco) History'. 2004. <http://www.fundinguniverse.com/company-histories/manila-electric-company-meralco-history/> [accessed 17 April 2019].

'Manila Today Is No Longer Known as Tropical Paradise'. 1957. *The Catholic Advance* (Wichita, Kansas), 10 May <https://www.newspapers.com> [accessed 28 January 2019].

Mashinsky, S. 1972. *The Works of I.A. Goncharov in 6 Volumes* (Moscow: Pravda Publisher).

Matthew. 2011. 26:56, *New International Version* <www.biblegateway.com/versions/New-International-Version-NIV-Bible/#booklist> [accessed 27 June 2018].

McGeown, Kate. 2012. 'Call Me: Tech Powers Philippines Call Centre Success', *BBC News*, 15 May 2012 <https://www.bbc.co.uk/news/business-18061909> [accessed 5 April 2019].

McKenzie, Duncan Alexander. 2012. *The Unlucky Country: The Republic of the Philippines in the 21st Century* (Balboa Press: Carlsbad), Amazon Kindle e-book.

McKinley, William. 1899. Quoted in James H. Blount, *The American Occupation of the Philippines 1898–1912* (New York: G. P. Putnam's Sons).

McKinley, William. 1900. Quoted in Jessica Hagedorn, *Dogeaters* (London: Penguin, 1991).

McKinley, William. 1898. 'War Message', in (ed. unnamed), *Papers Relating to Foreign Affairs* (Washington, DC: US Department of State), 750–60.

McKinley, William. 2011. 'William McKinley: Benevolent Assimilation." Letter, December 21st 1898", in Spencer C. Tucker (ed.), *The Encyclopedia of the Spanish-American and Philippine–American Wars Vol. 1* (Santa Barbara, CA: ABC Clio).

McKirdy, Euan. 2019. 'Philippines Vows to "destroy" Islamist Extremism. Here's Why That Won't Be So Easy', *CNN*, 31 January <https://edition.cnn.com/2019/01/30/asia/duterte-islamist-extremism-problem-intl/index.html> [accessed 20 February 2019].

McLeod, Alan. 2018. 'Facebook also Censoring the Left Isn't Just a Worry—It's a Reality', Truthdig.com, 23 August <https://www.truthdig.com/articles/that-facebook-will-turn-to-censoring-the-left-isnt-a-worry-its-a-reality/> [accessed 8 June 2020].

McMahon, Jennifer M. 2011. *Dead Stars: American and Philippine Literary Perspectives on the American Colonization of the Philippines* (Quezon City: University of the Philippines Press).

McNamara, Kevin. 2013. 'Introduction', in Kevin McNamara (ed.), *The Companion to the City in Literature* (Cambridge: Cambridge University Press), 1–13.

Mészáros, Edina Lilla. 2016. 'The EU-Russia "Uncommon Spaces" Stereotypes and Growing Russophobia: Does Cultural Diplomacy Stand a Chance in Shaping Future EU-Russia Relations?', in Alina Stoica, Ioan Horga and Maria Manuela Tavares Ribeiro (eds), *Culture and Paradiplomatic Identity: Instruments in Sustaining EU Policies* (Newcastle-upon-Tyne: Cambridge Scholars), 52–67.

Mignolo, Walter D. 2009. *The Idea of Latin America* (Oxford: Blackwell).

Mijares, Primitivo. 2016. *The Conjugal Dictatorship of Ferdinand and Imelda Marcos* (Manila: CreateSpace Independent Publishing Platform).

Miller, George A. 1929. *Interesting Manila* (Manila: Philippine Education Company).

Miller, Jonathan. 2018. *Duterte Harry: Fire and Fury in the Philippines* (Brunswick and London: Scribe).
Mishra, Pankaj. 2015. 'Bland Fanatics', *London Review of Books*, 37.23: 37–40.
Mishra, Pankaj. 2013. *From the Ruins of Empire: The Revolt against the West and the Remaking of Asia* (London: Penguin).
Mishra, Pankaj. 2018. Quoted in Francis Wade, '"The Liberal Order Is the Incubator for Authoritarianism": A Conversation with Pankaj Mishra', *Los Angeles Review of Books*, 15 November <https://lareviewofbooks.org/article/the-liberal-order-is-the-incubator-for-authoritarianism-a-conversation-with-pankaj-mishra/> [accessed 30 February 2019].
Mo, Timothy. 1997. *Brownout on Breadfruit Boulevard* (London: Paddleless Press).
Mo, Timothy. 2000. *Renegade or Halo²* (London: Paddleless Press).
Monbiot, George. 2004. 'Empire of Denial', *Guardian*, 1 June. <https://www.theguardian.com/world/2004/jun/01/usa.comment> [accessed 3 April 2018].
Moon, Krystyn R. '"There's No Yellow in the Red, White, and Blue": The Creation of Anti-Japanese Music during World War II', *Pacific Historical Review*, 72.3: 333–52.
Moore-Gilbert, Bart. 2000. *Postcolonial Theory: Contexts, Practices, Politics* (Verso: London and New York).
Morse, Jedidiah and Richard C. Morse. 1823. *A New Universal Gazetteer*, 4th edn (New Haven: S. Converse).
Mydans, Seth. 1996. 'Kidnapping of Ethnic Chinese Rises in Philippines', *New York Times*, March 17, Timesmachine.com <https://www.nytimes.com/1996/03/17/world/kidnapping-of-ethnic-chinese-rises-in-philippines.html> [accessed 8 June 2020].
Narayan, John and Leon Sealey-Higgins. 2017. 'Whatever Happened to the Idea of Imperialism?', *Third World Quarterly*, 38.11: 2387–95.
National Census and Statistics Office. 1982. '1980 Census of Population' (Manila: Republic of the Philippines National Economic and Development Authority) <https://psa.gov.ph/sites/default/files/1980%20Census%20of%20Population%20-%20Special%20Report%201.pdf> [accessed 13 March 2019].
Nelson, Raymond. 1968. *The Philippines* (London: Thames and Hudson).
Netzorg, Walton J. 1990. 'The Philippines in Mass-Market Novels', in Robin W. Winks and James R. Rush (eds), *Asia in Western Fiction* (Manchester: Manchester University Press), 175–95.
Nguyen, Mimi Thi. 2011. 'The Biopower of Beauty: Humanitarian Imperialisms and Global Feminisms in an Age of Terror', *Signs: Journal of Women in Culture and Society*, 36: 359–83.
Nightingale, Carl H. 2012. *Segregation: A Global History of Divided Cities* (Chicago: University of Chicago Press).
Nirenberg, David. 2013. *Anti-Judaism: The Western Tradition* (New York: W. W. Norton & Company).
Norton Kyshe, James William. 1898. *History of the Laws and Courts of Hong Kong* (London: T Fisher Unwin).

'Noted Soldier Author Coming'. 1905. *The Post-Crescent* (Appleton, Wisconsin), 17 March, Newspapers.com <https://www.newspapers.com/image/408148570/?terms=%22charles%2Bking%22%2B%22ray's%2Bdaughter%22> [accessed 29 April 2020].

Nuttall, Nick. 2007. 'Cold-blooded Journalism', in Richard Keeble and Sharon Wheeler (eds), *The Journalistic Imagination: Literary Journalists from Defoe to Capote and Carter* (Oxford: Routledge), 129–52.

Obama, Barack. 2011. 'Remarks by the President in Address to the Nation on Libya' <https://obamawhitehouse.archives.gov/the-press-office/2011/03/28/remarks-president-address-nation-libya> [accessed 25 February 2018].

O'Brien, Fergal. 2017. 'China to Overtake U.S. Economy by 2032 as Asian Might Builds', Bloomberg News, 26 December <www.bloomberg.com/news/articles/2017-12-26/china-to-overtake-u-s-economy-by-2032-as-asian-might-builds> [accessed 16 April 2019].

O'Rourke, P.J. 1989. *Holidays in Hell* (New York: Grove; repr. 2012), Amazon Kindle e-book.

Pagan, Andrew. 2012. 'From the Darkness to the Family: Evolving Orientalist Representations of the Katipunan in Euro-American Travel Literature, 1899–1917,' *The Forum: Journal of History*, 4: 87–102.

Palmer, Blanche. 1966. *Pilgrim of the Night* (Nashville, TN: Southern Publishing Association).

Panda, Ankit. 2020. 'In Sudden Step, Philippines Reverses Course of Ending US Visiting Forces Agreement – For Now', *The Diplomat*, 4 June < https://thediplomat.com/2020/06/in-sudden-step-philippines-reverses-course-on-ending-us-visiting-forces-agreement-for-now/> [accessed 3 July 2020].

Parry, Benita. 2004. *Postcolonial Studies: A Materialist Critique* (London: Routledge).

Peace, Roger. 2010. 'Cultivating Critical Thinking: Five Methods for Teaching the History of U.S. Foreign Policy', *The History Teacher*, 43: 265–73.

Pearson, Tamara. 2019. 'Everything the Western Mainstream Media Outlets Get Wrong When Covering Poor Countries', Counterpunch, 11 January 2019 <https://www.counterpunch.org/2019/01/11/everything-the-western-mainstream-media-outlets-get-wrong-when-covering-poor-countries-2/> [accessed 17 April 2019].

Peel, Michael. 2017. 'Drugs and Death in Davao: The Making of Rodrigo Duterte', *Financial Times*, 2 February <https://www.ft.com/content/9d6225dc-e805-11e6-967b-c88452263daf> [accessed 12 February 2019].

Peel, Michael. 2016. 'Philippine Leader Rodrigo Duterte mines seam of anti-US Sentiment', *Financial Times*, 5 October <https://www.ft.com/content/def867ce-8aca-11e6-8cb7-e7ada1d123b1> [accessed 27 March 2019].

Peng, Zengjun. 2004. 'Representation of China: An across Time Analysis of Coverage in the *New York Times* and *Los Angeles Times*', *Asian Journal of Communication*, 14.1: 53–67.

Perkins, Senator George C. 1904. Quoted in 'Senator Perkins Tells of Work in Congress', *Oakland Tribune* (Oakland California), 12 May <https://www.newspapers.com/image/71561537/?terms=filipino%2Bhappy> [accessed 22 February 2019].

Phillips, Claire "High Pockets" and Myron Goldsmith, *Manila Espionage*. 1947. (Portland, OR: Binfords & Mort; repr. Los Angeles: Enhanced Media Publishing, 2017).

Pilger, John. 2016. 'The Coming War on China', *New Internationalist*, 30 November <https://newint.org/features/2016/12/01/the-coming-war-on-china> [accessed 11 December 2018].

Pilger, John. 1998. *Hidden Agendas* (London: Vintage).

Pinker, Steven. 2013. *The Sense of Style: The Thinking Person's Guide to Writing in the 21st Century* (New York and London: Allen Lane).

Pratt, Mary-Louise. 1991. *Imperial Eyes: Travel Writing and Transculturation* (London: Routledge).

Pullum, Geoffrey K. 2014. 'Fear and Loathing of the English Passive', *Language and Communication*, 37.2: 1–6.

Quismundo, Tarra. 2015. 'Japanese Lawmakers Give Aquino Standing Ovation', *Philippine Daily Inquirer*, 4 June <https://globalnation.inquirer.net/123973/japanese-lawmakers-give-aquino-standing-ovation> [accessed 14 May 2019].

Rafael, Vicente. 2016. 'Duterte's Hobbesian World', *Philippine Inquirer*, 13 June <https://opinion.inquirer.net/95185/dutertes-hobbesian-world> [accessed April 15 2019].

'Readable Books'. 1900. *The Indianopolis News*, 17 December, Newspapers.com. <https://www.newspapers.com/image/40043165/?terms=%22charles%2Bking%22%2B%22ray's%2Bdaughter%22> [accessed 29 April 2020].

Remollino, Alexander Martin. 2009. 'Victims of Martial Law See in Arroyo a Tyrant Worse Than Marcos', *Bulatlat*, 21 September <https://www.bulatlat.com/2009/09/21/victims-of-martial-law-see-in-arroyo-a-tyrant-worse-than-marcos/> [accessed 29 January 2019].

Revilla, Linda A. 1996. 'Young Filipinos Lack Strong Ties to Culture', Honolulu Star-Bulletin, 20 April, Newspapers.com <https://www.newspapers.com> [accessed 28 January 2019].

'Rev. John Bechtel To Speak at Pavilion. 1944. *The Morning Call* (Paterson, New Jersey), 14 August. Newspapers.com <https://www.newspapers.com/image/552802457/?terms=%22john%2Bbechtel%22%2Bpig's%2Bbirthday> [accessed 27 April 2020].

Rizal, José. 1912. *The Social Cancer (Noli Me Tangere)*, trans. Charles Derbyshire (Salt Lake City: Project Gutenberg; repr. 2004), Amazon kindle edition.

Robb, Walter. 1926. *The Khaki Cabinet and Old Manila* (Manila: Sugar News Press).

Roberts, Michael. 2012. 'A World Rate of Profit', in *11th Society of Heterodox Economists Conference* (Sydney: Society of Heterodox Economists).

Robson, Seth. 2019. 'Facility for US Forces Opens on Philippines' Main Island; Another Slated for Palawan', *Stars & Stripes*, 31 January <https://www.stripes.com/news/facility-for-us-forces-opens-on-philippines-main-island-another-slated-for-palawan-1.566695> [accessed 16 April 2019].

Rockoff, Hugh. 2012. *America's Economic Way of War: War and the US Economy from the Spanish-American War to the Persian Gulf War* (New York: Cambridge University Press).

Rodriguez, Dylan. 2010. *Suspended Apocalypse: White Supremacy, Genocide, and the Filipino Condition* (Minneapolis: University of Minnesota Press).

Roh, David S., Betsy Huang and Greta A. Nui. 2015. 'Technologizing Orientalism', in David S. Roh, Betsy Huang and Greta A. Nui (eds), *Techno-Orientalism: Imagining Asia in Speculative Fiction, History, and Media* (New Brunswick: Rutgers University Press), 1–20.

Romein, Jan. 1962. *The Asian Century: A History of Modern Nationalism in Asia* (Berkeley and Los Angeles: University of California Press).

Romero, Alexis. 2018. 'Duterte: No Joint Expeditions with US during My Time', Philippine Star, 21 March <https://www.philstar.com/headlines/2018/03/21/1799010/duterte-no-joint-expeditions-us-during-my-time> [accessed 6 February 2019].

Roosevelt, Theodore. 'Special Message, January 4,' in Gerhard Peters and John T. Woolley (eds), *The American Presidency Project* <http://www.presidency.ucsb.edu/ws/?pid=69417> [accessed 5 April 2018].

Rowland, Dr. Henry C. 1902. 'Fighting Life in the Philippines', *McClure's Magazine*, July.

Rufo, Aries C. 2013. *Altar of Secrets: Sex, Politics, and Money in the Philippine Catholic Church* (Manila: Journalism for Nation Building Foundation).

Said, Edward. 1994. *Culture and Imperialism* (London: Vintage).

Said, Edward. 1985. *Orientalism* (London: Peregrine Books).

Said, Edward. 2003. 'A Window on the World', *Guardian*, 2 August 2003. <https://www.theguardian.com/books/2003/aug/02/alqaida.highereducation> [accessed 12 February 2019].

San Juan, Jr., E. 2007. *U.S. Imperialism and Revolution in the Philippines* (New York and Basingstoke: Palgrave MacMillan).

Savage, Luke. 2014. 'New Atheism, Old Empire', *Jacobin*, 2 December <www.jacobinmag.com/2014/12/new-atheism-old-empire/> [accessed 16 April 2019].

Sayles, John. 2011. *A Moment in the Sun* (San Francisco: McSweeney's), Amazon Kindle e-book.

Sayson, I. 2018. 'World's Largest Ikea to Open in Manila as Company Bets on Asia', Bloomberg.com, 20 November <https://www.bloomberg.com/news/articles/2018-11-20/world-s-largest-ikea-to-open-in-manila-as-company-bets-on-asia> [accessed 10 April 2019].

Scheffer, David J. 1992. 'Towards a Modern Doctrine of Humanitarian Intervention', *University of Toledo Law Review*, 23: 253–74.

Schult, Volker. 2002. 'Revolutionaries and Admirals: The German East Asia Squadron in Manila Bay,' *Philippine Studies* 50.4: 496–511.

Sevastopolu, Demetri and Michael Peel, 'Duterte Plays Cat-and-mouse Game with China', *Financial Times*, 8 May 2017 <https://www.ft.com/content/4375d4ee-340c-11e7-bce4-9023f8c0fd2e> [accessed 1 April 2019].

Seymour, Richard. 2017. 'Modi and Duterte', *Media Review*, teleSUR, 12 May <https://www.youtube.com/watch?v=sT65Nuh8OKc> [accessed 10 April 2019].

Seymour, Richard. 2019. *The Twittering Machine* (London: The Indigo Press).

Shaheen, Jack. 2001. *Reel Bad Arabs: How Hollywood Vilifies a People* (New York: Olive Branch Press).

Shakespeare, William. 1999. 'Hamlet', in *The Complete Works of William Shakespeare* Vol. 3 (Ware: Wordsworth Editions).

Singh, Amrik. 1997. 'Asia Pacific Tourism Industry: Current Trends and Future Outlooks', *Asia Pacific Journal of Tourism Research*, 4: 1–5 <https://www.hotel-online.com/Trends/AsiaPacificJournal/AsiaPacificTourismOutlook_1997.html> [accessed 15 October 2017].

Smith, Tom. 2016a. 'President Duterte's anti-US populism Is a Dangerously Isolationist Path', *Guardian*, 7 September <https://www.theguardian.com/commentisfree/2016/sep/07/duterte-anti-us-philippines-isolationist-foreign-policy-insult-barack-obama-china> [accessed 27 February 2019].

Smith, Tom. 2016b. 'Those Standing Up to Duterte Are from a Long Line of Strong Filipinas', *Guardian*, 7 December <https://www.theguardian.com/commentisfree/2016/dec/07/rodrigo-duterte-strong-filipinas-philippines-cory-aquino-gloria-arroyo> [accessed 29 January 2019].

Smith, Thomas A. 1999. 'The Pleasure of Hell in *City of God*', *Augustinian Studies*, 30: 195–204.

Sobiesky, Alexander. 2018. 'Corbyn Spy Smears Highlight Ruling Class Panic', *Socialist Appeal*, 2 March <https://www.socialist.net/corbyn-spy-smears-highlight-ruling-class-panic.htm> [accessed 8 June 2020].

Son Hing, Leanne S., Winnie Li and Mark P. Zanna. 2002. 'Inducing Hypocrisy to Reduce Prejudicial Responses among Aversive Racists', *Journal of Experimental Social Psychology* 38: 71–8.

Spear, Andrew. 2017. 'Hypocrisy and Responsibility: On the Uses and Abuses of tu quoque for Life', in *Grand Valley State University News* <https://www.gvsu.edu/seidman/ethics/module-news-view.htm?storyId=CD0BC3F2-D254-A741-C4495405CDC5B795&sitEModuleId=9C6681B1-92E9-F4F1-7B4DF17EDBE5D2DC> [accessed 27 July 2017].

Special Dispatch to the Chronicle. 1895. 'Reminiscences of Early San Francisco: Close of the Life of a Popular Writer of Adventures on Land and Sea', *San Francisco Chronicle*, 7 March. Newspapers.com < https://www.newspapers.com/image/27547168/?terms=%22william%2Bhenry%2Bthomes%22> [accessed 27 April 2020].

Spurr, David. 1993. *Rhetoric of Empire: Colonial Discourse in Journalism, Travel Writing and Imperial Administration* (Durham, NC: Duke University Press).

Steinberg, David Joel. 1969. *The Philippines: A Singular and Plural Place* (Boulder, CO: Westview Press).

Stevenson, DeLoris. 1956. *Land of the Morning* (St Louis: The Bethany Press).

Steward, T.G. 1902. 'Haven for Negroes', *The Cambridge City Tribune* (Cambridge City, Indiana), 26 June, https://www.newspapers.com/image/15178351/?terms=filipino%2Bhappy [accessed 22 February 2019].

Stratemeyer, Edward. 1900. *The Campaign of the Jungle, or Under Lawton through Luzon* (Boston, MA: Lee and Shepard).

Stratemeyer, Edward. 1898. *Under Dewey at Manila or The War Fortunes of a Castaway*, (Boston, MA: Lee and Shepard).

Stratemeyer, Edward. 1902. *Under MacArthur in Luzon or Last Battles in the Philippines*, (Boston, MA: Lee and Shepard).

Stuntz, Homer Clyde. 1904. *The Philippines and the Far East* (New York: Jennings and Pye).

Sussman, Leonard R. 1991. 'Dying (and Being Killed) on the Job: A Case Study of World Journalists, 1982–1989', *Journalism & Mass Communication Quarterly*, 68.1–12: 195–9.

Syjuco, Miguel. 2010. *Autoplagiarist: An Exegesis of the Novel Ilustrado* (Doctoral thesis, University of Adelaide, Australia). Retrieved from https://digital.library.adelaide.edu.au/dspace/bitstream/2440/77856/6/04whole.pdf [accessed 3 July 2020].

Tadiar, Neferti Xina M. 2004. *Fantasy-Production: Sexual Economies and Other Philippine Consequences for the New World Order* (Hong Kong: Hong Kong University Press).

Tan, Samuel K. 1987. *A History of the Philippines* (Quezon City: University of the Philippines Press).

Teixera, Pedro. 1610. *Relaciones de Pedro Teixera del Origen, Descendencia y Succession de los Reyes de Persia y de Harmuz* (Manila: publisher unknown).

Temprano, Pablo Feced. 1888. Quoted in Paul A. Kramer, *The Blood of Government: Race, Empire, the United States, & the Philippines* (Chapel Hill, CA: University of North Carolina Press).

Todorov, Tzvetan. 1975. *The Fantastic: A Structural Approach to a Literary Genre* (Ithaca, NY: Cornell University Press).

Todorov, Tzvetan. 1993. *On Human Diversity: Nationalism, Racism and Exoticism in French Thought* (Cambridge, MA: Harvard University Press).

Tolentino, Francis. 2013. Quoted in Kate Hodal. 'Manila Less Than Thrilled at Dan Brown's Inferno', *Guardian*, 24 May <https://www.theguardian.com/world/2013/may/24/manila-thrilled-dan-brown-inferno> [accessed 13 December 2018].

Tolstoy, Leo. 1869. *War and Peace* (London and New York: Penguin; repr. 2009).

Tonkin, Boyd. 1999. 'The Books Interview: Timothy Mo – Postcards from the Edge', *The Independent*, 9 July <http://www.independent.co.uk/arts-entertainment/the-books-interview-timothy-mo-postcards-from-the-edge-1105400.html> [accessed 25 September 2017].

Trading Economics. 2017. *United States Exports* <https://tradingeconomics.com/united-states/exports> [accessed 25 September 2017].

Tsygankov, Andrei P. 2009. *Russophobia: Anti-Russian Lobby and American Foreign Policy* (New York: Palgrave MacMillan).

Tubeza, Philip C. 2011. 'Aquino Back Home with $13-B Deals', *Philippine Daily Inquirer*, 3 September <https://globalnation.inquirer.net/11553/aquino-back-home-with-13-b-deals> [accessed 14 May 2019].

Turner, Janice. 2018. 'Is Sherin Khankan the Future of Islam?', *The Times*, 2 June <https://www.thetimes.co.uk/article/is-sherin-khankan-the-future-of-islam-wfrzfrwzd> [accessed 17 April 2019].

Turner, Mark. 1995. 'The Kidnapping Crisis in the Philippines 1991–1993: Context and Management', *Journal of Contingencies and Crisis Management*, 3.1: 1–11.

Turner, Scott. 2003. 'The Dilemma of Double Standards in U.S. Human Rights Policy', *Peace & Change: A Journal of Peace Research*, 28.4: 524–54.

Twain, Mark. 1900. 'A Salutation to the Twentieth Century', *The New York Herald*, 30 December.

United Nations. 2016. 'Delegations Accuse International Criminal Court of "Double Standards", "Selectivity", as General Assembly Adopts Resolution Welcoming Its Report', United Nations Meetings Coverage, 13 May <https://www.un.org/press/en/2016/ga11784.doc.htm> [accessed 9 January 2019].

Urban, Andrew. 2017. 'The Peaceful Majority Are Irrelevant', *The Spectator*, 1 July<https://www.spectator.co.uk/2017/07/the-peaceful-majority-are-irrelevant/> [accessed 20 April 2019].

Vartavarian, Mesrob. 2018. 'Imperial Ambiguities: The United States and Philippine Muslims', *South East Asia Research*, 26.2: 132–46.

Vonnegut, Kurt. 1969. *Slaughterhouse-5, or the Children's Crusade – A Duty Dance with Death* (London and New York: Vintage Classics; repr. 1991).

Wakabayashi, Daisuke. 2017. 'As Google Fights Fake News, Voices on the Margins Raise Alarm', *New York Times*, 26 September <https://www.nytimes.com/2017/09/26/technology/google-search-bias-claims.html> [accessed 8 June 2020].

Waters, Sarah. 2006. *The Night Watch* (London: Virago).

'W.D. Boyce Was Pioneer Yellow Journalist'. 1912. *The Bridgeport Times and Evening Farmer* (Bridgeport, Connecticut), 17 June. Newspapers.com <https://www.newspapers.com/image/336885604/?terms=%22william%2Bd.%2Bboyce%22%2B%22labor%2Bunion%22> [accessed 19 May 2020].

'Weekly Papers Are Being Hit Very Hard'. 1906. *The Labor World* (Duluth, Minnesota), October 27, Newspapers.com <https://www.newspapers.com/image/49590487/?terms=%22w.d.%2Bboyce%22%2B%22labor%2Bunion%22%2B%22newspaper%22> [accessed 8 June 2020].

Weidenbaum, Murray L. and Samuel Hughes. 1996. *The Bamboo Network: How Expatriate Chinese Entrepreneurs are Creating a New Economic Superpower in Asia* (London and New York: Simon & Schuster).

Wesling, Meg. 2011. *Empire's Proxy: American Literature and U.S. Imperialism in the Philippines* (New York: New York University Press).

West, Cornel. 2016. 'Goodbye, American Neoliberalism. A New Era Is Here', *Guardian*, 17 November <https://www.theguardian.com/commentisfree/2016/nov/17/american-neoliberalism-cornel-west-2016-election> [accessed 18 April 2019].

Wicher, Andrzej. 2014. 'Introduction', in Andrzej Wicher, Piotr Spyra and Joanna Matyjaszcyk (eds), *Basic Categories of Fantastic Literature Revisited* (Newcastle upon Tyne: Cambridge Scholars Publishing), 1–7.

Wickberg, Edgar. 1997. 'Anti-Sinicism and Chinese Identity Options in the Philippines', in Daniel Chirot and Anthony Reid (eds), *Essential Outsiders: Chinese and Jews in the Modern Transformation of Southeast Asia and Central Europe* (Seattle: University of Washington Press), 153–83.

Wilkes, Charles. 1849. *Round the World Embracing the Principal Events of the Narrative of the United States Exploring Expedition* (Philadelphia: Geo. W. Gorton).

Wilkes, Charles. 1842. *Travel Accounts of the Islands (1832–58)* (Manila: Filipiniana Book Guild; repr. 1974).

Williams, Maslyn. 1979. *Faces of My Neighbour: Three Journeys into East Asia* (Sydney: William Collins).

Williams, O.F. 1898. Quoted in 'To Govern the Philippines', *New York Times*, 30 May. <https://timesmachine.nytimes.com/timesmachine/1898/05/30/102562537.html?action=click&contentCollection=Archives&module=LedeAsset&region=ArchiveBody&pgtype=article&pageNumber=2> [accessed 1 March 2019].

Woods, Damon L. 2006. *The Philippines: A Global Studies Handbook* (Oxford: ABC Clio).

Workman, Daniel. 2020. 'Philippines Top Trading Partners', <http://www.worldstopexports.com/philippines-top-import-partners/> [accessed 21 May 2020].

Yap, Luisa. 1998. 'The Chinese in the Philippines.' *China Perspectives*, 20: 53–6.

Young, Robert J.C. 1995. *Colonial Desire: Hybridity in Theory, Culture and Race* (London: Routledge).

Young, Robert J.C. 2001. *Postcolonialism: An Historical Introduction* (London: Wiley-Blackwell).

Yu, Jing. 2016. 'Tibet, Xinjiang, and China's Strong State Complex', *The Diplomat*, 28 July <https://thediplomat.com/2016/07/tibet-xinjiang-and-chinas-strong-state-complex/> [accessed 7 April 2019].

Yuson, Alfred A. 1988. 'Confessions of a Q.C. House-Husband', in Cristina Pantoja Hidalgo (ed.), *Creative Nonfiction: A Reader* (Quezon City: The University of the Philippines Press, 2005), 39–44.

Zafra, Jessica. 2005. 'Dedma 101', in Cristina Pantoja Hidalgo (ed.), *Creative Nonfiction: A Reader* (Quezon City: The University of the Philippines Press, 2005), 27–30.

Zinn, Howard. 2001. *A People's History of the United States: 1492-Present* (New York: Harper Collins), Amazon Kindle e-book.

Index

Afong Moy 87
African Americans 59, 60, 138
Agrarian economy, nineteenth-century 10, 21
Aguinaldo, Emilio 39, 55–7, 91, 117
Alcazar Club 71–2
Alighieri, Dante 19, 25, 33
Anderson, Benedict 74
Anglo-Saxon exceptionalism 22, 38
'anti-Manilaism' 111–32
anti-Semitism 85–6
apophasis 62–3
Apostol, Gina 119, 127
Aquino, Corazon 28, 115
Arguilla, Manuel 120
Atlantic slave trade 8
Australia 84
'authoritarian populism' 17–18, 103, 109
Ayala Museum 10

Bailey, Muriel 89–90
Bamforth, Tom 123–4
Bartholomew, Rafe 120–2
basketball 120–1
BBC 95–6, 139
Bechtel, John 25–6
'Bell Measure' 27
Bello, Walden 104–5
Belloc, Hilaire 85
Bhabha, Homi K. 4, 71
Bildungsroman 49
Blackburn, Robin 8
Bowring, John 43, 86
Boyce, William D. 12, 15, 62–3, 66, 67, 70, 71, 90–1
British (English) imperialism 20, 45
  and occupation of Manila 20
Brown, Dan 34, 35
Bulosan, Carlos 131–2
Burnham, Daniel 15–16
Buruma, Ian 28, 29, 75
Bush, George W. 38, 39

cacique 17, 30–1, 60–1, 99, 101, 126
California 72, 80, 116
Carne Brothers 87
Carpenter, Frank G. 15, 61, 64, 66, 70, 71
Casmarines Sur 8
Chesterton, G.K. 85
China 7, 31, 92–7, 135
'Chinamania' in US 83
Chinese Filipinos 5, 8, *81–98*
  business clans 84
  coolies 65, 84
  exile from Philippines 83
  feminizing of 89
  immigration to Philippines 81, 84
  kidnapping 'crisis' 92
  massacres 81–2
  nationalization laws 91
  perceived as sexual menace 89–90
  Sangleys 81
  suspicious hybridity of 88, 90–1
Chomsky, Noam 105
Chu, Richard T. 8, 82, 89
climate emergency 135
Clive 'of India', Robert 49
colonial adventure genre 39, 44, 48–9
  deconstruction of 128–9
'commanding view' of Orientalist writers 40, 64, 69–70
comprador class 74
Conrad, Joseph 103
conspiracy theories 106
Constantino, Renato 8, 41, 43, 61, 75
Cooper, James Fenimore 38
Coronavirus pandemic 136
Coward, Rosalind 115
crime genre 100
cross-cultural communication 122
Crossley, John Newsome 9
Crush, Jonathan 5
Cuba 44, 47
cultural appropriation 119

Dalisay, José Y.   124
Dampier, William   6, 9
Davao   102
debt   96, 105
Defoe, Daniel   9, 82–3
de Legazpi, Miguel López   8
Deng Xiaoping   93
dependency theory   5, 28
'disparaging return'   61
Disraeli, Benjamin   85
Duterte, Rodrigo   7, 17, 94, 95, 96, *99–110*, 128–9, 131, 138–9

Eastwood, Clint   101
Edwards, Justin D. and Rune Graulund   111, 113, 121
Ermita   71
Estrada, Joseph 'Erap'   100
eugenics   86
euphemism   46
European Union (EU)   134
expressive modality   46–7, 62–3

Facebook   140
'fake news'   139
Fanon, Frantz   64, 90
'fantasy-production'   47
   resistance to   114–15
Fee, Mary H.   16, 67, 71, 118, 127
Feleo, Anita and David Sheniak   122–3
feminism   110, 137
Fenton, James   29, 74, 100, 104
Ferguson, Niall   6
Filipinas Heritage Library   10
Filipino literature in English   112, 115
First World War   135, 136
Flaubert, Gustave   79
foregrounding research in writing   115
Francia, Luis H.   8, 43, 81, 114, 123
Freudian projection   48, 126
Fujian   81

Gandhi, Mohandas Karamchand 'Mahatma'   111
Garcia, J. Neil   82
Garland, Alex   31, 32, 34, 35, 77, 100, 124
gender roles, deconstruction of   127–9
Genghis Khan   25, 83
German imperialism   11

Global rate of profit   135–6
'going native'   23, 57–9
Goncharov, Ivan   10–11
Google   140
Great Depression   136
Green, Martin   5, 10–11, 14, 39, 44, 48–9, 111, 138
Grosrichard, Alain   17, 19, 21, 23, 24, 57, 101–3
Guerrero, Madis Ma.   120
Gunter, Archibald Clavering   14, 15, 43–4, 51, 61–2, 65, 67, 87–8, 91, 96, 121, 125, 129

Hagedorn, Jessica   118
Hall, Stuart   102
Hamilton-Paterson, James   6, 32–4, 70, 73–6, 78
Hancock, H. Irving   88–9
Hau, Caroline S.   83, 91, 126
Hawai'i   60, 125
Hearst, William Randolph   50
hell   19, 23–4, 31, 33
Hispanophobia   23, 60
'history from below'   119–20
Hitchens, Christopher   29
Hobsbawm, Eric   119
Hollywood   31, 72, 89, 100, 101, 110
horror genre   31, 32
Horsley, Sebastian   103–4

Ileto, Reynaldo C.   29, 30, 37, 70, 99, 101
India   130
International Criminal Court (ICC)   108
International Monetary Fund (IMF)   105
intertextuality   118–19
Intramuros   10, 24, 25, 69, 122
'inverted patterns of travel'   130
Iraq War   38, 39, 107, 108
Iyer, Pico   78

Jagor, Fedor   11
Jameson, Fredric   32
Japan   6, 25, 31, 54, 71–2
Java   84
jeepneys   72
Joaquin, Nick   76, 117–18
Johnson, Lyndon B.   38, 73
José, F. Sionil   116–17

Kalaw, Maximo   120
Kelly, M.G.E.   94–5, 124
Kennedy, John F.   75
Kidd, Benjamin   57–8
King, Charles   55, 64–5
Korte, Barbara   130–1
Kramer, Paul A.   9, 63

Lacaba, Jose F.   119
Lacara, Cesar Hernandez   126
Lane, Edward William   42
Latinidad (Latin cultural consciousness)   22–3
Laya, Juan C.   131
Lee, Clark   25, 27
Lewis, Bernard   42
liberal identity politics   11
Lim, Alfredo   77
Lisle, Debbie   12, 111–12, 121
Loney, Nicholas   13, 20–2, 24, 40, 103, 113

Macapagal-Arroyo, Gloria   94, 110
MacArthur, Douglas   76
McKenzie, Duncan Alexander   93, 94, 129
McKinley, William   37–9, 53, 63, 136
McMahon, Jennifer M.   4, 131
MacMicking, Robert   10, 13, 15, 21–3, 40–3, 45, 84, 85
Mailer, Norman   125
Malay Filipinos
    exploitation of   8, 42–3
    infantilization of   56, 59
    perceived idleness   21–2, 54, 126
    US immigration   21–2, 55, 75, 106–7
Manila Hotel   71
Manilaism
    chronology   13
    feminization   16, 54, 61–2, 79
    genre   12–13
    geographical definition   7
Maoist armed struggle   7
Marcos dictatorship   16, 29, 30, 73, 75, 94, 113, 115, 119
masculinity   48–9, 102, 128–9
Mayhew, Henry   115
Meiring, Michael   106
Mignolo, Walter D.   4, 22–3
Miller, George A.   6, 24

Miller, Jonathan   94, 96, 99, 100, 102–7
Mishra, Pankaj   6, 100, 137–8
misogyny   44, 61–2
Mo, Timothy   31, 77, 91–2
Modi, Narendra   17, 109
Moro/Islamist armed struggle   7, 20, 29, 89, 106

Narayan, R.K.   130–1
NATO   131, 136
Nelson, Raymond   91
neoliberalism   99, 123, 137–8
    begetting authoritarianism   99–100, 104–5
'New Journalism'   125–6
new media   139–40
New York City   87, 92
New York Times   54, 92, 93, 139
Ninoy Aquino International Airport (NAIA)   123

Obama, Barack   38, 39, 109, 139
OFWs (Overseas Filipino Workers)   124
oppositional journalism   115–16
O'Rourke, P.J.   6, 28–9

parataxis   65–6
parody   119
Parry, Benita   4
passive voice   44–5
Perkins, George C.   59
Philips, Claire 'High Pockets'   71–2
Phillips, Caryl   131
Pilger, John   115
Pol Pot   99
polyphony in writing   111, 112, 129–30
postmodernist literature   31–2, 100–1, 118–19, 125
progress   24, 34, 41–2, 57–8
Pulitzer, Joseph   50
Putin, Vladimir   17

Rafael, Vicente   108
rationalism   30
Reagan, Ronald   29
Revilla, Linda A.   125
Rizal, Jose   107, 125–6
Robb, Walter M.   12, 14, 24, 60, 89, 90
Robredo, Leni   110

Roman Catholic Church
  appropriation of basketball   121
  conversion   8
  fetishization of suffering   103–4
  Manilaist vilification of   10, 23–4, 27
  Protestant antipathy towards   20
Roosevelt, Theodore   38, 51
Rosca, Ninotchka   127
Rousseau, Jean-Jacques   101
Rowland, Dr Henry C.   58
Rufo, Aries C.   115–16
Russian imperialism   11, 135
Russophobia   131

Said, Edward   3–4, 12, 18, 28–9, 34, 42, 80, 111, 112
San Fernando   104
San Juan, Jr, E.   105–6
Sayles, John   117, 126–7, 130
'scientific' racism   9, 54, 57–8, 86–7
Second World War   6, 25, 71–2, 76
'self-in-process' (Hunt and Sampson)   114
self-reflexivity   111–12, 114
sex tourism   1, 78–9, 123
Seymour, Richard   109
'shadowing' (Lisle)   76, 117–18
Shaheen, Jack   124–5
Smith, Tom   94, 95, 105, 110, 138
Social Darwinism   59–60
South Korea   6, 31
Spanish imperialism
  development of Philippines   61
  early discourses on Philippines   7–8, 37
  extinction of   6, 19–20
  Latin America   23
  Mexican viceroyalty   23
  neglect of Filipino culture   9
  perceived corruption and cruelty   20–21, 40, 54, 56, 60–1
  rebellions against   20
  re-settling Filipinos in North America   54
spatial assumptions, deconstruction of   120–1
Spivak, Gayatri Chakravorty   4
Spurr, David   40, 45, 65, 70
stereotypes, cognitive basis of   98, 134
Stevenson, DeLoris   6, 26, 35, 72–3

Stratemeyer, Edward   12, 45–9, 54, 58, 61
Stuntz, Homer Clyde   60–1
Supernatural, the   24, 33
surveillance   102
Syjuco, Miguel   115

Tadiar, Neferti X.M.   16, 74, 76–8, 94, 105, 114–15, 134
Tagalog ethnic group   8
Techno-Orientalism   33–4
Temprano, Pablo Feced   8
'third world blues' (Pratt)   28–9, 31
  and problematic whitewashing of   122
Thomes, William Henry   41, 87
Thompson, E.P.   119
Times (of London)   84
Todorov, Tzvetan   19, 33
Tolentino, Aurelio   63
Tolstoy, Leo   111
tourism industry   77–8
travel writing discourses   12, 24
Treaty of Paris   70
Triads   96
Trump, Donald   105
Twain, Mark (Samuel Langhorne Clemens)   48, 50, 53, 111
Tydings Rehabilitation Act   27

urban development of Manila   7, 70, 76–7
US imperialism
  'benevolent assimilation'   37, 53, 59, 63, 65
  Cold War   28, 134
  domestic resistance to   50
  early US colonial economy in Philippines   60
  flawed simulation of   71–80
  genocide   39, 47
  knowledge gathering   9
  linguistic colonization   66–7, 129
  missionaries   26–7
  neocolonialism   5, 7, 27–8, 75, 106
  'New Cold War' (Cohen)   135
  oppressive colonial rule   63–4
  pedagogy of (Campomanes)   136
  Philippine conquest (1898–1913)   24, 45, 55–8, 88–9, 116–17
  rhetoric behind   37–9, 56, 106

spatial inequalities 64–6
Vietnam War 38, 39, 45, 108

Vartavarian, Mesrob 7
visual description 41
Voltaire 101

'War on Terror' 94, 106, 108
Weinstein, Harvey 100
'whataboutism'/*tu quoque* fallacy 107–8, 114, 131, 138
Wilkes, Charles 13, 15, 16, 20–2, 40–1, 43, 54, 55, 84, 85

Williams, Maslyn 28, 30, 73, 113–14, 123
World Bank 105
World Trade Organization (WTO) 136

Yalung, Bishop Crisostomo 116
'Yamashita's gold' 123
'yellow' journalism 13, 50, 117
Young, Robert J.C. 4, 22, 48
Yuson, Alfred A. 127–9

Zafra, Jessica 130
Zinn, Howard 47
Žižek, Slavoj 47

www.ingramcontent.com/pod-product-compliance
Lightning Source LLC
Chambersburg PA
CBHW072236290426
44111CB00012B/2117